PLAYWRIGHTS

OF THE

NEW AMERICAN THEATER

PLAYWRIGHTS

OF THE

NEW AMERICAN THEATER

BY

THOMAS H. DICKINSON

Essay Index Reprint Series

BOOKS FOR LIBRARIES PRESS, INC.

FREEPORT, NEW YORK

First Published 1925
Reprinted 1967

LIBRARY OF CONGRESS CATALOG CARD NUMBER: 67-26731

PRINTED IN THE UNITED STATES OF AMERICA

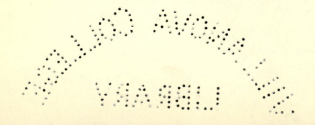

CONTENTS

PLAYWRIGHTS

OF THE

NEW AMERICAN THEATER

PLAYWRIGHTS OF THE NEW AMERICAN THEATER

CHAPTER I

THE PLAYWRIGHT AS PIONEER: PERCY MACKAYE

I

In 1897 there was delivered at the Commencement Exercises of Harvard College an oration on a theme at the time unusual for college affairs. The subject of the oration was "The Need of Imagination in the Drama of Today." The delivery of this oration deserves some notice, not alone on account of the nature of the subject-matter, but because the speaker represented in his own person a vigorous tradition in American drama and was himself on the threshold of a lifetime of activity in the theater.

"Is there not need of a higher standard in the composition and criticism of our modern dramas?" the orator asks. "Does the public possess a clear and just appreciation of what a play should be?" And he proceeds to discuss the principles that govern in the theater of the time and to test these by stand-

1

ards of his own application. He reminds his hearers that the mirror which, in the words of Hamlet to the Players, the art of the theater should hold up to nature, is not a dull, imitative looking glass, but a vitally reflective magic mirror. He surveys current successes to learn whether there is in them any trace of magic, and he concludes that, from the beginning to the end of the play, it is the purpose of the dramatist of the day not to fashion a world of the imagination, but "to keep the spectator in a state of excited expectancy, to draw from the audience the same breathless attention which they would bestow upon a runaway accident or an escaping thief, to appeal, in short, not to the imaginations of men but to their nervous systems." He concludes his oration with a plea for a new ordering in the American theater. Imagination, and then imagination and more imagination! This is the need of the American stage.

The speaker on this occasion was young Percy Wallace MacKaye. Looking back over the almost thirty years that have passed since this oration was delivered, it appears that the orator spoke better than he knew. Certainly he had pointed his finger at his own program of action. But he had done more than this. He had uncovered the doctrine by which a whole program of dramatic reorganization was to be motivated. He had elected himself spokesman, with all that thereto appertains of hard work and odium, of a new movement in the American theater. This position he has never relinquished. A something dynamic in the MacKaye nature, a certain combination in him of the warrior's obtuseness with the sensitiveness of the artist, has given him both the eloquence and the initiative of authority.

Percy MacKaye (in his early published work he dropped the middle name) was born in New York City, March 16, 1875, the son of a line which on both sides had been distinguished for intellectual attainments and strong convictions. His paternal grandfather had been an Abolitionist leader intrusted by Lincoln with responsibilities in connection with emancipation. His mother, as well as his father, had been a writer and playwright. He attended boy's school in New York, Groton, and Washington, D. C. Thence he went to Harvard, and after graduating in 1897, proceeded to Europe to continue his studies in Germany, France, England, and Italy.

Young MacKaye took with him to Europe a definite ambition to be a playwright. This ambition found its source in his own family tradition. Steele MacKaye is but a name to many to-day. A generation ago he was more than a name. He had been successfully painter, teacher, lecturer, disciple and exponent of Delsarte, author of dramatic works (of which "Hazel Kirke" and "Paul Kauvar" are remembered), theatrical manager, producer, architect and innovator. No justice can be done to the life work of the father in a hasty sketch of the life of the son. And yet the father cannot be ignored for two perfectly good reasons. He passed on to the son a

vigorous tradition of theatrical innovation. Like
the son, he never looked upon the drama as an art
of pure form; to him it was always an art in which
he saw realized an Utopian dream.

Percy MacKaye came to Harvard from his
father's death bed. He had spent the previous year
beside the drafting boards and work tables of his
father in Chicago. He had been confidant and sec-
retary to his father. Boyishly he had shared with
him the dream of a Spectatorium overlooking the
western lake; his first writing had been done for this
ill-fated enterprise. He had seen that dream go
down to defeat and his father to death. In the defeat
he had had his first taste of a fate too common
among those who would transmute dreams into
reality, whether in the form of Utopias or theaters.
When, four years later, he dedicated himself to his
father's work, it was with open eyes.

I find some interest in the fact that Percy
MacKaye, who was to raise his voice for an American theater, should have started his life work by
browsing in European libraries. A generation ago
few American playwrights had attended college.
Bronson Howard and William Gillette were college
men; Clyde Fitch, a college man, was just beginning
his career. But Augustus Thomas, David Belasco,
James A. Herne, Denman Thompson, Charles Klein,
had come to writing either through business or
through acting. The theater was alienated from the

bookish world. Writers for the stage acquired a hand-picked education that was by no means to be despised, but a college education as such was considered a handicap. Few have suffered more from this handicap than Percy MacKaye. He began his career by separating himself still further from the currents and interests of the American stage by burying himself in the myth and fable, in the classical tradition of the old world. It was as if he said to himself that as the way of preferment was closed in the popular avenues of stage activity, he would gather all forces for an attack upon the stage from the vantage ground of the accumulated tradition of the world of culture.

And indeed, for the task he had undertaken, there were advantages in the severely academic and classical equipment with which the young poet provided himself. I imagine that from his earliest youth MacKaye never deluded himself into thinking that he could write for the average commercial stage. I believe he was never interested in writing for this theater. From his childhood he had had another purpose, the purpose of writing for the theater as it is going to be. Nowhere could he gain a conception of the theater of the future so well as from a study of the theater as it had been in the golden days of the past. He was soon to learn that history does not repeat itself, that the theater of the future was to run on formulas of its own: he was himself to play his part in attempting to work out these formulas.

Meanwhile he found his support and inspiration, as so many others have done before him, in the past.

Of plays, MacKaye has written more styles than Polonius at his most garrulous ever dreamed of. The number of his published works comprises more than seventy titles, including collected editions of his works. There are six volumes of poems; four volumes of essays on the civic theater and on social ideals; fifteen volumes of plays, four volumes of operas, twelve volumes of masques and community dramas, and a score of miscellaneous works and editions. If these show the energy with which he has thrown himself into work, the themes of his earliest group of plays show the voracious appetite of the man for the old fables, the stored riches of world imagination. He started his playwriting as an Elizabethan with "A Garland to Sylvia"; moved back to the period of Chaucer for "The Canterbury Pilgrims"; thence to Scandinavian mythology for "Fenris, the Wolf"; over to France for "Jeanne d'Arc," and finally to the classical world for "Sappho and Phaon."

In 1896 MacKaye had begun, while still a student at Harvard, a play upon a theme derived from Elizabethan sources. Completed in Italy in 1899, "A Garland to Sylvia" was reserved for publication for some ten years and when finally published in 1910 had the advantage of a second preface in which the author expounded its history and some of the considerations entering into its composition. The play itself, taken in conjunction with the two prefaces, is a lucid document upon the whole career of the poet. Governing everything is the influence of Shakespeare. It would not be proper to say that the play is imitative of Shakespeare, but it is imbued with the spirit of the early comedies. The influence extended to the theme, the atmosphere and to some of the versification of the play, but not to its form. Of the hero of the play Mencken has said, "Felix, to put it in plain English, is Shakespeare-drunk. He has steeped himself in the gorgeous word music of the peerless bard as Thackeray once steeped himself in Addison's Haydnesque prose. . . . It is in fine, the Forest of Arden. I know of no more striking imitation, in this unpoetical age, of the 16th century Shakespeare—not the serious, self-conscious metaphysician of the bald dome and coat of arms, but the light-hearted devil of the 1590's and the early comedies."

MacKaye was always impressionable. The immediate influence, then, is not the most significant feature of a MacKaye play. Of greater significance are those persistent traits which, present in the first play, come to be the signs manual of the MacKaye technique. "A Garland to Sylvia" displays that artist consciousness, that theater consciousness, that is the peculiar mark of MacKaye's mind. In this work he seems always to be divided between two interests, his interest in the drama as an art of expression through form, and even more strongly his interest in the potentialities of the art of the theater in human affairs. It is the latter that gives his work that sense of *responsibility* that is a distinguishing attribute of most of his plays and a contributing reason for the failure of many of them in production.

To the world-old problem, "How is the artist to be true to human nature?" MacKaye adds another: "How is the artist to be true to evolutionary process? How can he be most useful to destiny?" Writing in his earliest preface the young author puts his finger on the trait that always distinguishes him. "As I began to write the play, this somewhat introspective—though I think not morbid—contemplation of my own relation to my characters fascinated, nay, I confess, weighed upon me." And he goes on, "I wished to portray—or rather, I saw portrayed before me mentally—first, a young *dramatist*, groping in the mists of his imagination, confronted and confounded by that personality of his own which he had unwittingly but inevitably wrought into the characters of his play."

This combined theater and social consciousness, this awareness of himself in all he does, this identification of himself with all his themes, controls the structure of this as of MacKaye's later plays. In this play the action is not only set in a containing plot. There is a double containing action and, as if to intensify the impression of the complications and involutions of life, characters move at will from one zone of the action to another. We shall see that

MacKaye never views the world simply. All reality is seen in a multiple aspect. Among these aspects the author moves freely now in one guise, now in another, inquiring and commenting.

The hero of the play is a young poet, Felix, who appears first in a prologue at Harvard College. He is writing a play. Speaking of Felix, another character in the Prologue says that he is always on "the wildest of speculations as to the relation of life to his imagination. The imagination, he believes, is a faculty of perception and creation. So, on the one hand, his imagination can perceive truths beyond mere eyesight; and on the other, it can create, from these truths, beings beyond mere flesh and blood—creatures which are henceforth indestructible, immortal; for whose existence he is responsible, as the good Lord, for him."

How the responsibilities of Felix work out in the play he writes, how the characters he creates prove as real, even more real than himself, so that they are substance and he is dream, provides the theme of the play. MacKaye would have us understand that while the problem of this play is essentially an artist's problem, it is not only an artist's problem; that all who dwell on the earth are concerned with the complex interrelations of things. "A Garland to Sylvia" has never been produced.

Before writing his next published play, MacKaye had collaborated with Evelyn Greenleaf Southerland in a romantic drama entitled, "A Maid of

Leyden," which was presented by the pupils of the
American Academy of Dramatic Arts at a matinée,
December 11, 1900. As far as known, this was the
first of MacKaye's works to find production. The
manuscript of "A Garland to Sylvia," shown among
the author's friends, secured for him the flattering
attention of Norman Hapgood, who was then writing on the *Commercial Advertiser*. It also elicited
from E. H. Sothern and Julia Marlowe a commission for a poetic play. For the theme of his next
play MacKaye went back beyond the age of Elizabeth to the more distant time of Chaucer. In the
composition of "A Garland to Sylvia," the author
had had the support of a vigorous dramatic convention. This was not the case with a subject chosen
from the fourteenth century. Here the author had
to dramatize materials not originally created for the
stage. This fact explains, perhaps, a certain stagi-
ness and excess of theatrical effect to be found in
"The Canterbury Pilgrims." Characters and atmosphere he found ready to hand. Action and plot had
to be invented.

The source material of this play is mostly to be
found in Chaucer's "Prologue" and "The Wife of
Bath's Tale" in "The Canterbury Tales." Many
features of the plot are derived not from extant
resources in fiction, but from the author's own imagination working upon historical characters of Chaucer's day, including the poet himself, as well as upon
the characters of the Tales. The play is in fact

MacKaye's tribute to the poet's poet, Chaucer. Not accepted by Sothern and Marlowe, it was first produced by the Coburn Players in Atlanta, Georgia, April 30, 1909, and was afterward acted by this company for six seasons in tour throughout the country.

Of all MacKaye's plays, this has had the largest measure of popular success. The reasons for this are not obscure. It is the most objective of the author's plays in plot, and shows fewer traces of social and æsthetic philosophy, of verbal and stylistic whimsy than MacKaye usually displays. For once the author forgets his passion for the theater in his interest in his characters. The action moves straight-away without prologues or other contrivances. The author does, however, permit his favorite confusion between the real world and the imaginary world by having Chaucer and other figures of history move about among the figures of Chaucer's—and MacKaye's—imaginations.

In two respects the play is a delight. MacKaye has always been an enthusiastic Chaucerian. In later days he edited and adapted to modern English the works of Chaucer. This enthusiasm for Chaucer is manifest in the atmosphere of the play. Never are MacKaye's characteristic faults less evident than in this play. He has laid aside his verbal super-facility, his disposition to make sound stand for sense. The verse of this play is instinct with the spirit of joy and adventure. The jocund sense of outdoor life so long associated with Chaucer is well achieved. Chaucer says he is in love.

> Mine own true mistress is sweet Out-of-doors.
> No Whitson lassie wears so green a kirtle,
> Nor sings so clear, nor smiles with such blue eyes,
> As bonny April, winking tears away.

The enthusiastic Squire, telling Chaucer of their trip, speaks as follows:

> Was ever such a ride
> As ours from London? Hillsides newly greened,
> Brooks splashing silver in the small, sweet grass,
> Pelt gusts of rain dark'ning the hills, and then
> Wide swallowed up in sunshine! And to feel
> My snorting jennet stamp the oozy turf
> Under my stirrup, whilst from overhead
> Sonnets shook down from every bough.

If we are pleased with the temper of the play we are also pleased with the characters. The cast of characters is large, including Chaucer, about thirty male Pilgrims, the Wife of Bath, the Prioress, the Nun, the Mistress of the Inn, and about a score of others. Well portrayed is the daintiness and sentiment of the Prioress, Donna Eglantine, who is put under Chaucer's protection, who tells her beads to keep the fairies from her feet for fear the bagpipes set them free. Beside the delicacy of the Prioress, the ribaldry of the Wife of Bath stands out clearly.

Delightful is the outbreak of the latter on womanhood:

> You men! God's arms! What ken ye of true women?
> You stuff one doll and name it Modesty,
> And bid her mince and giggle, hang her head
> And ogle in her sleeve; another puppet
> You make of snow and name St. Innocence:
> She sits by moonlight in a silver nightgown
> And sighs love-Latin in a nunnery.
> By Corpus' bones! Is not a mare a horse?
> A woman is but man; and both one beast——

In short the character and atmosphere of the play
are refreshing; the action is of a somewhat lower
order. The author's purpose seems rather to put his
characters through a large amount of gymnastics
than to tell a story that will be believed. The central
conception of the plot is artificial enough. The action
goes through many complications of a playful nature
in which the poet himself plays a far from dignified
part. He dances in an arbor with the Prioress. The
verses he had written for Eglantine reach a meaner
wench. There is an incredible number of misunderstandings and crossed personalities. We are expected to believe that characters which have been
traveling to Canterbury to meet each other would
go for days in the same procession without meeting.
Chaucer escapes marrying the Wife of Bath only by
the interposition of King Richard who is introduced
by the author for the purpose. If the play were to

be judged by the plot it would not require much consideration. Happily it possesses other and higher qualities of imagination which raise it to importance.

From Chaucerian England the poet now turns toward Scandinavian mythology. In northern myth Fenris, the water demon, was shaped like a wolf and grew to such tremendous size that the gods chained him up. Twice he broke his chains until it seemed that he could never be controlled. The chain that finally proved strong enough to hold him was made of the sound of a cat's footsteps, a man's beard, the roots of a mountain, a fish's breath and a bird's spittle.

This primitive myth offers ample material by which to suggest the strain of the beast that lies in all of us and the spiritual bond by which the inborn brute may be constrained. The conception of the power of magic to control both brute force and fate is dear to MacKaye's heart. To him imagination is the breaker of chains, man's liberator from the baser powers that hold him enslaved. But the play is not one of his best. The story is told in the form of a five-act tragedy, partly written in blank verse, partly in archaic Anglo-Saxon meter. As a tour de force the work is impressive. But the play offers nothing important to the understanding of human nature. Story and style are monotonous; the symbolism is trite. Again the author's interest in the theater is revealed when at the end it is shown that the building of toy houses (*i.e.*, plays and stories) is an important measure for the civilizing of man. This play has not been produced.

With the composition and production of "Jeanne d'Arc" Mackaye begins that close coöperation with the artists of music and design that has marked his active career as a playwright. "Jeanne d'Arc" was first produced by E. H. Sothern and Julia Marlowe in Philadelphia, October 15, 1906. Its New York production was at the Lyric Theater, January 28, 1907. In April of the same year it was produced in London. For this production stage designs were made by Barry Faulkner. An incidental music suite was composed by F. S. Converse, of Boston, the first of several collaborations. "Jeanne d'Arc" belongs to the older order of blank verse drama with music accompaniment and songs, a form much more common seventy-five years ago than to-day. The form derives on the one side distantly from the Elizabethan blank verse play; on the other it derives from the melody drama of a more sentimental generation. No admirer of MacKaye's tonic influence in turning the American stage toward imagination needs to claim that he has more than skimmed over the surface of this great theme. One cannot avoid comparing this play with two great plays on the same theme, with Schiller's "Die Jungfrau von Orleans," which had been written a century before, and with Shaw's "Saint Joan" which was written twenty years later. With neither play does MacKaye's work compare favorably. The appearance of Shaw's play only convinces us the more that for the treatment before modern audiences of the heroic legends that stand on the threshold of the modern era, no romantic dress of poesy is necessary or desirable. It is the author's duty to delve always deeper into the hidden sources of consciousness and decision. He must not be satisfied with words except as words escape like cries from distracted minds. MacKaye had not learned this lesson.

MacKaye's "Jeanne d'Arc" is graceful and, in a superficial way, theatrically effective. The play follows the career of the Maid from Domremy in 1428 through various scenes to the final event at Rouen in May, 1431. At no point in the story does the author seek to plumb the deeps of his theme. As a pageant or festival entertainment the play has its qualities. It has color, movement, songs, crowds, stage effects, now and then snatches of felicitous phrasing. It never moves as with an organ note of deep revelation, nor does it pretend to render with justice the aspirations and agonies of the Maid. Whenever the spiritual demands of the play become too deep to be easily handled, the author introduces a stage device. On one occasion the Emperor in the stained glass window turns toward the king and speaks with the voice of St. Michael. Again a voice speaks within a bell. This use of the trickery of the stage to represent the deeper motives of the playwright's theme is unfortunate.

In the early scenes the character of Jeanne is conceived with simplicity and directness. And yet when her hour of vision comes she is without inspiration. And her most sacred hours are cheapened by the allures of romantic love. Beside a passion like that of the Maid, a mortal passion seems irreverent. Certainly the author does not make the love of D'Alençon of any importance either to the Maid or to us.

In "Sappho and Phaon" we come to the end of the first phase of MacKaye's career. As heroine of this play MacKaye chooses Sappho, the Lesbian poetess of the 7th and 6th centuries, B.C. In many respects this is the most characteristic as it is the most ambitious of the author's poetic works. In his treatment of the unhappy love of the Greek poetess for Phaon he is consistently modern in temper, plot, intrigue and interest. He pays tribute to the past only in a certain regard for ancient types of production and for archæological externals of the action. MacKaye's choice of the old Grecian story and the manner of his treatment uncover again some of the deepest interests of his life. Only by the employment of an ancient story that runs through the ages can he give that sense of the complexity and involution of modern life that is his chief concern. In this play we have displayed again that "theater-mindedness" that is found throughout MacKaye's work. The story is involved in various planes of action and reveals many motives and objectives. MacKaye neither sees a situation simply nor can he trust his audience to follow it save through openings of successive draperies.

Very few plays have had a time scheme as extended as that of "Sappho and Phaon." Beginning with our days the action moves through various prologues and inductions backward for twenty-five hundred years. The action takes place on the site of a stage of a theater at Herculaneum. In the first Prologue a group of excavators are shown at work in the ruins of the Players' quarter of the private theater of Varius. The Induction then transports us to the same spot in the year 25 B.C., the theater then being standing. The Prelude and Interludes take place on the fore stage or orchestra in front of the curtain of the theater. The Play Proper is the tragedy of Sappho and Phaon, conceived as being played upon this stage of Varius' theater, during the first century B.C. The scene reveals a high promontory overlooking the Ægean Sea, near Mitylene in Lesbos with the exterior of the temple of Aphrodite and Poseidon. Such is the machinery of the play.

There is no need to tell again the story of the love of Sappho for Phaon. This story is every-man's material now. MacKaye makes it his own; puts the stamp of his hand upon it. Manifestly he is not interested in Sappho alone, and not at all interested in Sappho, the Greek. He is interested in the persistence among men to-day of the forces, the dreams, the sacrifices, victories and defeats that make up the record of man in the past. To him time is a dream.

He is interested, too, in the interchangeable values of the real and the ideal, the substance and the show, actor and audience, poet and figment of poet's brain. Of all these interests Sappho is a symbol and an instrument.

As treated by MacKaye, the play is the story of "the eternal maiden and her lover." It is handled with a free, romantic fancy, teems with complications, fabricated circumstance and coincidences. In plot the play is no more distinguished than a thousand plays of stage intrigue of the nineteenth century. It is a tragedy of crossed loves, pitiful contrivances, misunderstandings, partings, and death. The catastrophe grows from an external situation. The play makes little pretense to represent the Greek spirit either in the feeling of man for woman or in the attitudes of the characters toward the surrounding forces of their lives. Sappho says, "We must dare all to be ourselves." On Phaon's part he too speaks revolutionary words of "the tyrant's hate, the galley master's goad, the sordid trader's dreams of avarice." When they marry she hears the "chant of life," "world music." Phaon answers rightly, "These are but thou; and thoughts of thee are music."

If we judge this play as a modern attempt to make the past live again it does not succeed. The fable is not worthy of the theme. The author fails to evoke that terror of the wrath of the gods that alone can explain Phaon's killing of his child. The tragic denouement depends too much upon accident. Nevertheless the play is one of the most important of American verse plays, not only because of its emotional appeal, but even more because of the author's success in giving the impression of the unbroken continuity of dramatic art through the ages. True to the author's interest in the theater we are shown not only a play but the circumstances of dramatic production in Italy in 25 B.C. We see characteristic figures of the player, the pantomimist, the mime, the training master of players, and the audience. We see Prologus, who announces the tragedy before the curtain. And when the Induction opens we learn something of the conditions behind the scenes in the old Roman private theater.

Again the author's interest in the theater is shown when in reply to a slighting remark made by Horace, a spectator, Actius speaks for the Players:

> . . . Why, then, a player
> Is man epitomized, an ape
> Of glorious hypocrisy,
> Magnificent, because alone
> He shows the counterfeit his image,
> The hypocrite—himself.

II

With "Sappho and Phaon" we reach the end of the first phase of MacKaye's work. He had begun to write plays under the influence of the masters of

the verse drama of the past. Study of these masters
had brought two convictions to his mind. That
where work of the theater has been highest it has
tended always to express itself through old stories
which have been distilled through the imaginations
of peoples. That a work of dramatic art can achieve
long life only in case its expression rises to elevation
and beauty of language. In these beliefs he undertook his first work and in these beliefs he remained.
Considerations arose, however, which made him question whether the times were auspicious for the writing
of plays in verse, whether his own powers and convictions did not compel him to enter the world's arena
rather than dwell in the cloister of poetry.

MacKaye's first work had been based upon the
theory that language is the preponderant dramatic
medium. He learned that language, however refined
and beautified, is not of itself enough. A good play
involves other factors of expression, deeper and
more delicate than those of language. As human life
develops in complexity and intensity, the part that
words can play becomes always smaller, the part
played by other expressive mediums aside from
words becomes ever greater. It is not because the
stories of the past are not relevant to us that so
many ambitious projects for their dramatization
fail. A great story is always relevant. They fail
because the artist seeks to express an old story
through a medium that also is old. One of the signs
of the age of our civilization is that we have become

weary in the use of words. Words no longer have the joy to us that they had when the world was new. Whatever his theme, the artist must seek always the medium of joy. If words are dead, then he must seek the living line, the living color, the living music. Twenty years ago men had not learned that language was dead. The theater needed to break the shackles of language entirely in order that it might rediscover the true potencies and use of language. At the time that MacKaye began to write, Stephen Phillips was having his first successes in England with verse plays. Arthur Symons had said that no play could be considered a true play except it was written in verse. These men were not aware of it, but so far from speaking for the theater they were cutting themselves off from the theater. Whether by conscious judgment or not, MacKaye was to learn that the art of the theater was not to be re-created by refining its spoken language; that life was to be brought back into the theater by giving it an orchestra of languages of which speech and verse are but single instruments.

Summing up the work of MacKaye's first period, we find many characteristics that appear throughout his life. His early plays showed his unusual command of the resources of stage technique. They revealed a rich and luxuriant verbal gift, a gift too much concerned with the sound of words, too little concerned with their meaning and selection. They showed a comic sense of almost an antic type, with

little wit or humor of the higher order, much playfulness and jesting. They showed an ability to
handle the strands of a dramatic action so that it
arrived in full force at a foredetermined conclusion.
These qualities implied both merits and defects.
MacKaye's dependence upon stage tricks, upon
verbal facility, upon a forced comedy, is a defect.
Overcoming all defects is an imagination fecund in
power and majestic in scope. This is a rare and
valuable thing.

Inquiring more deeply into these plays, we find
that they reveal other interests of the playwright.
The first of these has to do with his conception of
the place of dramatic art in social life. This interest
leads him to identify the action of every play with
a social motive. Either his plot is symbolic and
suggestive of social meanings, or his dialogue is
pointed with social ideas, or both. As a rule this
social idealism of his is identified with a passion for
the theater as an agency of society. From his very
first work the young poet had a vision of the theater
not alone as a place of entertainment but as the
assembly room, the academy, the laboratory, the
temple of peoples. The theater was to him the most
effective agency of the free man's development into
his larger associations. It was the place at which
men could meet and exercise themselves on every
plane of their souls. MacKaye's conception of the
modern theater carries back to those dim origins
when the theater was ritual and worship; it carries

forward to the future when order and dignity and beauty will, we hope, be the marks of our common life.

This conception of the theater as social organism dominates all MacKaye's playwriting. It supplies the themes of many of his plays. He is constitutionally unable to consider life apart from the theater or the theater apart from life. The two are identical. As a result a course of dramatic action never presents itself simply. Life is a complex thing, a thing of interlocking circles, of varying planes. Therefore, the play must likewise be made up of interlocking circles and varying planes. So strong is the sense in him of the implications of a piece of imaginative work that his imagination ventures to include in the action all those who touch it and are influenced by it. Decidedly this is an interesting conception of dramatic structure. It is justifiable in the searcher for social formulas. It is justifiable also in the artist who would present a picture of truth through art. But it has disadvantages. One of these is that much of MacKaye's work gives the effect of confusion. At first view it would seem that he has not thought his way through to the end. He, of course, would answer that he has no wish to make simple that which is by nature complex. Nevertheless, this complexity of structure and thought is a positive barrier to the enjoyment of his plays.

In these considerations we have reason enough for

the unfortunate stage history of many of Mac-
Kaye's most ambitious plays. The successful
playwright must be dramatist and nothing else.
MacKaye has never been able to limit his interest to
the play. Beyond the play there were other interests upon which he could retire. He has never been
able to conceive of playwriting as the one and only
medium of expression of his ideas. I imagine there
are artists who are tongue-tied in other arts. I
imagine the artist exists who is so much in love with
the material of his own art that humanity itself
could go to the bonfire and he would be content,
given only that his work remained. MacKaye is not
such an artist. He has never yet forced his creative
imagination to the point of the inevitable once-and-
for-all. A certain lack of power of discrimination, a
certain powerlessness in rejection, is shown in different ways in different periods of his playwriting.
It remains characteristic of him throughout his
career.

By the year 1909 MacKaye had gone far enough
to reveal his qualities and to indicate his limitations.
We have already shown what these qualities and limitations were. We must now show how they guided
the succeeding steps in his career.

In this world art is the only thing that matters.
Art supplies the only true standard of values of
human effort and human life. Among the arts the
one that touches life most nearly and on the greatest

number of sides is the theater. Holding these views MacKaye's course was laid out for him. He must do all possible to make the theater live up to its high destiny. Though it masqueraded as an art, the theater was as a rule not in any respect an art. Art must again be given to the theater. Imagination must again crown the theater. Given a theater free, electric, incandescent, who can tell what it might not do? It might help to apply the standards of art even to life itself. No one can view the theater profoundly, as MacKaye has done, without seeing that the theater is itself an index of larger values and a larger truth. Enthusiasm for the theater is not enough. The theater implies communal organization. You cannot think in terms of the theater without thinking in terms of social bonds, disciplines and trends. In this sense the theater passion of these days—in Russia, in Germany, in the new countries of Central Europe as well as in America—is partly a youthful curiosity to see how the mechanism works, to tinker with it, and partly it is a millennial zeal. MacKaye has both this curiosity of experiment and this nostalgia for a society perfected by the tenets of art. He has these qualities with all the implied impatience, all the lack of balance, all the faith in shibboleths and patent nostrums. He differs from those who blow hot and cold by having his faith all the time.

With these ideals in view MacKaye proceeds to work for a new theater in America. He strives to

rebuild the theater from within. He strives to aug-
ment the professional theater with new movements
among amateurs. And as if to signalize his new
ideals he changes the forms of his own playwriting.
The young MacKaye now saw what so many others
have seen; that if he were to play his game to the
full he could not be writer alone. The stage was not
yet ready for the writers who composed their plays
solely as works of art. In order that it might be
made ready fundamental work must be done on the
structure of the theater itself. The structure of the
theater rests proximately upon the workers in the
theater, but its ultimate support is the patrons of
the theater. Brushing aside middlemen, the fetchers
and carriers of the theater, MacKaye addressed himself to the great public, to the audience which sup-
ports the theater.

Now there come to mind the words of kindly, clear-
thinking Charles Eliot Norton, upon reading that
commencement oration on "Imagination in Drama."
"Our American public," wrote Norton, "is an audience in which there are few who will listen to your
discourse, and fewer still to lay it to heart." Nevertheless, it was to this audience that MacKaye proceeded to address himself. If there was not such an
audience, then it must be created. MacKaye became
the prophet and ballyhoo man of the new American
theater in the open spaces. He spoke and wrote for
it through all the seasons of the year. He appeared
on platforms, in pulpits, and in college halls, from

one end of the country to the other. Always he appealed over the heads of the theater men to the people in the audience. A self-confident man, he forgot himself and his own interests in his passion for a new theater. He knew that even if his work succeeded the results would come too late to serve the purposes of his own art. I have talked with him about his plays and found him timid and hesitant, his mind abstracted and at a loss. Turn the conversation to the future of an American drama, to the vision of a new theater, and his eyes flash and words come in an eloquent torrent.

Without question MacKaye has paid a price for his faith and for his devotion to a great task. Men always pay a high price for anything that is worth having. The highest price that he has paid is in the quality of his own playwriting. His passion for stage reform has given to all his work an intense purposeful note.

MacKaye's theories of community drama are expressed in four volumes of essays and addresses entitled "The Playhouse and the Play, and Other Addresses Concerning the Theater and Democracy in America" (1909); "The Civic Theater, in Relation to the Redemption of Leisure: a Book of Suggestions" (1912); "A Substitute for War" (1915); and "Community Drama; Its Motive and Method of Neighborliness" (1917). There is no need to summarize the arguments of these books. These are well known. Viewing the arguments of these books narrowly and as a theater lover rather than as a social Utopian, I find in them much with which to agree, some ideas that compel reservations. If by community drama MacKaye means to throw the practice of the art of the theater over to the people, then I do not agree with him. The theater is not less a specialized art because it deals with humanity as a whole. Any attempt to introduce the bungling, political-minded compromises of common action into the theater can only end by killing the theater. I assume he does not mean that. If by community drama MacKaye implies, as I presume he does, a means of realizing the conceptions of creative artists, there being no other way of accomplishing this save by mobilizing the community, then I agree with him. But I cannot agree to substitute for the creative vision of the individual, the haphazard, chance commitments of group action. Nothing in the new art of the theater promises to dispense with the independent and responsible artist. However extended the theme may be, the artist must always pass it through his own soul.

Once MacKaye writes, "The civic theater idea, as a distinctive issue, implies the conscious awakening of a people to self-government in the activities of its leisure. To this end, organization of the arts of the theater, participation of the people in these arts (not mere spectatorship), a new resulting technique . . . these are the chief among its essentials." And again he calls the Civic Theater "the efficient instrument of the recreative arts of a community." This is well and good in so far as it applies to the theater as a social agency. It has little if anything to do with the theater as art. Art is not concerned with the people's leisure. It is very much concerned with the artist's crowded hour of intense life. As MacKaye's passion for democracy throws open to the artists new worlds of imagination he is serving the art of his time. I am sure he has no wish to withdraw the theater from the artist and give it into irresponsible hands.

When MacKaye's interest turned to the concrete features of theatrical organization there came a change in his playwriting. He dropped the poetic play entirely. His imagination now turned to those themes that lie adjacent to the current interests of his audience. In particular he began to conceive of a play as a part of the organic tradition of the race or nation that gives it birth. Here appears his interest in the American play as such. The three plays that follow "Sappho and Phaon" require little comment. These are "Mater, an American Study in Comedy" with incidental music by George W. Chadwick, produced by Henry Miller at San Francisco in 1908; "Anti-Matrimony, a Satirical Comedy," played by Henrietta Crossman in 1910 and 1911; and "Tomorrow," played by Frank Reicher in Philadelphia in 1913. Of these the first two were comedies of a forced and purposeful humor, workmanlike but dull. The third deals with the author's Utopian visions.

With "The Scarecrow" and "Yankee Fantasies" we come to a new and more significant phase of our author's playwriting. The latter, published in 1912, is a series of five one-act plays variously composed and produced. These are "Chuck, an Orchard Fantasy" (produced 1912); "Gettysburg, a Woodshed Commentary" (produced 1912); "The Antick, a Wayside Sketch" (produced 1915); "The Cat Boat, a Fantasy for Music" (produced 1921); and "Sam Average, a Silhouette" (produced 1912). Both "The Scarecrow" and the "Yankee Fantasies" display that playful quality of the imagination and leaning toward the grotesque that are characteristic of MacKaye's work.

The desire to create a drama that is distinctively American is as old as our stage. In recent years it has come to be fashionable to scoff at this desire. It is said, and with reason, that we should be willing to accept imaginative beauty from every source. Unquestionably this is true as far as applies to the production. But there is nothing for the American writer to do but write American plays. This has nothing to do with his own will and little to do with patriotism or with those external controls that bind a man to his parish, right or wrong. The urge to write a native play is the same urge that attaches a man to his own soil. It is fundamental to all art that the artist shall turn his hand to the materials that lie adjacent to him, not because these materials are better than other materials, but because these are the only materials he has. By the handling of these, will he, nill he, is his mastery displayed and known. True imaginative creation is an intimate thing. It works in secret with forces that are of the fabric of life. There is no other material with which an artist can deal than that which has passed through his own experience. How futile it is then to suppose that true imagination can go to far places for its inspiration. How can a man handle the symbols of the distant if he is helpless before the nearer symbols? The urge to create an American drama is not a political and nationalistic matter at all. It is not inconsistent with an international view. It arises from the inner necessities of the artist's own temperament. Mackaye was never on solider ground than when upholding the idea of an American substance in plays.

"The Scarecrow, or The Glass of Truth: A Tragedy of the Ludicrous," was completed in 1907. It was first produced by the Harvard Dramatic Club, December 7, 1909; later in New York by H. B. Harris at the Garrick Theater, January 17, 1911, and produced in England by Muriel Pratt at the Theater Royal, Bristol, November 30, 1914. Without question this is the most significant of MacKaye's dramatic works, both as a play and on account of the ideas that govern its composition. From Mackaye's Preface to the published edition of the play we learn that the fable of the play is derived from Hawthorne's "Feathertop," a tale in "Mosses from an Old Manse," which relates "how

Mother Rigby, a reputed witch of old New England days, converted a corn-patch scarecrow into the semblance of a fine gentleman of the period; how she dispatched this semblance to 'play its part in the great world, where not one man in a hundred, she affirmed, was gifted with more real substance than itself'; how then the scarecrow, while paying court to pretty Polly Gookin, the rosy, simpering daughter of Justice Gookin, discovered its own image in a looking-glass, returned to Mother Rigby's cottage and dissolved into its original elements."

Such in outline is Hawthorne's story. It would seem that this story could not be improved. This is not Mackaye's opinion. In the handling of this story he must needs modify it to a new, or at least, to his own view. In Hawthorne's story we have a theme of universality and simplicity, one of the native chunks of imagination chipped by Hawthorne from the New England rock. In treating this theme MacKaye displays that irrepressible, jocose spirit we have noticed before. He is unwilling to view a simple theme simply, even when it is handed down to him from a master. He even admits "many radical departures from the conception and treatment of Hawthorne." Naturally there is no law to compel the author to dramatize Hawthorne literally, but if he takes the theme of a great writer, he must recognize that any changes he makes in the handling of the original will call for and receive very close scrutiny. In Hawthorne's romance the scare-

crow is an imaginative epitome or symbol of human
charlatanism. Coxcombry and charlatanism are the
butt of the satire. MacKaye believes that the theme
of the scarecrow that became a man is susceptible to
a wider development. Indeed, he indicates that
Hawthorne himself had had intimations of this wider
meaning which he had failed to cultivate, and he
quotes in proof the last sentence in which Mother
Rigby exclaims: "Poor Feathertop! I could easily
give him another chance and send him forth again
to-morrow. But no! His feelings are too tender—
his sensibilities too deep." From this last sentence
MacKaye seeks to draw the conclusion that Hawthorne had not grasped the theme fully, that it is a
theme in which pity and sentiment have a strong
part. For my part I should draw the contrary conclusion, that Hawthorne had grasped the theme
fully, and that with his marvelous artistic tact he
had decided upon the limits of his treatment. These
limits lay within the bounds of irony. For MacKaye
there are no such limits. He does not accept irony.
The words that end Hawthorne's story serve as the
starting point of MacKaye's play. Says MacKaye,
"The element of human sympathy is here substituted
for that of irony, as criterion of the common absurdity of mankind." The play becomes a *tragedy
of the ludicrous*.

In these words quoted from the Preface to the play
we have Mackaye's commentary on its temper. In
the opinion of this critic Hawthorne's story has

been sentimentalized. In introducing human sympathy into the play MacKaye introduces something that has nothing to do with the case. Human sympathy is not a criterion of absurdity. Human sympathy is not a criterion of anything. Pleasant and important enough in its place, it is certainly not an instrument in art. When the artist takes sympathy or pity into his hand, judgment fails. To the extent that a man is shown to be worthy of pity he is shown to be something that he is not of himself but only is in the mind of the observer. The matter is quite other with satire or irony. To the extent that a man is shown to be incongruous, false, insincere, he is shown either in himself or in his relation with other men. Pity does not exist of itself; incongruity does. Irony is the art of observing an objective incongruity and keeping it poised objectively. But the eye of pity cannot be trusted to see nor the mind of pity to judge.

With the exceptions here set forth, the dramatization of Hawthorne's story is expert and effective though fantastic and over-adorned. Now again in plot construction MacKaye allies himself with the school of intrigue and forced situations. It would have been better for Dickon had the author not been so well acquainted with the jestings and chop logic of the Elizabethan clowns. The play is called a "tragedy of the ludicrous." Ironically enough, MacKaye's "tragedy" touches the emotions less than did Hawthorne's irony. The action depends too much upon tricks, too much upon externals of character and deportment to engage the sympathy. In my judgment the play fails of absolute greatness but it will outlive many successes of smaller magnitude.

MacKaye returned to an American theme many years later in "Washington, the Man Who Made Us." This play was produced by Walter Hampden on Washington's Birthday, 1920; later at the Lyric Theater, New York, March 1, 1920. It was called by the author a "ballad play."

In developing the action of "Washington, the Man Who Made Us," MacKaye discards entirely the biographical and chronological method. It is his idea that Washington, the man of history, has passed out of the confines of personality. He has become a figure of legend and is woven into the fabric of the country. Properly to present him, therefore, as he is to-day, the author employs all those factors of folk myth by which the deeds and character of a great man are kept alive among men. These are ballads, anecdotes, pictures of action, songs and folk ceremonials. In employing these to make up his play, MacKaye returns to his favorite plan of prologues and epilogues, inductions and transitional actions. The play is broken up into fifteen episodes set within prologue and epilogue. And each one of these is connected with the following by a transitional song, ballad, or dance. The intent of the author is manifest. It is to show Washington embedded in the life of his countrymen. Needless to say, the idea is more interesting as a conception than it is in execution. The figure of Washington seldom emerges from the cloak of ballad and ceremonial by which it is surrounded. And though the idea that a great man lives eternally in the generations that follow him is impressive, the entire work has the air of frivolity and inconsequence of a torchlight procession.

III

The narrow confines of the professional theater could not long contain a worker of the resourcefulness and energy of Percy MacKaye. He must either broaden the practice of the theater or he must go outside the theater entirely. He did both and herein lie the activities from which his lasting fame will be derived. Within the theater MacKaye early began to contrive a larger synthesis of the arts than had usually been permitted on our little stages. This began when he called into collaboration in his compositions practitioners of the arts of painting, sculpture, and music. MacKaye has been a promoter in selling the theater to artists who had before found in it no outlet for their talents. His dependence upon other artists began in 1906 when he called into coöperation Barry Faulkner as scene designer and F. S. Converse for incidental music for his "Jeanne d'Arc." Since then the list of artists collaborating with him reads like a roll call of the foremost artists of the day. These include among musicians Prof. A. A. Stanley for "Sappho and Phaon"; Geo. W. Chadwick for "Mater"; F. S. Converse for "The Immigrant"; "Sinbad, the Sailor," "Sanctuary," and "St. Louis"; William Furst for "A Thousand Years Ago"; Reginald de Koven for "The Canterbury Pilgrims, an Opera," and "Rip Van Winkle"; Walter Damrosch and Charles A. Stafford for "The Gloucester Pageant"; Arthur Farwell for "Caliban" and "The Evergreen Tree"; Clarence Dickinson for "The Roll Call"; Harry Barnhart for "The Will of Long." Among artists of design MacKaye's collaborators include Maxfield Parrish for "Sappho and Phaon"; Arnold Genthe for "Anti-Matrimony"; "Washington, The Man Who Made Us," "Sanctuary," and "The Roll Call"; Robert Edmond Jones for "Washington," "Caliban," "The Evergreen Tree," and "The Roll Call"; Joseph Urban for "Sinbad, the Sailor" and "Caliban"; John W. Alexander for "The Pittsburgh Pageant"; Joseph Lindon Smith for "Sanctuary" and "St. Louis"; Richard Ordynski for "Caliban." The collaborators from the arts of acting, dancing and production are too numerous to mention. These lists are impressive and significant. In a period in which the theater was enlarging its resources they go far to justify MacKaye's title to greatness.

Comparatively little of this coördination of the arts found a place on the professional stage. Among the dramatic forms of twenty years ago the only one

which demanded a synthesis of the arts was grand
opera. But grand opera is far too convention-bound
to offer promise of becoming the supreme art of the
theater. Too many objections to grand opera as an
art form stand in the way. One may grant, as many
critics do, that the highest criterion of the art of the
theater lies in music without granting that grand
opera achieves these standards. Grand opera is
indeed in essential opposition to the true spirit of
music generally applied. It is a form of mechanical assembling. The most sensitive artists of the
theater have long been aware of the need of subjecting their art to a regimen as exact and intensive
as that of music. They have not been able to convince themselves that grand opera is anything more
than a dignified parody of the dramatic, sometimes
impressive, sometimes sublime, and often ridiculous.

As an artist MacKaye was aware of the demand
for a synthesis of the arts. As an experimenter he
was willing to take a chance with grand opera. In
fact he took four chances. None of these succeeded,
for very good reasons. The music provided by his
collaborators was not adequate to carry the works in
the sense in which grand opera is now understood;
that is, great or appealing music applied to puerile
dialogue and a fable that is twaddle. MacKaye
lacked the strength—naturally—to raise by his own
powers these works to a higher level of synthetic
creation.

MacKaye's first experiment in opera was "The

Immigrants, a Lyric Drama," written as a commission for the Boston Opera House, the music being composed by Frederick S. Converse. The work was never produced. In the preface to this play MacKaye calls attention to the fact that traditions of opera have been handed down from times when "pure romance, or fairy fancy, or courtly intrigue, or symbolic mythology" held sway. He decides "that the uses of opera in English need not be confined to a mere rendering into English words of the imaginative concepts of foreign artists, nor to imaginative concepts which are themselves aloof from the passionate problems of our modern life, but that those uses ought to be extended even more widely to increase the creative opportunities and creative works of English speaking artists of the theater in expressing the realities of human passion and aspiration which cry out for expression now and here in our midst." Without questioning the validity of the author's ideas, it cannot be claimed that he succeeded in his task. Leaving the music aside—the writer knows nothing of this—the lyric drama composed by MacKaye was in the last degree trite and mechanical. It was written in an antique form. The intrigue is without distinction. The theme is the American assimilation of the foreigners, but the play never grasps the subject. The author's view of America is sentimental. The lyrics are of the style of the light opera of fifty years ago. The hero is very good; the villain is very bad.

Like "The Immigrants," the following opera, "Sinbad, the Sailor," called "A Lyric Phantasy," was also written for the Boston Opera House. The war prevented its production. MacKaye next prepared "The Canterbury Pilgrims" for music composed by Reginald de Koven and the opera was produced for seven performances at the Metropolitan Opera House. His last work in this style was "Rip Van Winkle," a folk-opera in three acts, with music by Reginald de Koven, produced by the Chicago Opera Company in Chicago and New York, January, 1920.

MacKaye's experience proved that nothing could be accomplished in enriching the resources of the stage by surrendering to the domain of music as now administered in opera. There were, however, other resources and agencies of the imagination by which the theater could be enriched. These applied to the theater the standards of rhythm, color and design. It is generally assumed that the creative impulse of the arts of design was first applied to the modern theater by Gordon Craig. In some of the formalized types of theatrical art these arts had always had a strong influence, in the ballet, the dance, in the puppet play, in the forms roughly covered by the term Commedia dell' arte. But these had almost expired in the world of false face that grew up in the nineteenth century. With the opening of the new century there came a renascence that carried forward the imaginative potentialities of design to points undreamed of in the previous history of the stage. The growth of this movement is by many considered the most important event in the history of the modern theater. The artists of mass and design and color came to the stage with new enthusiasm. They had a new world to work in. Design had become dramatic. Movement had entered into design. The reverberations of daily discoveries extended not only throughout the theater but into the studios as well. The designers were remaking the theater but the theater was having its revenge. The theater was introducing new dimensions into design. We are interested chiefly, of course, in what happened to the theater. With heads turned by the grand new world they lived in, the designers began to set up extravagant claims. They began to de-personalize the theater, to take language from it, even to relieve it of plot, theme, and sequence. They began to promise the day when the playwright would disappear. Plays would be "studies" in mood, color, circumstance; plays would be grotesques, nocturnes. In all this there was some truth and much stimulation. There was also some falsehood and overstatement.

Much of this hardly touches MacKaye at all except to the extent that his acquisitive brain, always looking around for new worlds to conquer, pounced upon the new effects of the designers and proceeded to use them for his own purposes. In one respect he never surrendered to their view. He had no intention of relinquishing his place as playwright to a draftsman, a sculptor, or a draper. He was willing to employ the resources provided by them. He was too much a language lover to dispense with words; but he was willing to string his words in a different pattern, and to seek his dramatic pattern in the studios of the designers. In two cases the works so composed were made for the professional theater. By far the greater number of such works were composed for production outside the professional theater by community organizations expressly created for the production of masques and pageant rituals.

"A Thousand Years Ago, A Romance of the Orient," was produced with Henry E. Dixey and Rita Jolivet, December 1, 1913. The story of Turandot, Princess of China, has a long history. The old Persian tale, "Turandot" was taken over into Italian comedy by Carlo Gozzi, and thence adapted by Friedrich Schiller to the German stage. This work was recast by Karl Voellmoeller for Reinhardt and the modern German form was translated into English by Jethro Bithell. It was this translation that MacKaye was called upon to adapt to the American stage. MacKaye is careful to indicate that while his work refers back to these sources, it is in effect an original composition.

The task undertaken by MacKaye in this comedy was an ambitious one. For the substance of his fable and for the manner of its treatment he went back to different sources. The substance is derived from the Persian tale, the manner is a free adaptation to modern conditions and stagecraft of the resources of the Italian Commedia dell' arte. The chief male character of the play, Capacomico, is entirely MacKaye's. He it is who provides the unity of plot and sentiment. More significantly it is he who, as the spokesman of the author, makes the direct appeal to the modern audience for that cessation of disbelief, for that fine fervor of romance, that it is the chief aim of the author to awaken in his audience. There is, in fact, no law that would forbid the Commedia dell' Arte to invade old China. The universality of the stuff of dreams is a favorite article of the author's creed. The attempt to apply the formal-informality of the Italian method to the materials of a Chinese imagination is undertaken with all of MacKaye's daring and fecund fancy.

When we come to the consideration of MacKaye's work on the masque we reach his most important contribution to the drama of our time. MacKaye was not the first to present masques in this country. He did, however, carry the masque farther than it has gone in this or any other country in our time. MacKaye's masques must be distinguished from the pageants which have been popular during the same period. The masque as a rule deals with generalized and sometimes allegorical symbols. The pageant, on the other hand, deals with a progressive historical action. In one respect both the pageant and the masque as now practiced are similar. They represent the tendency of the theater to break its bounds, to incorporate into its action large numbers of those who were before spectators, to diversify its structure and to bring the subject home to the simple interests of people. These are forms which find their greatest expression in the play spirit of crowds.

When we consider the essential nature of the masque, important differences of opinion should be noted. On the one side there are those who assume that drama is the expression of a community aspiration and that, therefore, the masque is one of the highest forms for the release of this aspiration. On the other side there are those who do not believe that society in itself has any such aspiration. They hold that in so far as this aspiration exists it has been implanted by individual men and women of vision, and that the ultimate achievement is always the result of individual initiative and administration. People in general have 'the play spirit, they are gregarious and sportive. But the people cannot create a work of dramatic art. To assume for the people en masse the possession of creative powers would be to falsify all that we know of the creative process. Society of itself never has made anything beautiful and never has tried to make anything beautiful. It has never perfected anything. Whatever beauty or perfection is achieved is the work of an individual. It comes because of the labors of a man or a woman. MacKaye has never made his own position absolutely clear in this respect. He speaks often of the desire of society for expression, once of "the desire of a democracy, consistently to seek expression through a drama *of* and *by* the people, not merely *for* the people." But it is not without significance that the New York which MacKaye says is anxious for expression has not even a place in which to express itself, unless we can say that it expresses itself in ball grounds and boxing arenas and the Great White Way. The most pessimistic thought that one can permit himself is the thought that Boyle's Thirty Acres and the New York Yankee Stadium truly represent our people.

In some respects this question is theoretic and irrelevant. But it has its aspects of pertinence. Let us distinguish once and for all between those things that can be done by means of popular coöperation and political arrangement and those things that can be done only by a man clothed with authority. We tell ourselves that we can be governed by the methods of accommodation. But we cannot find truth by a referendum or create beauty in a caucus.

The best justification of the community masque lies in the fact that it is a training school for the creative dramatic artist in handling material not yet adapted to stage use and on a larger scale than any heretofore imagined. Incidentally, the masque provides good entertainment for the crowd, and a means of getting together for creditable purposes. But nothing accomplished in the masque so far even approaches the precision and harmony of art. Even the best masques—and in these high imagination and

skill have been lavished—have been but bungling
tentatives toward an art that has hardly yet been
glimpsed. The difficulties that lie in the way of this
super-dramatic art are such as to make it very difficult even to prophesy what the future may bring.
The problems of sight are far more easily handled
than the problems of sound. If this art of the hundred thousand is to achieve itself, there must be some
cruel rejections or some rich accretions in the resources of the art as they are at present. The graces
of language are valueless. Even music is under a
heavy handicap. Personality is dwarfed and insignificant. The theme must be the simplest. Sometime amplifiers and radio will join to bring sound to
the hundred thousand as electric light brings vision.
But this is not yet.

It is not my purpose to sketch the future of this
magnified art form of the theater. I am impelled
only to apply the work already done to some absolute standard and to point out the difficulties in the
way of the development of this art. No one living
has done more than MacKaye for this super-art form
of the people's theater. And yet MacKaye is bound
to forms of expression that have shown themselves to
be utterly futile in production. He is a poet of
remarkable facility of phrase. His great masques
are built upon a framework of literature. This
means simply that they are built upon a structure
that is out of sight and out of mind of the audience.
The use of megaphones to magnify speech has so

far only introduced an element of the grotesque. MacKaye has been quick to seize every new expedient and to give it imaginative use. The effects of lighting, of massing, of chorals, the use of great puppets have been justified in his work. Nevertheless, he would be the first to admit that everything achieved so far is but the first draft of an experiment toward a new form.

MacKaye began his work in the masque by writing the Prologue to Louis Evan Shipman's "St. Gaudens' Masque," presented at Cornish, June 23, 1905. Four years later, "The Canterbury Pilgrims" was expanded and presented with fifteen hundred people as The Gloucester (Massachusetts) Pageant. There followed in 1910 "A Masque of Labor," projected with John W. Alexander for Pittsburgh, Pa.; and "Sanctuary, A Bird Masque," presented with a distinguished group of collaborators at Meriden, N. H., September 12, 1913. From this time forward MacKaye's work in the masque falls into two orders: first, that order in which he seeks to express his vision of a new society in a form of imaginative beauty; second, that order in which he seeks to create for the use of social groups a ritual of common life and aspiration.

The first order, expressly called "Masque," attaches itself to the Jacobean form of masque and more distantly with the Greek forms of drama and with opera. "I have called it a Masque," writes the author, "because—like other works so named in the past—it is a dramatic work of symbolism involving in its structure pageantry, poetry and the dance." To this class belong "St. Louis, a Civic Masque," presented at Forest Park, St. Louis, with seventy-five hundred citizens of St. Louis, before half a million spectators, May 28–June 11, 1914, and "Caliban By the Yellow Sands," devised and written to commemorate the tercentenary of the death of Shakespeare, produced in New York and Boston, May–July, 1916. In the Masque of St. Louis the author employs the events of history, half legendary, half factual, of a middle western community to create a magnified allegory of the community life of man on the globe. In "Caliban" he returns to the theme of his first enthusiasms and dreams, the theater. "The art of Prospero," he writes, "I have conceived as the art of Shakespeare in its universal scope, that many-visioned art of the theater which, age after age, has come to liberate the imprisoned imagination of mankind from the fetters of brute force and ignorance." Caliban is "the passionate child-curious part of us all, groveling close to his aboriginal origins, yet groping up and staggering . . . toward that serener plane of pity and love, reason and disciplined will, where Miranda and Prospero commune with Ariel and his spirit."

In "St. Louis" and "Caliban" we have the art of the masque reaching its highest point. These represented the work of a single artist handling vast forces of men and materials for dramatic effect. Though they brought into play large organizations they were not in the structural sense community affairs as MacKaye employs that term. They showed the community under the artistic generalship of a man. But he dreamed, as we have seen, of the community supplying its own initiative and creating its own formulas of group action. MacKaye was nothing if not consistent. Imaginative artist himself, he conceived that the highest point of his art would be reached when he could surrender his own prerogative. Studying social groups he found that they were bound together by customs, habit, atavistic memories which found expression in folk rituals. These folk rituals provided the first sketches for the greater solidifying of the race in its movement forward. As a servant of the community he began to set down these rituals, to perpetuate them for the use of groups. Here the activity of the man goes definitely outside the limits of the theater and I shall not seek to follow him save to enumerate the leading rituals. These include:

"The New Citizenship, a Civic Ritual" devised for places of public meeting in America (New York and St. Louis, 1916); "The Evergreen Tree, A Masque for Christmas," for Community Singing and Acting (1917); "The Roll Call, a Masque of the Red Cross," for Community Acting and Singing (1918); "The Will of Song, a Dramatic Service" of Community Singing (1919); "The Pilgrim and the Book," a Dramatic Service of the Bible, for use in

Churches. The logic of the situation had drawn the author from the participation of large numbers of people, to the participation of all members of the community. The community had swallowed its theater.

IV

The Great War put a punctuation point in the creative work of many careers. To some it meant the placing of the final stop. To some it meant a colon or semi-colon. There were few who were able to continue the sentence begun before the war without either a comma or a dash. MacKaye was not one of these. After the first enthusiasm and confusion MacKaye was able to discipline his forces better than he had done for many years. He was the same man, with the same visions, the same tendency to break into verbal and mental spindrift, but he was better anchored.

In 1920 MacKaye was appointed American fellow in Poetry and Drama at Miami University at Oxford, Ohio. He had always been interested in the backgrounds of his country. Hitherto the folk element had come to him filtered through the hard crust of an overlying civilization or in a thin stream of literature and legend. Now he was able to drink of the primitive life of America from a living spring. Oxford is in the Ohio Valley. Just across the river in the mountains of Kentucky, the Virginias and Tennessee there persist, almost as if insulated from

the currents of progress around, the original pioneers of the country. They are of English, Scotch,
and Irish extraction; their schooling has been of the
most elementary type. They are inbred. In the
century in which they have lived in the mountains
they have taken on some qualities, lost others. Nevertheless, they constitute to-day a living storehouse
of tradition, a storehouse which will soon be exhausted as civilization beats its way into the mountains. It is this storehouse that MacKaye tapped
when in 1922 he and his wife made a sojourn among
the mountaineers.

In this essay I am interested in MacKaye, the
playwright, only incidentally in the explorer into
folk myths. MacKaye proceeded to make himself
the master of the language, legend and history of
these mountain people. His records of speech forms,
ballads, jests, stories, myths, are almost unbelievably
full. They are all indexed and cross-indexed for
future use. They will be a museum of folk speech
and folk lore. He is now busily engaged in dressing
up for future consumption many of his records.
Some of this material is appropriate to be put into
dramatic form. He has sketched a series of mountaineer plays, of which two have appeared, "Napo-
leon Crossing the Rockies," and "This Fine, Pretty
World." Few plays of recent years have won the
critical praise given to this latter play, yet it failed
in production. It failed with the audience on account of those qualities that have marked MacKaye's

work from the beginning, lack of discretion, of selective power, lack of the ability to assess the fine line of popular approval. Under these external traits the play has all the qualities of popularity and many of the qualities of greatness. It is more objective than any other of MacKaye's works. Imaginatively it belongs with the great works of joyous fancy of this and other centuries, with Synge, with Mark Twain at his best, with Cervantes and Le Sage. It has nothing to bar it from this comradeship save only a riot of language which places it almost beyond the understanding of even the most intrepid of diggers and delvers. With all its difficulty the language has a haunting beauty of phrasing and sound.

Percy MacKaye has all the defects of his virtues, the virtues of his defects. No man can be all things. He has tried to be all things. I hold for him that he is possessed of the most fecund imagination in the American stage of to-day. Against him I hold that this very imagination, this superfluity of energy, this belief that he can set all things right has led him into activities that have ill served his cause. He has surrendered to the fallacy that by lecturing the people he can create a people's art. With much of the patience of greatness he has much of the rashness too. He would see all in his own lifetime.

The work of Percy MacKaye symbolizes the course of American drama during a generation. With half the energy, and with twice the judgment he could have accomplished ten times as much. And so could our theater. But when we have said this we have said nothing. For judgment demands experience, and Percy MacKaye and men like him supply the data by which judgment is made. We know now, better than we knew when MacKaye started, that the theater will not be remade by creating institutions. In the strictest sense the theater is not an institution at all. It is an ever renewed creation of men of genius. If the vision remains the theater lives; without the vision the theater perishes. So we prove nothing when we say that Percy MacKaye lacks selection, that the gift of rejection fails him. It is quite true that not everything that is thrown off from the heated brain is artistic imagination. If it were then our dreams, our fears, our fancies would be imagination. But when MacKaye began to write it was not selection that was called for: there was nothing to select from. What our theater called for was creation, fecund and without limits. The base metal of our life must be transmuted. Creation is prodigal. We shall see that others who come after have a finer sense of discrimination, a judgment more keenly poised. The possession of these gifts ·implies merit in them without question. It implies also, and this must not be forgotten, the existence of stores of material quarried from the living rock ready for their selective hand. No man has done more to quarry this material and make ready the way than Percy MacKaye.

The pioneer rôle which he has been elected to play has made MacKaye always conscious of himself as personality and artist, conscious of himself in relation to the drama and in relation to his age. This thing which might be called subjectiveness, is, in fact, objectiveness. This subjective-objectiveness (if you please) is shown in the Preface to "A Garland to Sylvia," written fourteen years after the play was begun. It is displayed in the play itself, the first play he composed. The young poet sees himself in a new and terrifying rôle. He is a poet, that is, a "maker" who would be a dramatist. What does he face? To what guidance shall he turn? There is no better guide than the greatest of all, Shakespeare. And the young poet writes, "I saw portrayed before me mentally—first a young *dramatist*, groping in the mists of his imagination, confronted and confounded by that personality of his own which he had unwittingly but inevitably wrought into the character of his play . . . secondly, a young *man* groping in the mystery of our life."

This is the key to the exploits of a rich and busy life.

CHAPTER II

THE PLAYWRIGHT UNBOUND: EUGENE O'NEILL

I

It is now only ten years since the first of Eugene O'Neill's plays was published. His first play was produced eight years ago. He is still a young man. What place he may occupy in the annals of our stage, with what forms of dramatic composition his name will be associated, it is still too early to say. It would be a poor service to the man himself to treat as if it were complete a career that has just begun. Anything written here must therefore be considered but a preliminary survey of an early phase of a career that may go on through many years and many phases. And yet were he never to write another play, O'Neill's place in the history of our drama would be secure. It is assured not alone by the qualities of the plays that he has produced, but even more by the fact that he has brought to playwriting an artistic integrity, a disciplined craftsmanship that have established playwriting in America among the fine arts.

Such an achievement as this, flowering in the nox-

ious air of America's post-war spiritual slump, must
have had deep roots. No combination of chances,
no mere "assembling" of personal and social factors
would explain the vitality and validity of this phenomenon that appeared full grown in the American
theater. Certain factors of this phenomenon appear
in the hereditary and environmental resources to
which the playwright was born. By all odds the
most significant factor lies in that mysterious element of character by which the resources available
were intuitively weighed and judged, discarded or
appropriated. Eugene O'Neill is debtor to his heredity and to his environment for a rich endowment;
the nature of the endowment is but a measure of the
manner in which he has magnified the talents which
have been given him.

Like Percy MacKaye, Eugene O'Neill was born
to the theater. The association of his father, James
O'Neill, with the sensational success, "The Count of
Monte Christo," has made us of a later generation
forget that he was an actor of all-round training and
skill, playing his hundreds of parts on the stage
when to do so meant not to serve the metropolis alone
but the length and breadth of the country. Through
his father Eugene O'Neill has that Celtic strain in
him from which has come a large share of the creative dramatic imagination of the English-speaking
stage in the last two centuries. In his young years
he traveled with his father on tour, and at the moment that he was beginning as a playwright he rep-

resented one of his father's last theatrical ventures. It is idle to deny that this association with the practical theater is important to the playwright. Popularize the theater as we will, adopt it into our society, it still remains a secret society, a world within a world. O'Neill had to undergo neither the extreme illusion nor the extreme disillusion that are involved in lack of acquaintance with the stage. In his hereditary endowment O'Neill was blessed by the fates.

What, now, of the environment of the young playwright? Again the fates were kind. Eugene O'Neill appeared in the American theater at precisely the moment when the stranglehold of the old theater was released by the persistent blows of the insurgents and experimenters. Partly by fortuity, because he was too young, partly by wisdom, because he was too wary, he took no part in the confusions of the early campaigns for a new ordering in the theater. The experimental theater of fifteen years ago was just that and nothing more. It was experimental, inexpert, ill equipped. As a rule it was built and managed by men and women who did not know the stage, who were supported in their efforts largely by their enthusiasm, their ignorance, and their insight. With all its faults it had one inestimable advantage. It was not mortgaged to preconceptions. Among many notions that were brash and sophomoric there were some that would not fade in the wash. These were the idea of the stage as an instrumentality of a creative impulse, a clear conception that this creative impulse employs money for its ends but cannot be employed by money, a disrespect for awkward stage traditions and the hocus-pocus of stage wizardry. By the time O'Neill appeared on the scene, little instruments were ready for him. They were the keys upon which he could play. He did not have to try his new notes on the wheezy old instrument of the professional stage.

Up to this point, in outlining those elements of fortuity, of good luck, if you please, that enter into the makeup of the O'Neill creative machine, we have been fair enough. But any review that lays emphasis alone on the external factors of O'Neill's career fails to do justice to the qualities of character and decision possessed by the man himself. Not the least index of this character lies in the intuitive reactions of the young man, long before he became a playwright, toward the established institutions of society. Between that day when Percy MacKaye spoke on "Imagination in Drama" before his commencing classmates at Harvard, and the day when Eugene O'Neill shook the dust of Princeton from his shoes and went out on dustless lanes to seek life in strange harbors, only ten years had passed. But there was a generation, a long generation crowded with revolt and disillusion and iconoclasm, between the worlds of the two young men. Whereas Percy MacKaye began his career with the support of schools and employing the resources of the classic theater, O'Neill began his career by throwing overboard both school and theater. MacKaye began as classicist and became revolutionary, projected himself into the mêlée, and in swinging the sword lost sometimes the skill of the craftsman. O'Neill kept himself serenely aloof from the machines, contrivances and policies of a world he already despised, and protected his artist's fingers. In the confusion of the world around him many men were losing their bearings entirely and were scattering their energies. Young O'Neill had no disposition to be a dweller in a social maternity hospital. He settled the matter by running away from all institutions, and he ran away to the quietest place he could find, to the place where the hand of man makes no changes, and on the face of which man leaves no records. He ran away to sea.

The story of O'Neill's *wander-jahre* has often been told. There was in him the lure of the places "beyond the horizon," controlled by a something hard and disciplined and ironic. I quote the words of E. A. Baughan in the *Fortnightly Review* for 1923: "He tried his hand at all kinds of occupations; a clerk in a New York office, a gold prospector in Honduras (where he fell ill of fever), and an assistant manager of a theatrical company. The call of the sea came to him from Conrad's '*The Nigger of the Narcissus*' and he shipped on board a Norwegian barque bound for Buenos Aires. He remained in the Argentina for eighteen months, made a voyage to

South Africa and back, and finally returned to
New York on a British tramp. Afterwards he
shipped for several voyages as able seaman on the
American Line. Work as a dock laborer and as an
actor and newspaper reporter finally culminated in
an attack of tuberculosis. The attack gave him
leisure for setting down his experiences in the form
of dramas."

When we come to study this record we are struck
both by what he had missed and by what he had
gained. He had missed books and second-hand
things. He had missed the confusions of criticism,
the imperatives of definitions. He had missed the
hurrying of little men back and forth with blueprints
in their hands. He had missed the loud-voiced men
(and women) who drag their little boxes to public
places to harangue idle crowds. Instead of these he
had gained something. I was going to say that he
gained Reality, except that Reality is but another
of those terms by which criticism begs the question
of life. Reality is but an attribute; it is not a thing
in itself. Who could imagine an artist going out
after Reality any more than after bricks? What
O'Neill went forth for and found was a knowledge of
Pain and a vision of the magnitudes of the world.
The days and nights on the open sea, among the
beach combers, in the taverns of Buenos Aires and
New York and London, the weary round of ribaldry
of common men, had so brought home pain to him
that its odor had become no longer a sensation but a

suffusion. And pain is the little brother of beauty. No man who has not had sensitive nerves beaten down by the weights of fatuous, only half-deceived vulgarity, could have the keen, almost tragic sense of beauty that O'Neill has, could present the impression of spirit, stunted and gnarled but aspiring, as he does.

When he came to playwriting he had eight years of world-wandering behind him. He had literally gone to school to the world. World-wandering means not alone meeting up with strange and hard characters. It means meeting up with yourself. It means loneliness, the opportunity to test one's soul. O'Neill had gone through all that, and then as if to counterbalance the more lusty reaches of his experience he had spent six months hand in hand with sickness and face to face with death. More than any other American playwright, O'Neill has been absorbed into the reality of life, not in the form of problems but in the form of moral and personal stresses. To him the sea always took first place. Behind the sea loomed up other realities no less majestic, no less inspiring. He started to write plays with no vague imitative itch to do something in the theater. Much writing of plays is like much art of other types. It is undertaken as a compensation for the life that has passed the artist by. The impulse is nostalgia. It is not so that great works of art are created. Great works of imagination come from an overflowing of life. The creative vitality is so strong

that what we call reality is pallid.   Only the vision
of the artist is real, a reality so intense, distilled,
that it turns into a super-reality.   Here we have all
the difference between being stage-struck and world-
struck.   O'Neill was world-struck.

II

Eugene O'Neill was born October **16, 1888,** in
New York City.   At the time these lines are written
he is in his thirty-seventh year.   His productive
period has all been comprised in the last ten years.
In this period he has written about fifty plays.   Of
these about one half are short plays, the others are
full length plays.   Of the plays written, say thirty-
five have had some kind of production.   Of those
produced, twenty have had some kind of success.
The movement and tempo of his career have been
healthy and ascendant.   Beginning deliberately, he
has moved to a crescendo of his powers.   By all
means his greatest productiveness has been during
the last five years.   Following the production of
"Beyond the Horizon," O'Neill has composed fifteen
or sixteen works.   Of these all but one or two have
been produced.   On the side of productiveness alone
O'Neill has already set a new standard in our theater.
And this energy of production has been accompanied
by no lowering of imaginative force.

Few playwrights owe less to the conventions of
the professional theater than does O'Neill.   He has
always made it a point to run athwart conventions

or to create new ones. As a consequence he has had
to work things out for himself through experiment
and failure. It was natural that O'Neill should start
by writing one-act plays, because this was the only
form his prentice hand could handle. He has to see
a theme clearly before he begins to write. His mind
strives for simplicity. The one-act play as O'Neill
began to write it is the simplest of all dramatic
forms. It deals with a tabloid situation, a single
phase or aspect of an action. There is no variation
of space or time. As a rule the action is comprised
within a period between the rising and the falling
of the curtain. During six years of intense labor
O'Neill did not succeed in breaking through the
narrow limitations of the one-act form.

In 1914 there was published in Boston, at the
expense of the author himself, a volume of short
plays entitled, "Thirst and Other Plays." In addition to the title play the volume contained "The
Web," "Warnings," "Fog," and "Recklessness." It
is not on record that any of these plays have been
produced, nor do the plays give evidence of the
artistic qualities that distinguish his later work. But
of the characteristic slant of his mind there are evidences, in their misanthropy, their biting resentment
against the cheats and shams of civilization, and
their dependence upon the sea as a background of
the human tragedy. The plays in this volume demand no further review than is necessary to reveal
the early development of the author's mind. The

title play of the volume, "Thirst," is a tragic episode enacted on a raft of a steamer floating becalmed on the ocean after a wreck. On the raft are two men and a woman. One of the men is a West Indian mulatto; the woman is a dancer. The third is a product of "higher" culture. The growing terror of death by thirst is suggested in a Maeterlinckian dialogue which is, however, not so dramatic as it is narrative in form. In her desperation the dancer offers herself to the negro sailor in return for a swallow from his flask. In the strain of madness with which the play ends and in the character of the negro we have the first signs of characteristic O'Neill features. "The Web" represents the tragic skein in which the life of a consumptive prostitute is tied. The action of the play reveals the various passions and loyalties of her character, her love for her man, her passion for her child, her relation toward the other man. "Warnings" in two scenes tells of a wireless operator who has become deaf. On account of the needs of his family he conceals his affliction and keeps his job. A wreck results and he kills himself. In "Fog" appears a mystical note. The scene is a lifeboat in a fog. Unseen a poet and a business man discuss life and human problems. They approach an iceberg and are saved from death by the warning cry of a child which is later found to be dead. "Recklessness" deals with a story of reckless love between a chauffeur and his mistress and ends in a suicide.

In this volume we have indeed little of the later O'Neill. And yet this volume justifies itself if for nothing else than that it shows in crude form the characteristic substance of O'Neill's interest and provides a measure by which the rigid discipline of his later work can be valued. The world we have here is a simple world and it is viewed in a sardonic way. Already the world is divided into two classes, those who are contemptible and those who belong. The contemptible are, as a rule, those with the well-tailored clothes of convention upon them; they are variously weaklings, welchers, birds of prey. Those who belong are as variously recruited. They may be prostitutes, West Indian negroes. Here we have in crude form the characteristic O'Neill predilections, the backgrounds of the immensities of nature and of human experience; we have the collapse of poorly tempered minds under heavy pressure into madness; we have the first sketches of the incisive studies into the psychology of races; we have sensitiveness slinking and hiding behind brutality. O'Neill's art had not developed in his first book. But the work was his own.

Between the publication of "Thirst" in 1914, and the publication three years later of "The Moon of the Caribbees and Other Plays," a significant development had taken place in O'Neill's art. Certainly in the plays comprised in the latter volume O'Neill's art had come of age. Something is due, no doubt, to the fact that these latter plays had had the advantage of production. But production will not explain the change that had taken place in the author's technical management and his outlook on the world. I have no hesitation in saying that the appearance of "The Moon of the Caribbees" and its companion plays is the most important event in the recent history of our theater. It introduced to the stage a new genius and sounded a note of new promise. O'Neill himself has done nothing better than the title play of this volume. He has done other more ambitious things on a larger canvas. He has done nothing that is more nearly perfect in its class. This play takes rank with Synge's "Riders to the Sea" as a study in mood, a nocturne of glamour and irony.

All the plays of this group are placed on the sea or near the sea. At least four of them are placed in the same boat—the S. S. *Glencairn*. In the forecastle or on the deck of this steamer there gathers a motley group, the tag-ends of humanity swept up from the seven seas and the seven sea-faring nations. There is a Yankee, a Cockney, a high-class Englishman, a Scotchman, a German, an Irishman, and a Swede. Frequently negroes come into the action. The author shows these men to be derelicts each in his own way from civilization and with an irony as sure as it is biting shows their follies, their frailties and their sins to be the heritages of the civilization they have left behind. In "The Moon of the Caribbees" he shows them as their boat floats under the disintegrating spell of the southern moon. The play tells no story. It is a symphony of mood. The past histories, the pitifully broken characters of the sailors weave themselves through dialogue and action into a fabric of sensation in which the moonlight is an overtone. The action begins slowly enough on a note of mingled melancholy, resentments and yearnings. The sea is the refuge from the land and the land alternately is the haven of the seafarers. As the ship approaches the harbor of the island in the Caribbees the stored-up passions quieted by days on the sea begin to be released. The passions of common men everywhere are objectified in drink and in woman. O'Neill intensifies the latter passion by introducing into it race lures and repulsions. A negro had been the dominant character in "Thirst," his first play to be published. In "The Moon of the Caribbees" he definitely adopts the psychology of the black into his theater. Now for the first time as always afterward in his work he shows up the black as the victim of the follies and crimes and debased lusts of the dominant white race. O'Neill has the gift of pity in generous measure, but always bound about with irony. This pity is never so strong as when he shows the black child of nature struggling toward the light of the white man's gods and caught in the storm of the white man's return to barbarism.

When the men come to port they must have rum. Rum and women are smuggled on board by a black woman while the officers are conveniently on shore in pursuit of their own pleasure. The men need but maintain a decent semblance of order and no harm will be done. But they cannot. Brawls ensue. Knives are drawn. The officers return and the women are bundled off to shore, sans rum, sans their store of provisions and sans money. The innocent native is the only loser.

Throughout the entire action of this play the strains of character are maintained in their integrity. And as if to supply the spiritual motive, Smitty, the sensitive young Englishman, sits apart and broods and the Donkeyman philosophizes. The action is projected to us through the medium of the refined perceptions of these two men. While the men about them are degrading the thought of womanhood, they have other pictures in their minds. "Gentlemen don't hit women," says Smitty, and the Donkeyman answers placidly, "No; that's why they has memories when they hears music." Smitty too gets drunk, but he gets drunk in order to shut out the present and live in the past. The others get drunk in order to intensify the present orgy. The play is not compounded alone of character and action. The whole mood of the summer sea, the pervasive opium of the southern moon, the intoxication of sounds and smells and rhythms are themselves factors of the play. A negro chant over the waters, the songs, the clashes of instruments on shore, the punctuating bell, mingle in "the saddened voice of the brooding music faint and far off, like the mood of the moonlight made audible."

In "Bound East for Cardiff" we meet again many of the same characters now on the sea lines between New York and England. Before, the action had been seen through the perceptions of refined or thoughtful spirits; now the bent, brutalized lives of those who go to sea are shown against a greater reality even than that of the sea, the reality of death. The smutty jokes of the forecastle, the stories of the loves of nigger wenches in out-of-the-way ports, the nameless exploits of the sailors' night on land take on themselves an aspect grotesque and unreal beside the fact that death is contending with a man behind the curtains in a lower bunk. It is not a heroic death that Yank is to die. He has missed the ladder and fallen through. A sick man is out of luck and out of place. That is all there is to it. And sympathy would be as much out of place. The sick man expects no sympathy. He must get well of himself or he must die. The author makes no effort to stimulate the action or to intensify the moods. The real subject is not the dying man any more than the subject is the sea that is tossing in the murk outside. The subject is men—seen under conditions which magnify all their traits as if by a pantograph. The sailors are grumbling, grumbling. It is the kind of night that brings stories of shipwrecks. The dying man expresses the general opinion when he says, "This sailor life aint much to cry about leavin'—

just one ship after another, hard work, small pay,
and bum grub; and when we get into port, just a
drink endin' up in a fight, and all your money gone,
and the ship away again. Never meetin' no nice
people; never gettin' out of sailor town, hardly, in
any port; travelin' all over the world and never seein'
none of it." His mind turns away from the sea to a
farm " 'way in the middle of the land where you'd
never smell the sea or see a ship."

The sailor is by nature a man who "yearns beyond
the sky-line where the strange roads go down." The
sea is his means of escape; but even before he reaches
the sea escape is in his blood. Escape is the key to
his character and to his sins. And so he dreams no
less while on the sea than while on the land. On the
sea he dreams of far harbors, and the strange chances
that will bring fortune into his lap; he dreams of
booze and of women. Nothing is more clear than
that in these characters that dream "beyond the
horizon" we have the key to the greatest strength
and the greatest weakness of human nature, its most
sublime victories, its most degraded defeats. Success and failure are not as opposite as the poles.
They are separated by but a hair's breadth. O'Neill
is interested in the sea as revealing these qualities of
character. But before he is interested in the sea he
is interested in the aspiring and blundering man.

O'Neill's next play, "The Long Voyage Home," is
more sardonic than the other plays, in that while
showing the sailor's yearnings in all their weakness

and strength, he shows how the harpies of the land fatten upon the weaknesses of the sea man. The scene is a London waterfront where a group of sailors have just landed. Olson has saved his pile in order to buy a farm back in Sweden. He has determined to be good, to take only ginger ale. But the land is lying in wait for him. What drink cannot do is done by the seduction of women. Only less revealing than the study of Olson himself, the simple-minded man seduced by the soft friendship of women, is the study of the girl who is used as the tool of his downfall. So closely identified are the wiles of sex with the characters of these women that it is difficult to bring a hard judgment against them. For after Olson is doped and robbed and shanghaied onto a crazy tub that may sink in the next storm, the girl too loses her reward at the hand of the hard villain whose master mind constructs the plot. Olson is the victim of an inner aspiration losing itself in the muck of his own degraded appetite and the sins of the world. Is Freda any the less the victim of the power of that womanhood which she has not yet learned to redeem, which is used for base purposes by others?

Few plays of first rank dealing with war appeared during the great conflict. The value of "In the Zone" arises from the fact that this play subjects war emotion to a test of absolute values. In this play we have carried to the ultimate the conception that a steamer at sea is a microcosm. The situation is well arranged. The *Glencairn* is approaching the danger zone of submarine warfare. In the fore-castle the men are lashing themselves to a frenzy of fear and suspicion against one of their number whom they accuse of plotting to sink the ship. Smith has been hiding a black box under his mattress; against orders he has left his port hole open. Pretending to sleep he has prowled around looking at the contents of his box. It takes but a bit of fancy to convince the men that he has been signaling a submarine. So after a desperate fight they get the box and find only letters in it. When they read the letters they learn that what he has been hiding is a letter revealing the tragedy of a drunken man who has lost the woman he loved.

The first four plays in this volume are among the best short plays written in English in our time. Within short compass they achieve emotional effects of great intensity. The emotion arises from no single dominating source in character or circumstance but from a blending of factors. The author intrudes neither his conceptions nor his artistic method. As much cannot be said of the following three plays. In these the author indulges a personal predilection toward the stark, the melodramatic or the bizarre, which we must presume is always present in his consciousness but is as a rule kept under rigid control. Heretofore the action developed out of a complex circumstance. In the next three plays it develops out of the intense characteristics of the protagonist.

"Ile" is one of the strongest and yet one of the least satisfying of O'Neill's plays. The play deals with conditions on a steam whaling ship two years out in search of oil under the command of a dogged sea captain who brooks no opposition in his determination to find oil on this voyage. To do so he puts down a mutiny among the men, and drives his wife, whom, against all precedent, he had brought on the voyage, into madness. Naturally this play could not exist except in the character of the captain. Keeney is a strong man with one idea; Mrs. Keeney is a woman broken by that idea. In a few tense moments of decision the author gives the effect of two years' quiet struggle of wills. Keeney withstands the attack of force; he withstands his wife's plea. When he learns that the ice is breaking up to the northward he orders the men to push full steam ahead. At the moment the whales begin to blow his wife's reason gives way.

Again, in "Where the Cross is Made," we have a study of a character with an obsession. The obsession is now gold. The sea-faring man has come home. But he is still in his "cabin" erected on a lookout post on a high point of the California coast. The structure of this play varies from that of former plays in that while those were developments of a single situation which was complete in itself, this depends upon an anterior situation which must be developed by narration. Old Captain Bartlett's eyes are busy on the sea. He has the reputation of being mad. Years before his ship had been wrecked on an island in the Pacific. There treasure had been found, murder had been committed, some of the crew had succumbed. Finally the Captain had escaped. Now he has sent a schooner to bring back the treasure from the point on the chart "where the cross is made." To the thought of this treasure he has given his life. The ship is mortgaged; his wife is dead; his son has the same obsession of gold that the Captain has. And then it is shown that the treasure is all paste and false.

In this play we have the first effort of the author to express a general idea in terms of drama. In fact this play provides the nucleus of the author's first long play entitled "Gold," which was made by prefixing two acts dealing with the antecedent action. The play displays as well that sardonic irony, that distrust of all the pretensions of man that are characteristic of the author's temper.

Irony appears in the next play combined with another element that is rarer in O'Neill's work. O'Neill has been accused of being a misanthropist, a pessimist, an ironist, and an expressionist. He has never yet been accused of being a humorist. And yet I suspect that this strain runs also in him, concealed only by that grotesquerie and irony that make him flee from the flippancies of wit as well as from the softness of sympathy. The satirical twist in "Where the Cross is Made" has elements of humor in it. In the next play this humor is made more explicit but more cruel. "The Rope" is one of the most interesting of O'Neill's short plays in that it shows the trend of his mind away from the sea into the more isolated regions of psychic oppressions and confusions. O'Neill had all along been interested in the minds of men as they were crowded and stunted by natural forces. "The Rope" is a study of senile dementia and idiocy, as ugly a piece of work on sex repression as our language has seen. It forecasts "Diff'rent" and "Desire Under the Elms" in uncovering the noisome back-currents of provincial life. Strangely enough it incorporates into the action a jest of a cruel and insane imaginativeness. From the degraded *milieu* only one character has escaped, and he only by fleeing to a life of crime. The grandfather has promised the departed youth only a rope to hang himself. The prodigal returns to torture the old man for his gold and at that moment by an accident the rope is pulled disclosing the sack of gold at the end. It would be hard to find a meaner play than this. It is the very triumph of perverse fancy. Those who pursue the horizon and stumble over a dunghill are saints beside these provincials who remain in their cranny and rot.

III

O'Neill's art has never gone beyond the standards set in "The Moon of the Caribbees," "Bound East for Cardiff," and "The Long Voyage Home."

It has been widened to cover a broader scope of subject matter; in some respects his interests have been particularized, but the sane balance, the absorption and blending of all factors in the theme, the rigorous, even militant, independence of artistry that mark the later O'Neill are found in this first volume of plays. There is found also the same hatred of the world.

Much soft twaddle has been written about the sea. One hesitates to broach the subject lest he, too, be led to sentimentalize about the least sentimental of subjects. And yet one cannot write of O'Neill without swallowing the sea in a mouthful. Like Conrad, who was his first master, O'Neill was neither a sea man nor the son of a sea man. The sea was employed by neither Conrad nor O'Neill as the element to which he had been born. Such writers there have been, but they do not represent the modern uses of the sea in literature. To the modern writer the sea offers a simple and specific set of measures by which man may be tested, of tools by which he may be presented. On land we cannot see humanity for the people. On the sea we gain perspective and poise and background. The sea is, then, the most tangible, the most accessible of the immensities. It is a symbol of all the other immensities within the heart of man and beyond his reach. Essentially the sea is no more an immensity than the land or the air or the light of the sun. But it is more apprehensible. The sea is the living mother of myths. The explorer crosses the continent once and for all. Every ship that sets sail on the ocean is an adventure into the unknown. There has, therefore, been built up about the sea a tradition that gives it a super-personality.

Naturally the sea offers a specific to those who view life fundamentally. It offers as well a bundle of tricks to those who view it superficially. Perhaps the best test of a writer's use of the sea is to ask whether beyond the sea he discerns other and vaster immensities. Besides Conrad, the imaginative writer among the moderns who has delved most deeply into the immensities is Hardy. As it happens, Hardy is not drawn to the sea so much as to the vastness of stellar space. In a memorable passage in the preface to "Two on a Tower," he shows how the physical immensities of the world are dwarfed beside the inbred moral codes, the bonds of love and duty, the furies of appetite and of sex passion of the human heart. Of this novel he writes that it "was the outcome of a wish to set the emotional history of two infinitesimal lives against the stupendous background of the stellar universe, and to impart to readers the sentiment that of these contrasting magnitudes the smaller might be the greater to them as men." To this test of the employment of the physical immensities in art O'Neill responds satisfactorily. He first discovered magnitudes when he discovered the sea. As his art develops he does not so much leave the sea as incorporate it in the greater magnitudes of men's minds.

Here, then, we have a key to O'Neill's treatment of

character. It is admitted that O'Neill possesses unusual skill in sketching the elementary differentiations of character. He easily passed over most of the technical difficulties involved in characterization. But character to him is not a matter of dress, of deportment, of dialect, even of personal history. To be significant character must have deep roots. It must not reflect a theatrical conception; it must reveal an ingrained inclination toward life. Here we find explained the large place that race divisions take in O'Neill's plays. Few modern writers show such a wide catalogue of races as does O'Neill. The differences between the Cockney and the high-born Englishman of "The Moon of the Caribbees" are memorable. And in particular O'Neill has a leaning toward those elementary qualities of character that are revealed in races that lie below the line of high civilization.

Allied with this characteristic is his tendency to intensify character in a single dominant motive that sometimes rises to obsession. In the O'Neill theater character is like the strings of a violin, which do not give forth music until they are placed under strain. And not infrequently the pressure is made so great that the cord breaks in madness or in suicide. I have no doubt that this quality in the O'Neill play rises from his conception of the theater as a place for the display of the abnormal, the unusual. I am sure that it arises from his conception of life. It is only when we are under strain that we are truly ourselves.

When the string hangs loose custom and habit rule. When the string is tightened character is shredded into atavistic strains; forgotten memories sing in the sound. By showing character always under pressure O'Neill introduces another dimension into character portrayal. We see not alone what the character is; we see suggested the various steps by which the character has come to be.

By some "Beyond the Horizon" is held to deal with the degeneration of a New England farm. Accepting this as the theme of the play, one critic objects that the deterioration is shown to have taken place within too short a period of time. I cannot believe that degeneration represents the author's chief interest in writing the play. For one thing, the idea that a community degenerates is false. Communities change front; they change uses. But the community does not deteriorate; men deteriorate. O'Neill had a deeper theme to treat in this play than that of the downfall of a neighborhood.

In this play the young playwright for the first time turns on the world a full-sized lens of creative imagination. The man behind the lens is the same. The attitude of this man toward the world has been fixed. He loves the great natural beauties of the world; of the ways of men he is cynical when not contemptuous. O'Neill's plays teem with men and women who despise the world so much that they fall ah easy victim to it, men and women who fall in the mire while pursuing a star. But he is careful to show that the pursuit is necessary to us if we are to live. The fall, too, is a necessary consequence of the pursuit. Not the striving but the very fall itself is a sign of the vitality that is within us. To the extent that you aspire, reality will get you. Yet there is nothing else to do but aspire.

And so in "Beyond the Horizon" O'Neill has a larger stage than a farm set amid imprisoning hills. The theme is the human soul with yearnings beyond its power, with reach beyond its grasp. If I read O'Neill correctly he means that we all dream beyond our power, and that often the bad men, the failures, are those who have dreamed most bravely, most richly, and most passionately. How often the good and great are merely those who have refused to dream, who have played safe with their souls. With hero worship of such as these O'Neill will have no part. Nor will he have any part in throwing roses on the pathways of the dreamers. For it is these who fall confused among choices, blinded by visions. In reading this play let us get out of our minds that it makes any difference whether the dreamer goes or comes, whether he pursues the rainbow across the world or hugs his vision to his breast in his own village. In neither case will he find what he seeks.

There has grown up what may be called a "frustration" school of literature, which identifies man's failures with great external forces, the wrath or indifference of the gods, the pressures of circumstance, the injustices of social organization. O'Neill does not belong to this school. He lays on man the burdens and responsibilities and joys that belong to him. Of these the chief responsibility is to live with all the life there is in one, to live extensively, even though so living means that you fail. Any one who wishes to find in this story an argument for the disciplined life, for the steady hand controlled by policy, may do so and take his joy in the lesson. I cannot read any such message in the play.

"Beyond the Horizon" is the story of Robert Mayo, his brother Andrew, and Ruth who becomes his wife. Robert and Andrew live on a New England farm that overlooks the sea. From childhood Robert has been set off from the others by a something finer, more wistful in his nature. Their own objectives are at home in the immediate task. Robert's mind is far off in a world of distant achievement. He has never been well, he has never done his share of the tasks of the farm, he has not even been successful at school. He lives always in dreams, in visions, distant and alluring, of lands beyond the sea, and the great deeds he will sometime perform.

So far it appears that this is merely a study of a weak character, self-deceived. It is this, but it is more. The play opens on a country highway on a spring evening. Here we see Robert and Andrew in conversation. Apparently Andrew is in every way the opposite of Robert, but is he? Let us see. Robert is a fantasist or illusionist. Andrew is a realist. He takes what is near at hand, does his job.

Speaking to Robert about his plans to leave the farm and go to sea he says, "You might as well stay right here, because we've got all you're looking for right on this farm. There's wide space enough, Lord knows; and you can have all the sea you want by walking a mile down to the beach; and there's plenty of horizon to look at, and beauty enough for any one except in the winter."

Of the two it would seem that Andrew would be the one to succeed, Robert the one to fail. The author's conception is not so simple as this. Both boys fail. Andrew loves Ruth and is going to marry her. When he comes to say good-by to Ruth, Robert discovers that there are other horizons no less appealing than the skyline. In a scene of real intensity and beauty Robert confesses his love to Ruth; she surprises him by confessing her love for him. Robert's illusions are breeding illusions; his lawlessness is sowing lawlessness. It is decided that Robert shall stay at home, marry Ruth and manage the farm, while Andrew goes to sea with his uncle.

After Robert's marriage to Ruth the horizon contracts and hems him in. The last three acts present a pitiful picture of sordid decay. We are not to suppose that if Robert had gone with his uncle he would have found the far regions to his liking. Certainly he soon finds that the farm is not to his fancy, even with Ruth. He is unfit for farming or any other work. The illusions of love are soon embittered by duty. In this situation the interest centers in Ruth.

She, too, is a dreamer, but she has but one dream, the dream of love. And so we now find her thoughts turning "beyond the horizon" to the discarded brother whose image takes alluring shape in her mind. The author wastes no time in showing the results of the characters of these two dreamers upon the environments of their lives. The farm runs down, Robert's illness increases. Their child is a weakling. The credit of the family in the neighborhood is reduced to the vanishing point. No detail is spared in showing the external signs of an internal shiftlessness. Robert potters around, half-heartedly doing things in the wrong way, continually late, continually the sport of nature which delights to attack a weak man in his weak spot. Both Robert and Ruth turn to books for a narcotic from the pitiful disillusion of their lives, the failing crops, the increasing debts, the sickly child, the sneering neighbors, their own sordid decline. And through it all Ruth cherishes the letters from Andrew and looks forward, hoping and fearing, to the day when he will return. In an impassioned scene she throws up his failure to Robert and confesses her love for Andrew.

What now of Andrew? Upon his return we get a picture of what life beyond the horizon is like. Life there is a matter of work, of problems faced, of decisions made, and of discontented dreams as well. In other words, it is just like life at home. The dangers there are the same as the dangers here. And Andrew has succumbed to these dangers. He has become ruthless and cunning and crooked. In the dull drab of the end of the play there enters no ray of light. Five years have passed. The processes of deterioration of all three are complete. Father and Mother and little Mary have died. Robert is broken with disease. Ruth is broken by the denial of her last illusion of love. In production the play ends with Robert's death and a cruel bickering scene between Andrew and Ruth in which he denounces her for not lying to the dying man.

Certainly no such scathing an assault upon false ideals has been seen on our stage in many a day. But the play does not therefore give sympathy to the man without vision. Tragedy belongs to the man of vision who aspires. But the great mass without vision, without aspiration, deserve only scorn and irony. Technically the play has some remarkable qualities not the least of which is the impression it gives of the passage of time, the slow attrition of years. This play is the artist's heartless analysis of the ills to which, more than any other class, the artist himself is heir. The play was produced at the Morosco theater, Feb. 2, 1920, at special matinées, Richard Bennett playing the part of Robert Mayo. It was successful in New York but unsuccessful in Chicago and on tour.

IV

The awarding of the Pulitzer Prize to "Beyond the Horizon" in June, 1920, sealed in popular esti-

mation the judgment of the few enthusiasts who had
felt since 1916 that a new force had arrived in the
American theater. Not only had the young playwright made himself a master of the stage; others
had done this to an equal or even a superior degree.
His unique achievement had been that he had through
the medium of a play made a real contribution to the
knowledge of life. We have had beautiful plays,
imaginative plays, entertaining plays, plays display-
ing wit, wisdom, and resource, but how rare in American drama have been those plays which have been
constructed of deep-lying materials of human character. George Jean Nathan has said, "The essential
difference between O'Neill and the majority of his
contemporaries in the field of American drama lies
in the circumstance that where the latter think of
life (where they think of it at all) in terms of drama,
O'Neill thinks of drama in terms of life."

In 1916 Frank Shay published for O'Neill a short
play entitled "Before Breakfast." This play is
pretty bad, and yet, bad as it is, it is significant as
showing the direction in which the playwright's
thoughts were turning. Only one character appears,
that of Mrs. Rowland, a slovenly, formless woman of
spiteful nature in her early twenties. Her husband,
Alfred, is understood to be in an adjoining room and
is not seen. The story transpires through the speech
and action of the woman, who is characterized by
stealth, malignity and cunning. From her words
we learn that the two are down to their last nickel,

that he has pawned everything, that she is going out to sew while he spends his time with artists. Through her taunts we see him a sensitive, over-wrought soul unequal to the pressure upon him, slipping deeper and deeper into insecurity. Once we see a nervous hand with long, sensitive fingers reaching through the curtain for a bowl of water. At the end of her cruel harangue a noise is heard off stage. He has killed himself and the dripping of the blood is heard on the floor.

This play must be read as a first rude sketch of "Beyond the Horizon" and of many of O'Neill's later plays in which sensibility is shown to be synonymous with tragedy and defeat. All the sins of life, according to O'Neill, grow out of civilization, rightly or wrongly so called. Be callous and brutal, live like the ox, and the world will take care of you. But woe be to you if you would live beyond the ox! Hell exists for you in this life in the flames lighted in your flesh.

Some critics have said that O'Neill lost his interest in the sea. I think it more just to say that his interest was never limited by the sea. It was as if he said to himself, "There is an intensity in the human soul beside which the storms of the sea are as nothing. Nature has neither heights nor depths save as these are ascribed to her by man. Only man can intensify experience, make it significant. This, then, is the mark of the man, that he live deeply, that he feel profoundly. If he do not then he is not a man. He is an indivisible part of dead matter." As O'Neill saw his task before him as artist and man, I imagine it appeared to be to delve always more deeply into the roots of human experience, to push ever farther and more venturesomely his pursuit of the knowledge of man.

Given O'Neill's nature and interests he could not have lived through the second decade of the twentieth century without coming under the influence of psycho-analysis. His relation with this subject is typical of that of the better class of writers of our time. He appreciated the value of the new theory to the understanding of the mind of man. He was alive to the contributions it could make to the subject matter of plays. But the implications of the science itself were too profound, the zones of human experience thus opened were too widespread to be readily incorporated in the substance or the technique of plays. Playwrights did indeed turn their attention to the subject. Not unnaturally the general run of plays finding their inspiration in psycho-analysis have been superficial and unsatisfactory. As far as the playwright is concerned, psycho-analysis offers two uses. It offers a code of scientific method to be applied to all researches into hidden phenomena in human nature. And it brings into the view of the playwright various zones of experience, including dreams, memories, atavistic strains, repression areas, which are of technical use in his craft. It may be said at once that scientific method as applied to the researches of the playwright is a delusion and a snare. No playwright has as yet succeeded in overcoming the initial handicap to his imagination entailed in the attempt to enforce upon it scientific method.

O'Neill is no exception to the rule. His attempts to apply scientific method to the underlying situations of his plays have been unsatisfactory. He has written only a few plays under this influence, and as I do not consider them representative of his art at its best I am going to dispose of them out of their order.

"Diff'rent" was produced at the Provincetown Theater, Dec. 27, 1920, and taken uptown to the Princess Theater in January, 1921. The action of the play takes place in a seaport village. In the element of suppressed desires, and in certain features of the background the play is reminiscent of the short play, "The Rope." This play is a thoroughly drab and disillusioned study of the compensations demanded by nature for sins against nature. In the first of the two acts we see the Crosby home in 1890. Emma Crosby is a romantic dreamer like Robert Mayo in "Beyond the Horizon." She places impossible burdens on reality. She has built up an ideal of Caleb, the man she is pledged to marry, as different from other men, purer, cleaner, not subject to human appetites. Caleb, on the other hand, who has tested his dreams, is good-natured, practical, a human vessel that rides on even keel. These are the two central characters of the play. The others are futile, self-deceiving, the caricatures of men and women who grow up amid fears and repressions. In the play O'Neill subjects the Victorian doctrine of "appearances" to a searching analysis. If things are not good they must at any rate be made to seem so. For a true standard of conduct one looks beyond reality to something "diff'rent" from reality. Experience failing her, Emma Crosby finds her standards in an imagination fed by romance and religion. The man she loves must live not by the standards of reality but by standards "diff'rent" from reality. So when she finds that on his voyages he has departed from these standards she is adamant. She will not marry him.

The only character of real interest in this play is Emma, the daughter of long repressions whose mind is locked in an obsession of self-torture. The true fabric of her mind is indicated in the vulgarity of her environment, the frank lasciviousness of her family, and her own insistent nagging to get at the truth regarding Caleb's sin. The first act of the play is of great length. The author is so anxious to present all the data on Emma's condition that the first act is like a clinic.

As is to be expected the second act shows the price at which Emma's "difference" has been bought. Water seeks a level. The passion repressed for years finds an outlet in demands no less diverse from reality than those of Emma's youth. Thirty years have passed. Caleb is still true to Emma and is waiting for her. The change in the room reflects the change in the woman. Varnished hardwood floors, oak furniture, painted seascapes on the walls provide a fit setting for a woman rouged, dyed and frilled, "revoltingly incongruous in a pitiable sham, a too apparent effort to cheat the years by appearances." Emma's affections have now gone out to the scapegrace son of Caleb's sister. She makes herself the dupe of this vulgar fellow, spends money on him, and is contemptuously discarded. Shamed by the fall of the woman he has loved Caleb hangs himself and Emma follows him to death.

The force of the play is beyond doubt; nor can its truth be questioned as far as Emma is concerned. All that can be questioned is the central conception of the author, who by main force bends all the factors of a play out of shape in order to center these around the fortunes of a vulgar woman. One can admit that a change would have taken place in the person of Emma without admitting that the whole group should for thirty years remain subordinated to her story. The author makes this a tragedy only by forcing social relations to hang upon individual qualities. To make the story of Emma's repression of significance to a group, to make Caleb hang himself for anything Emma did or failed to do is to force the stresses of the dramatic beyond their powers.

It will be remembered that after he returned from his wanderings at sea O'Neill spent six months in a sanitarium for tuberculosis patients. While there his mind had been at work. Often in his subsequent career he returns to the observations of the human spirit as it reveals itself in sickness. We shall note how he early repudiates the "banality of surfaces" in behalf of a deeper reality. His interest in sickness is but another aspect of his interest in madness, in obsessions, in repressions and in the struggles of alternating love and hate. O'Neill is by no means of the school that accepts the compensation theory of illness and sacrifice. And yet just as he holds that man is not man save as he lives intensely, albeit painfully, so also he holds that sickness isolates or points up the native qualities of character. It does not follow that because a person is physically ill he is therefore spiritually heroic and virtuous. Often physical illness itself is but the expression of a psychic lesion. Robert and his mother-in-law in "Beyond the Horizon" are both ill and both are scathingly presented. Illness intensifies and purifies the dominant strain. It does not change it.

"The Straw" was produced at the Greenwich Village Theater Nov. 10, 1921. Though not successful in production it is one of the most admirable of O'Neill's works. Interest in this play is divided between two features. It is first of all a remarkably lifelike and sympathetic depiction of life in a sanitarium for the consumptive. All the characters, professionals and patients, are closely observed. The selfishness and heartlessness of health toward sick-

ness, and of the sick toward each other, the flinchings,
the irritations, the monotonies of institution life are
faithfully presented. But the play is more than an
etching of life. It is a study of the intense, un-
selfish spiritual nature of one character, Eileen Car-
mody, a character of such strong spiritual powers
that her soul quickens her flesh. We are prepared
for seeing Eileen sick by seeing her amidst the
family to which she is little mother. Eileen's mother
had died of tuberculosis. When Eileen is taken down
her father, sisters, lover, fight the idea that she should
go to the hospital. She also is more interested in protecting others than herself. But also she wants to
get well. And when she goes to the infirmary she is
determined to live up to its rules. But she ignores
her own nature, that maternal strain in her that
makes her find someone to mother even in the hospital. There she no longer has her family to mother
but she has Murray. Murray is a young man who
has never made much of himself, who needs but the
inspiration of Eileen to discover hidden powers. And
so she proceeds to give him her little bit of life. They
draw together into what they call love; but love is
in fact the joy of giving on her part, the joy of re-
ceiving on his. When she helps him to sell a story,
his eyes turn again toward the outer world and he
forgets her. He rapidly improves in health while
she declines. She is retarded by home troubles, dis-
spirited by the heartless visits of her family who are
forgetting her. A scene of pathos and beauty is her

meeting at night against all the rules of the hospital with the now recovered Murray to bid him good-by.

The last act shows her with the last bond to life broken. She has given her all to the living and the living have passed her by. Her father is no longer willing to pay the little sum necessary to keep her from the poor farm. When it seems that she must die one straw is thrown out to save her. It is a weak straw and the author himself does not know whether it is strong enough to serve. Through the instrumentality of a nurse Murray is given to understand what he owes to Eileen. She had given him back his interest in life. He sees, too, that without her even his ambitions are nothing. Driven first by duty, then by a full recognition of the truth of his words, he tells her that he needs her. She is finally convinced that she is necessary to him. This is the straw that is to save her. Will the straw hold? A remarkable little tragedy without even passion to move it, without a flaw in its psychology.

In two plays O'Neill has explored the zones in which the soul of a man meets the soul of a woman in friendship and in marriage. The first of these, "The First Man," was produced at the Neighborhood Playhouse, March 4, 1922. Of all the plays O'Neill has written, "The First Man" shows evidence of the most toil in the composition. This toil was demanded not alone by the subject he had chosen to treat but by something imposed and arbitrary that he chose to add to the symbolism of the play. The matter of greatest importance was the question whether a man and a woman could collaborate in their deeper mental interests at the same time that they were collaborating in love and parenthood. O'Neill shows the woman striving to maintain sympathetic contact with her husband in all the latitudes of their characters. The man is apparently not so generous. He is willing to believe that his partner in the deepest interests of his brain can be at the same time his mistress. He cannot believe that she can be mother of his child. In other words passion does not contend with friendship but maternity does.

This theme is involved with another which the author holds to be connected with it. Assuming that the motives out of which he creates his play are the deepest and most elementary in life, the author assumes also an association between these and the race history of man. The hero who in his own family is seeking the secret of the most fundamental of associations, that between husband and wife, is at the same time an archæologist seeking the origins of human life on the globe. He is interested in finding the traces of the first man, and the desire that his wife shall join him in this pursuit makes him insist that they shall have no child. The result of this situation, her demand for a full marriage, that is a marriage with children, his demand for an incomplete marriage, that is one in which she shall be free to follow his mental interests, makes up the play. In the region of abstract thought the idea is a good one. It is not good theater. The situation is almost entirely one of the intellect that broods on life, rather than a composition of life's factors. For this reason it is difficult to realize in play form and is brought to action only through much forcing of the wills of the characters, reiterations of the validity of past oaths, and other expedients of a hard pressed author. Forced by the desire to make drama of what is only thesis the author externalizes the situation between husband and wife and draws the entire emotional force of the play out of the relations between these and an intrusive family. Jayson desires his wife to go exploring with him; she desires a child. She cannot have a child and go exploring too, so she has the child. Jayson is angry, treats her unsympathetically and she dies in childbirth. There should be enough here for a life-sized play, but in order to intensify the action O'Neill calls in as misunderstanding a crowd of relatives as ever appeared in fiction, and he practically puts an accouchement on the stage. In this play O'Neill's artistic discretion, usually fine, fails him entirely.

"The First Man" fails because it falls between two stools. Its real plane of action lies in the tortured minds of a man and woman who, while bound to the world-old task of physical procreation, are aspiring to find a way toward a higher form of procreation. The uses of this theme for drama lie in the deep and ever deeper probing of the secret places of the soul.

O'Neill does not treat it in this way. He treats it as a drama of social groupings. A theme as intimate as that of "Rosmersholm" is developed in a treatment as diffuse as that of "The Thunderbolt."

Evidently the author took this lesson to heart for when next he came to treat subjects of this kind he limited the action of the play to the characters concerned. In "The First Man" Jayson and his wife had welded their lives together so closely that there was no room for a third, even their own child. In "Welded," produced in 1924, the same theme is pushed one step further. The wife in "The First Man" was not in a position of equality with her husband. He needed her, but her needs could be filled only at the price of her death. The wife in "Welded" is in a better position. Strategically she is either equal or superior to her husband. She is a creative artist in her own right. Moreover, she has lived her own life before meeting her husband. In the former play the only thing that kept Jayson from devouring his wife alive was her power to get a child into which to draw herself as into a retreat against his assault. In "Welded," on the other hand, there is no question of a child. Nor is there any hope of unity between these two unless one or the other surrenders. This neither will do for each has in his art an armor and a weapon. And yet the sex passion between them draws them both continually. The problem is one for which there is no solution. Neither unified nor entirely separate the two must remain forever "welded" in a bond that is a rapture and a torture.

There are in the world two zones of creation. One is individual and lies within the domain of the arts as heretofore understood. For want of a better term we shall call the other "social"; of this sex is the key. This, too, is an art, but it is an art of which the confines and definitions are not yet worked out. In the association between man and woman there is a womb of the spirit. In this the works which time will bring forth are conceived. Such works can come to birth only when man and woman stand co-equal, welded yet free. The man and woman in "Welded" are both free and yet not free. The important thing is that in relation with each other they are equal. Appropriately enough it is among the artists that these experiments toward a better poising of the forces of the soul are made. Because they have most concerned themselves with the testing of the world's values alone it is they who must suffer the pangs of the testing together.

In form this play is as economical as the former was diffuse. Again the husband and the wife are the primary characters. The only other characters are the former lover of the wife and a street girl, companion for a night of the husband. No attempt is made here to outline the simple plot of this play. It is of importance only in motivating the theme. In these new economical structures there is one severe drawback. In order to uncover the action there is

required an articulateness on the part of the characters, a completeness of self-revelation and open discovery that are inconsistent with the psychology of
the situation. For it is precisely in these matters of
sex contest that men and women are most inarticulate. They are represented rather by their silences
and refusals to speak than by their speech, rather by
inversions of meaning than by directness. This is
the paradox of the theater, that an art that depends
upon speech should in its higher reaches rapidly be
tending beyond the confines of speech. In this play
O'Neill makes few efforts to dramatize the unspoken.
Instead he forces speech upon situations which would
in all human probability be speechless or at best
inarticulate.

V

In these plays there is displayed the influence of
the only man who may fairly be said to have exer-
cised a dominating influence on O'Neill's art and
outlook. Just when it was that O'Neill became aware
of Strindberg I do not know. His early plays up to
and including "Beyond the Horizon" show few
marks of influence of any kind. In the Irish family
of "The Straw" and in Mat Burke of "Anna Christie" there is an almost disconcerting influence from
the Irish dramatists. Happily O'Neill nowhere else
displays such clear evidences of borrowed strains.
The effect produced on O'Neill's art by his association with Robert E. Jones and the disciples of the

new systems of staging cannot so much be called an
influence as a widening of his resources of expression
in the theater. But Strindberg had a marked effect
on his technique and on the content and inclination
of his mind. More than any other living playwright
Eugene O'Neill has been content to permit his work
to speak for him. He indulges in no press campaign
on his own behalf, he issues no pronouncements and
apologies. All the more significant is it then when
he once breaks silence to pay tribute to the great
Swede. He does this upon the opening of the Provincetown Playhouse with "The Spook Sonata" in
1923. The composition is worthy of quotation
in full as an interpretation of the work of Strindberg and as an index of the aims and standards of
O'Neill himself.

"In creating a modern theater which we hope will
liberate for significant expression a fresh elation and
joy in experimental production it is the most apt
symbol of our good intentions that we start with a
play by August Strindberg: for Strindberg was the
precursor of all modernity in our present theater,
just as Ibsen, a lesser man, as he himself surmised,
was the father of the modernity of twenty years or
so ago, when it was believed that 'A Doll's House'
wasn't—just that!

"Strindberg still remains among the most modern
of moderns, the greatest interpreter in the theater of
the characteristic spiritual conflicts which constitute
the drama—the blood of our lives today. He car-

ried naturalism to a logical attainment of such poignant intensity that, if the work of any other playwright is to be called 'naturalism' we must classify a play like 'The Dance of Death' as 'supernaturalism' and place it in a class by itself, exclusively Strindberg's, since no one before or after him has had the genius to qualify.

"Yet it is only by means of some form of 'supernaturalism' that we may express to the theater what we comprehend intuitively of that self-obsession which is the particular discount we moderns have to pay for the loan of life. The old 'naturalism'—or 'realism,' if you prefer (would to God some genius were gigantic enough to define clearly the separateness of these terms once and for all!)—no longer applies. It represents our fathers' daring aspirations toward self-recognition by holding the family kodak up to ill-nature. But to us their old audacity is blague; we have taken too many snapshots of each other in every graceless position. We have endured too much from the banality of surfaces.

"Strindberg knew and suffered with our struggle before many of us were born. He expresses it by intensifying the method of his time and by foreshadowing both in content and form the methods to come. All that is enduring in what we loosely call 'expressionism'—all that is artistically valid and sound theater—can be clearly traced back through Wedekind to Strindberg's 'The Dream Play,' 'There are Crimes and Crimes,' 'The Spook Sonata,' etc.

"Hence 'The Spook Sonata' at our playhouse. One of the more difficult of Strindberg's 'behind-life' (if I may coin the term) plays to interpret with insight and distinction—but the difficult is properly our special task, or we have no good reason for existing. Truth in the theater as in life, is eternally difficult, just as the easy is the everlasting lie."

There were in Strindberg two strains. One was intense and introspective. It made out of his own agony a catalogue of life's values. The other was venturesome; it wandered far afield. It incorporated in his art new worlds which, because they were so far removed from the cold world of conventionalized surfaces, appeared to be fantastic and bizarre. But this world was not fantastic. Were we but able to follow our own minds and motives through their various planes we would know that Strindberg never ceased his search for an understanding of the commonplace world in which we live.

After Strindberg in the treatment of this disjointed cosmos of many planes came Wedekind. Naturally this new conception of reality demanded a new technique of expression. It was impossible any longer to force a story into the Procrustean bed of the "well made" play. Cold intellectualism no longer served at all. Speech had come to be a means of concealing rather than revealing thought. Neither motive nor action nor speech was simple. It was no longer possible to set down a set of circumstances, assume that these represented the total, and reason from these. Even the illusion of free will was lost in the theater. Behind every action, every motive, every impulse, there were trains of action, motive and impulse reaching back to the beginnings of time. In such a world as this there was no place for propaganda. The conception of "society the villain" disappeared into the limbo to which the personal villains, devils and gods had long ago been consigned. Above all, nothing was so futile as reason. Neither the nicely shaped doctrines of the art philosopher nor the ratiocinations of the raisonneur were worth more than the wind by which they were blown away. Life was sensation, infinitely diversified, infinitely intensified. Life was a sentient, eternally aware vital experience in which there was never a break between birth and death. Even sleep did not break the stream of living, for in sleep one simply continued his dream.

For such a drama as this the conventions of the old staging would not serve. Fortunately there appeared just in time groups of new artists of the stage, who based their method upon the appeals of sensation rather than of formalized reason. These artists, who have supplied the instruments, have worked in close association with the composers of plays. One result of this collaboration has been the drama of expressionism, sometimes held to be a pursuit of the extravagant but in fact the result of the application of sincerity to the treatment of emotional materials. Materials which were formerly treated from the outside are now treated from the inside. That which was objective becomes subjective. It is the business of drama to get under the surface. Under the surface we find layer after layer of reality. Ibsen dimly suggested this deeper reality by giving to his plays "overtones." Strindberg stripped away the veil entirely. Life was not two-dimensional like a surface or three-dimensional like a solid, it was four-dimensional as time came to be a factor of every situation. Every event had its far sources. The science of mind covered a wider field than had before been considered. If the theater were to represent life it must cover this field, too. As the dead past lives again in the present the artists began to seek out the expedients of the past art of the theater, the choruses, masks, puppets, dances and harlequinades of yesterday.

It is still too early to say just what expressionism represents. Three factors are, however, noteworthy in it:

1. Atavistic race strains; the hidden factors of heredity;

2. The duality or multiplicity of life as between illusion and reality, or various planes of illusion, and reality;

3. The disposition to summarize the world of appearances into expressive categories, representing the application of man's systems to natural phenomena.

Needless to say the driving impulse of such a play as this can never be the desire to "reconcile the ways of God to man." The passion of the artist is ironic or revolutionary. For the first turning of his mind in the direction of this kind of play O'Neill has to thank Strindberg. For providing the instrumentality by which his conceptions can be realized he has immediately to thank Robert Edmond Jones, ultimately Gordon Craig.

"The Emperor Jones" was first produced at the Provincetown Playhouse, November 1, 1920. It was moved to the Selwyn and thence to the Princess Theater in January, 1921. It was revived with success in 1924. In production "The Emperor Jones" was one of the most successful of O'Neill's plays. In the strict sense the play is a comedy, not the less so that Jones dies at the end of the play. Jones is never made to appear important for himself. We never follow his fortunes with an individual sympathy. He is always a futile, half contemptible figure, gaining glory only from his own vaunting. As such a figure he is a fit subject for the irony with which he is pursued. Again in his writing O'Neill shows the ill equipped trying to play the game of civilization without the password. And again he shows the effort failing. "The Hairy Ape" is conceived in the same irony as is "The Emperor Jones." Civilization provides certain slogans, catch-words, doctrines of safety and salvation. Are these true? Certainly, if they are they must be useful to the poorest and the most humble. Again and again O'Neill shows the poor and the humble coming into contact with civil-

ization and retiring worsted. So it is always with
the "inferior" races. It is not so much that these
races are exploited by the white race; that would be
bad enough. But the white man preaches a doctrine
to the black that he doesn't practice in his relation
with the black. He preaches a doctrine to the black
that does not work in the black's experience. The
white man in "The Moon of the Caribbees" teaches
the savage that there is law and then violates the law
and cheats the savage. If left to himself the savage
would not have submitted to such a law. The law
is therefore a snare to him. Brutus Jones has learned
from civilization the laws of "bluff" and "double
cross." He tries these on the children of nature and
nature gets him. O'Neill has no scorn for the savage
except as he apes the ways of civilization but for
the hypocrisies of civilization his scorn is bitter.

"The Emperor Jones" is both good drama and
good theater. It is good drama because through a
concrete action it is interpretative of society as a
whole. It is good theater because the action is realized directly through sensation and the emotions. It
must be remembered that in the composition of this
play O'Neill was not handling well worn symbols. He
was creating new mediums to reach ends as yet uncommon in our drama. Seldom have the instrumentalities of the theater been employed so effectively for
terror, and to deepen the knowledge of the hidden
traits of primitive man. The use of the reverberat-
ing drum to imply the deeper rhythms of life from

which the Emperor was seeking to escape by his trickery of civilization, a rhythm that was to swallow him up as the tide laps the sand, is one of the creative achievements of the modern theater. Let no one dismiss it as a mere stunt. Creative, too, is the reappearance in the mind of the fleeing man of the phantoms of the past history of his race, phantoms which are so much more real than reality that his foolish bullets are wasted in them. The Little Formless Fears, the Prison Guard, the Planters, the Auctioneer, the Slaves, the Congo Witch Doctor, the Crocodile God are effective as phantoms. But they are more than phantoms; they are reality to Jones, they *are* Jones.

O'Neill's tendency to give the "better classes" the short end of the horn is revealed in the contrast between Jones and the white man Smithers. At the point where the white race touches the colored races it is mean-spirited, shifty and ignoble. Smithers is unscrupulous and cowardly; Jones, as a full-blooded negro, possesses an underlying strength of will and self-reliant confidence. Above all he has a hearty contempt for such low-down white men. Jones is a good-tempered Nietzschean. "Dere's little stealin' like you does, and dere's big stealin' like I does," he says. For the little stealing Smithers will go to jail sometime. For the big stealing he is Emperor. Thus he has the secret of the white man's morality. He is a realist, too. When he learns that his guard has deserted him, "Feet, do yo' duty!" he says. He has three hours before sundown. He will be across the plains before dark, and then into the woods and to the seacoast. But he never reaches safety; the little nameless fears get him and the beating of the drum.

"The Hairy Ape" was produced March 9, 1922, at the Provincetown Playhouse. Thence it was taken for a run to the Plymouth Theater. Maintaining O'Neill's established attitude toward an institutionalized world this play shows a great advance in the mastery of the stage. Irony which had formerly been more implicit than explicit now becomes the controlling impulse of the play. As long as the author bases his theme on differences of race his conclusion can be palliated. But the Hairy Ape belongs to the master race. Moreover, he seeks to do what the leaders of civilization pride themselves upon doing. He seeks to "think through." And he, too, learns that the codes by which we live and thrive are not the codes which we profess.

"The Hairy Ape" is called "a comedy of ancient and modern life." Let us drop once and for all the idea that the hero is, or is assumed by the author to be, a study of an individual. In this play the author has frankly gone beyond the limits of a personal complication and has made his play out of generalized actions and characters. "The Hairy Ape" is shaped like a man but is more than a man. Like sculptors' figures of "Death," "The Thinker" and "The Discus Thrower," he is modeled after a man, but he transcends man. "The treatment of this scene, or of any other scene in the play, should by no means be naturalistic," writes the author of one of the scenes. Such a play as this has many of the qualities of allegory. Each character, each action carries a general meaning.

There are eight scenes in the play. The first scene is in the fireman's forecastle of a transatlantic liner; we are back at sea among common men. But there is a difference between these men and the men of the sailing vessels. These latter had come into contact with forces too strong for them; and fleeing from these forces had achieved for a little while the freedom of the sea. But on this transatlantic liner men are under the pressure of more highly organized, more terrible forces. For the organization of civilization is now carried onto the ocean, and these men are subject to it. The liner is a microcosm of our industrial civilization. The men we see there have almost ceased to be men. At the first glance we get of them we see men bent not so much by their own follies as by the system which crushes down upon them. Civilization is resting upon these men. They are the living primitives. And as if to carry out this idea the author shows that they have the appearance of Neanderthal man.

Among these men there is one, the master of them all, Yank, in whom there is moving a vague discontent, a pricking of responsibility, an ability to discriminate values. The minds of the men are poisoned by "goil" stuff and old ideas that are dead. He breaks in on the din. "Can't you see I'm tryin' to t'ink?"

He has made a discovery. He is thinking through. He is learning to discriminate between lies and truth. Some things that might be true are always on the side of the lies. These are sentiments, home, love, religion, beer, equality, the worship of the past. But some things are always true. They are power, they are the sources of energy, the things that run the ship and run the world. If power stops then the ship stops. They are down there in the hold to keep power working. They are necessary to it. They belong. Paddy sums up the new conception when he says, "Is it a flesh and blood wheel of the engine you'd be?" and Yank answers it is. In this way he belongs. They move, have speed, smash through. He's through with the crazy tripe about nights and days, hitting the pipe of the past. He means the thing that is the guts of all this. It takes a man to work in hell. "I'm de t'ing in coal dat makes it boin, I'm steam and oil for de engines; I'm de t'ing in noise dat makes you hear it."

It is a tremendous first scene of one of the most searching, thought impelling plays written in America. O'Neill poses for Yank a characteristic problem of our day. Does Yank belong? It is a combined problem in drama and in thinking. O'Neill thinks through. The next scene shows a glimpse of the sea that Paddy had never seen from his sailing ship. The sea now is only a bit of colored background for a floating mechanism of man's handicraft. On that ship are beings never seen on Paddy's ships. They are delicate, pale, anæmic or gross and surfeited. Mildred is the expression, not of life energy "but merely of the artificialities that energy had won for itself in the spending." Mildred sums herself up when she says that she would like to touch life somewhere but has neither the vitality nor the integrity.

What is needed now is to bring these two worlds together and we shall have the first jolt to Yank's idea that he belongs. As a feature of the game Mildred determines to go to the stoke hole and the third scene shows us the heart of the ship. The great machine is taking its toll of human power. But even in the sweat and the blinding glare of the furnaces there is joy for Yank in the thought that he "belongs." Then there comes to him the apparition of a thing in white from another world fainting with horror at the sight of him.

The contact is a shock to Mildred. But that is unimportant. The real blow is to Yank. For he sees that while he belongs, while he keeps the engine going, he has never before inquired what he belonged to. He must think that through. Deep under his muscles, those muscles that are such a burden, there is a spark. The spark must glow and shine. In his thinking he is confused by voices that repeat like phonographs words like "love" and "law" and "government." He shakes his shoulders and buries his mass in thought.

There is this other world that thinks itself better than his world. Though it does not belong it controls those who do belong. He must explore every nook and cranny. The first explanation that comes to him is the obvious one of his radical friend Long. They are slaves, the living are slaves to the dead. His thoughts become confused with blind brooding resentments. He'll show her that he is better than she is. But his ideas of revenge are curiously crude and ineffective, like breaking her face.

The scene is a corner of Fifth Avenue, "magnificence made grotesque by commercialism, a background in tawdry disharmony with clear light and sunshine of the street." Yank comes with Long; Long is trying to get him to make this a class matter, to make war on those who enslave the makers and builders of the world. There passes a "procession of gaudy marionettes, yet with something of the relentless horror of Frankenstein in their detached mechanical unawareness." Can these be the people he must fight? Are these his masters? He tries to engage them head on, to break through their reserves, to come to grips on the problem that is eating him. Magnificent in sardonic humor is the scene in which he seeks unavailingly to bring himself to their attention. He does land himself in jail but the procession passes on unaware.

Yank is in a cell at Blackwell's Island. He is much beaten but he is still thinking. The Judge has given him thirty days to "think it over." That is all he has been doing for weeks but he has not been able to think through. Can the Judge? It is doubtful. Voices come to him from other cages in a phantasmagoria of the cries, catch-words, clichés of civilization. He thinks that this prison has been made to hold him down, to bind him in. Very well. If he cannot think through, he will break through. He is out of his cage and in an I. W. W. local near the water front. Here is the implement with which he will break the cages of the world to bits. In this I. W. W. he looks to find the power that can grapple with and control the mysterious domination of those who "do not belong." Here he must find the key. He is seeking someone to break laws, to crash through. He is ready to use his power, to blow up the steel works, to set a fire under the house. He will have revenge. But the I. W. W. is breaking no laws. It is operating strictly by the rules of the game. Protesting and surprised he is seized and bound and thrown aside.

Again he muses in a greater maze than ever. What is the great mystery that is devouring him? The thing is in your insides but not in your belly. And when you ask questions all men do is to lock you up. Put you in a cage—that is the only answer of the world. He stumbles from cage to cage. Even when free of the steel cage he is in one of his own. He wanders around until he reaches the zoo. Still inquiring he faces the gorilla. The gorilla too is in a cage. But his cage is worse than the gorilla's, for the gorilla can break out of his cage. How can the

Hairy Ape break out of his cage? Suppose he and the gorilla talk things over. Perhaps they have things to say to each other. "Christ, where do I get off? Where do I fit in?" he asks. He opens the gorilla's cage. The beast crushes him to death. Perhaps, as the author says, the Hairy Ape at last belongs.

VI

In 1921 there was produced a long play entitled "Gold," developed from O'Neill's short play "Where the Cross Is Made." The play was not successful in production. Nevertheless, it is significant in that it is the only play of O'Neill's composition that deals with passion as crude force. The world of the inner life came to O'Neill with a shock of discovery. In fact, it saved his art. In "Thirst," "Where the Cross Is Made," "Gold," he went as far as he could in sheer, unmixed brutality. In the latter there was, as we have seen, a note of the sardonic. But eventually primitive life of itself comes to be irrelevant. The men of the sea, the savages of the islands mean nothing save as they are seen alongside the more complex structure of civilized society. Like civilization itself, the men in "Gold" carry around with them visions of a precious metal which is, in fact, but brass. For this they kill men and poison their own souls.

The mingling of spiritual values with crude passion, the probing even of brute appetite until some flavor of beauty is found in all longing, is a mark of O'Neill's later work. No man living has a more powerful repulsion from softness than O'Neill. And yet the very honesty of his search leads him to find under the ugly mess that man has made of his mind, the instinctive lure of beauty. This is the latest phase of O'Neill's work. It is found in hints in three or four of his later plays. It is found in full, free and magnificent expression in only one, "The Fountain." This recognition of an underlying hunger for beauty is by no means to be confused with reconciliation. Nothing in the author's work so emphasizes the essential tragedy of his outlook as the discovery under passions and appetites and tangled growths of falsehood, of a soul-plant of purity and aspiration.

"Anna Christie" was first produced on November 21, 1921. One of the most successful of O'Neill's plays before the broad public, the play cannot be considered among O'Neill's best, either as conception or theater. More than in any other play of his composition the situations seem to be entangled, the ends he is striving for are in doubt. As a rule O'Neill well escapes the charge of generalization about natural forces. I cannot think that he fully does so in this play. As he left the sea behind him the sea assumed a symbolic meaning that it had not carried before. The provisional title of "Anna Christie" had been "That Ole Davil Sea." Hints of this title still remain in the passion of the old barge master to keep his daughter from the sea that he had come to hate, and in the fact that it was from the sea that the cleansing of her sick soul was to come.

Structurally the play is unsatisfactory. The framework of the action over-reaches the drama. As drama the play is complete with the fall of the first curtain. Everything that happens afterward is theatrical surplus that is given vitality only by the energy of the author. Few plays in the recent theater are richer with drama than this first act. Old Chris has followed the sea all his days. Now he is old and has become captain of a coal barge, and is living with Martha of whose status the less said the better. Hidden under the sordid reality of his life he carries a dream. He cherishes the thought of his daughter. To him the sea symbolizes everything ugly that he has known. So in protecting her from the sea he thinks he has protected her from ugliness. But he is mistaken. When she comes she is a pathetic land wreck as he is a sea wreck. Under the sad disillusion two strains of beauty stand out, the persistent ideal of Chris, the good-natured understanding of his discarded Martha.

As I have said, the author extends a situation which is complete in one act, over four acts. In order to do so he must make another point. It is that however bad Anna may be there is in her, too, a spark of the divine that will save her. He does this in an action of undeniable force and intensity, though in it he treads somewhat closely upon the heels of his predecessors in the popular theater. Out of the fog there comes Mat Burke, a sea-going character from the Irish bogs. And between these two there develops a situation in which the tearful Magdalen of the old drama repeats herself in a new setting. No one will deny the theatrical power of the play, but it is not O'Neill at his best. Only by playing the persistent prejudices of Old Chris against the love story of the two young people does the story continue at all.

Mention has already been made of O'Neill's interest in the black race. To the members of this race he was always ready to grant a hidden spring of beauty in character that he denied to the dominant white. In "The Dreamy Kid" (1919) he shows a negro desperado, hounded by the police, who permits himself to be captured on visiting his mother. In "All God's Chillun Got Wings," the author rises to the treatment of the race problem as it involves both whites and blacks. In fact, this play sets a new standard for such plays. As a rule these concern only the sentimental aspects of the problem, confusing the issue by giving the members of the dark race a strain of the white. In this play the negroes are black. The author shows again how the burdens of civilization fall upon the submerged race. In revealing the strivings of the negroes to raise themselves by means of an honest application of the white man's abstract morality, against the treason of the white man to his own standards, the author makes a document of the first value. The play was produced in 1923.

In "The Fountain" we have a work entirely unlike anything else that O'Neill has done. This is the only play in which the inner beauty which is usually denied, and despised, is permitted to come to the surface and dominate the structure and the language and the conception. The theme of the quest for the fountain of eternal youth is a recurrent one. The quest is a favorite theme of the author himself. Seldom is the theme developed with such majesty and beauty as here. Seldom is the slow sweep of tragedy so intense and moving. The author has employed in this play a substance finer than the crude material of intensified experience. This substance is here true poetry. Irony is eliminated; in its stead there is a brooding melancholy.

O'Neill had always been interested in the compressed psychology of New England character. In "Desire Under the Elms" (Nov., 1924) he returns to the dour outlines of "Beyond the Horizon" and "Diff'rent.". This play is in many respects the most closely knit of the author's works. Again the note of frustrate longing appears in many forms. The best qualities of men and women are used for their damnation. The love of Eben for his dead mother, the vulgar lust of the older brothers for the free, open road and promised gold of California, above all the magnificent passion of Eben's step-mother for the boy, a passion so strong that she will murder her child for it, are the materials of Greek pity and terror. And more memorable than these is the hardness of the old man, a better man than any of his sons, who has made his home among the stones and at the end contents himself to go out to sleep with the cows. God can be lonely. So can he. In this play, as Walter Prichard Eaton says of "Beyond the Horizon," the character spiral "goes neither up nor down, but onward to the point of annihilation."

These are hungry men and women. They are hungry for the beauty of the sky, for gold and distant places; they are hungry for home, for companionship, for mother love, for love of child, but all their hunger is dominated and overcome by sex passion. And when they get food they gorge themselves and die.

VII

Summing up the qualities of O'Neill as a craftsman, we find two qualities overleaping all others. These are:

1. A rigorous selectiveness, an ability, even brutal, to discard his own work if it does not please him;

2. A diversity of formula in composition.

More than any man of his time O'Neill is heartless to his own work. Of the fifty plays he has written to date, twenty have been destroyed without trace. As important as this ability to discard work that does not suit him is the willingness of the man continually to experiment. An O'Neill style there is, manifested in intensity, honesty and lack of humor. But O'Neill has not tied himself up to any form of writing or to any field of interest. He is aware of the danger of

the untraveled road, but to him it is never so dangerous as the traveled road. So he is continually adventuring into new forms. If by chance he deals with a
theme that has been treated before he so intensifies
or inverts that theme as to make it new. A large
factor of O'Neill's success as a dramatist goes back
to the fact that he makes himself master of his materials. He commands attention because he is the
man who knows. It is simply a quality of his mastery
of his materials that he insists on treating them in a
hard way. Sentimentality is not so much a substance
as it is a quality. It is a characteristic of half-
knowledge, of the myth-making phase of knowledge.
All such things O'Neill despises.

Modern criticism has sadly confused thinking by
adding new definitions and formulas. For my part I
should like to see the time when every art creator may
be called a poet. And then I should like to see the
term "poet" interpreted in its only true and broad
sense. Even discussion of reality, or super-reality,
gets one nowhere unless one combine in this consideration those creative and universal factors that constitute a man a poet. Given all the qualities of
discrimination and insight, of a sense of form and an
aspiration for beauty, there still remains one factor
that distinguishes the true creator from others. I
do not know how better to denominate this than as
energy, the power to make out of oneself and one's
works a contemporary legend. This power O'Neill
has. His years of wandering helped to provide the

great essential of a successful career. Combined with something highly sensitized and passionate there is in him a driving force of creative energy that has permitted him to wield adequately subjects of great gravity and weight.

Without striving to be so, O'Neill is American. It is a strange commentary on the mind of our own and other countries that his plays have not been markedly successful abroad. European countries are still under the spell of what they think us to be. They have little conception of what we are. And so the crude, apologetic, awkward, parvenu attitude is what they see and want to see, not a civilization that has developed a discipline that permits it to view itself with irony. The best of O'Neill is that, seeing the world and not illusioned, he is not disillusioned either. There is only one thing more puerile than illusion and that is disillusion. O'Neill will have none of either. And he snaps no little doctrinaire whips over society to conceal a lack of imagination.

One fault to be found in him, but not recently so much as before, is his disposition to permit his work to break up in madness. Now madness is not for the dramatist at all. It is an avoidance of the issue. It is as if he said, "Thus far I can carry my situation and isolate the currents of motive and feeling. After this point they become too strong for my hand." Where dramatic imagination stops madness is likely to begin. Madness is but like the other worlds of myth, that disappear when the light of knowledge is turned on them.

O'Neill appeared on the scene after the busy workers had come to their first stage in the building of a new theater. It was fortunate for him that he appeared just then. As it is he has never been compelled to take sides, he has never been drawn to make those analytical judgments between tweedledee and tweedledum that confuse the minds of many creators. The theater to him is not a thing to think about and preach about. It is a house to work in. Its instrumentalities and institutions were ready when he needed them. When he came to play-writing there was a little theater ready to hand, a nondescript theater, but it served his uses. The very nondescript quality of the Provincetown Players was an advantage to a poet creating in a new way. And the men he came in contact with were helpful, too. They were artists of other arts, collectors of foreign influence, experts, pioneers, free spirits. The statement that the great artist is an individual creator should be taken with understanding. His work is his own, but the instruments of his work belong to others. These instruments have been made by hundreds who are forgotten. Under the limitations of life it is inconceivable that the artist should both create the tools and the work itself. Eugene O'Neill did not create his own tools. These had been created by artists and theater builders and experimenters. As we saw in the last chapter, Percy MacKaye and those following his lead had done much to provide a new social basis for drama in the United States, and to establish drama among the arts. They had in fact liberated the various factors of the stage. O'Neill was the first playwright to be a free agent in the theater. He is the playwright unbound.

And O'Neill is the first playwright of the new science. It would be too much to say that O'Neill treats nature outside of man as if it possessed character. And yet he endows it with those expressive qualities by which character is implied. Certainly the sea does not exist for man. Nor is it only a framework of man. The sea speaks a thousand tongues, and would speak these many tongues were there no human ears to hear. The same thing is true of the great woods of "The Emperor Jones" and of "The Fountain." It is true of the stars. Perhaps it is true of the great machines which man has made to be his servants, machines which are so rapidly becoming his masters. O'Neill's plays teem with the language of inanimate things, a language spoken not to man alone, but a language spoken nevertheless. One does not understand his plays if he does not gain from them the sense of a very wide tapestry woven of many strands, of which man, with all his complexities, his anxieties and aspirations, is but a thread that is often hidden in the pattern.

CHAPTER III

INTERPRETERS OF THE AMERICAN SCENE

I

THE ROOTS OF AMERICAN DRAMA

IN what is in many respects the most acute study of the work of Eugene O'Neill yet written, Hugo von Hofmannsthal calls attention to O'Neill's custom of driving straight through to a predestined conclusion without paying much regard to grace or to those fantastic interpositions of chance that give the most sincerely logical work something of the surface of experience. From the point of view of the continent this criticism is apposite. Our playwrights have not yet learned to be at once intense and gracious. They can grit their teeth but they naturally are not yet able to smile while doing so.

To do our playwrights justice they had to learn one lesson at a time. First, they had to think through. In so doing they achieved intensity and lost grace. But is this not better than grace without truth? The more I study the manifestations of a living theater, the less faith I have in those values that are derived from the cant of *a posteriori* criticism. If the terms "romanticism," "realism," "naturalism"; if the phrases "return to nature" and "reflection of life" ever had any value for estimating the worth of a play, that value is past. The only proper way by which a contemporary work of art can be judged is to regard it as a task set before an artificer and to consider, therefore, the blending of motive and skill that have gone to its completion. The American playwright has been under an inner compulsion to get at and to tell the truth. This task is in itself one of first magnitude. But the very fact that the task was undertaken has made the work of American playwrights intense and purposeful, has given it an air of awkwardness and self-consciousness.

In choosing the works to be treated in this volume it is not enough that we make our selection on the basis of artistic value. This critic for one is not ready to weave a rope by which to hang himself. Artistic quality would supply a serviceable enough formula of inclusion and exclusion could we suppose that there would be any agreement as to what constitutes the artistic play of the time, or that our terms were so clearly defined as to be generally acceptable. I question whether any such agreement is possible; and I question the ability of any man to establish the standards and content of the art of his time. What we can do is to center our interest rather in the playwright than in the play, in the performance rather than in the task performed.

Then many efforts that appear to be futile take upon themselves significance, many lives that appear to have been failures are seen to have been careers of important achievement.

It is in fact a noteworthy commentary upon the theater of our time that of the playwrights who can by any stretch of definitions be said to belong to the new American theater, only two have been able to pursue a consistent career over many years. Percy MacKaye, though still in middle life, has had a career in the theater covering thirty years. Eugene O'Neill has pursued an unbroken career for something over ten years. The records of all the other men we can mention have been made up of broken tentatives, of advances and retreats. A surprising number have died in youth; others have been incapacitated by illness or mischance. It would be ridiculous to charge this fact to the nature of the men who write plays. The truth of the matter is that the theater of our time has been a killer of men and women. It has taken the best from men and has sent them into the dark house with empty hands, without even the satisfaction of magnificent failure to comfort them.

In a recent book Isaac Goldberg employs a term by which to denominate the more vital and significant drama of the day. He calls this the "drama of transition" and defines this as not so much that drama that lies between two forms, as the drama that derives from the electric moment of change in human affairs. Ashley Dukes in his "Modern Dramatists" employs the term "modern" instead of "transition" and asks, "What is it that distinguishes modern dramatists, modern novelists, modern poets from the mob of dramatists, novelists and poets of their own period? The answer is clear enough. It is simply that they are in touch with, or in advance of, the thought of their own time; that their work breaks new paths, offers new forms and modes of expression; that the men and women they create do not merely reflect the conditions under which they live and the spirit of their age, but are dynamic, developing, continually offering a criticism of those conditions, and so projecting themselves into the future and making history."

Here we have under different terms a common touchstone for the testing of the living art of the theater. All life, and therefore all art, is change. What we need to guard against is the tendency, common among critics, to treat the last change as the most important, the last age as the pinnacle of all time. And yet we must not be blind to the true conditions of the world in which we live. After all possible regard has been given to the demands of a historical perspective we still know that our times stand out from others for the peculiar intensity with which we have tried all values. It has been indeed a time in which all conventions have been tested, all norms have been tried. Whatever has occurred in the theater has been but an index and a reflex of the activity in the life behind. For years the theater played but a little part in the testing of the values of life. It held itself within the norm. The old political maxim of China, "Amuse them, tire them not, let them not know," served as the formula of the theater of yesterday, serves indeed as the formula of a large part of the theater of to-day. But it does not serve for the best of the theater to-day. The theater to-day is engaged in the breaking of norms both in the arts of life and in the arts of the presentments of life. If it is to do this the first requirement is that it shall know this life well and present it faithfully. A large part of the activity of the American theater has been given to this elementary research. The playwright has sought to make himself master of the life around him, its habits, customs, characteristic manifestations, surfaces, clichés of thought and action and speech. Observation has been elevated to first place.

But observation pushed far develops for itself a conscience. In some playwrights, like Percy Mac-Kaye, observation developed a social conscience, a sense of responsibility of art toward society. In others, like O'Neill, observation developed into artistic conscience, the sense of the responsibility of the art with respect to truth.

In studying the relation of drama toward its deep-lying roots, I have had no interest in differentiating the American strain from any other. Recent events in the theater represent one phase of the ferment in the Great Society. And yet in a peculiar sense America is taking the lead in the establishing of the functions of the new theater in society. It is important that we clarify in our minds the true source of what we know as American drama. In spite of much temptation to find the source in the imagination of poets and the fancies of draftsmen, neither my reason nor my knowledge of the facts of the case permits me to do so. We shall have occasion to study the contributions of the poets as well as of the designers. We shall find that while these stimulated the fancy and released a creative urge, the validity of their creations was always tested by referring back to the more homely strains derived from the native storehouse. Indeed, the poets and the "new stagers" themselves found that their work gained significance only as it attached itself to the discoveries of those who were exploring the facts of our native life.

America has not been blind to the influence of the innovations from the continent. Our theater has extended a welcoming hand to the bizarre, the experimental, as it came across the ocean. But the true work for an American drama has not been done by the disciples of Gordon Craig and Reinhardt and Stanislavski, great as their contribution has been, but it has been done by those playwrights within the professional theater and outside its ranks who have thought deeply and thought through in an effort to identify dramatic expression with the motives and temper of American life. The free creative imagination is more important than free form. Imagination breaks through to form. And we are in error if we count form an external manifestation. It is an inner quality of the imagination. It is because form and substance are one that I seek the roots of the new American drama not in the ateliers of Florence and Berlin and Moscow, but in the homespun fancy of American playwrights who now and again felt the urge to write a play "the best way they knew how."

II

PLAYWRIGHT AS POET: JOSEPHINE PRESTON PEABODY —WILLIAM VAUGHN MOODY

When the poet commences playwriting he brings to his task a fine set of tools. Not that he always uses his tools. One of the recurrent perversities of the stage is the bad plays written by good poets. The plays are not bad because the authors are poets. The plays are bad because the author has not been able to apply to construction for the stage the standards and creative insight that presumably governed his work as poet. We have now to consider the work of two poets who wrote their names in the history of the American theater of the twentieth century. The first of these remained a poet to the end, achieving by her mastery of the subjective forms of verse a structure framed indeed like a play, with much of the appeal of a play and more of beauty of design and language than most plays can show, and yet lacking that objective self-motivating quality essential to a play. The other also began as a poet of subjective imagination. But his imagination ranged, and came to compass the interests and responsibilities of his people. The world pressed in upon him until he took the world to himself, identified himself with it, and became a dramatist who handled with unusual power the hidden qualities of character that reveal themselves to a poet's vision. Both playwrights died at the height of their powers.

In 1909 American pride was stirred by the award to an American poet and dramatist of a signal honor. Josephine Preston Peabody's play, "The Piper," was awarded the first prize from among fifteen hundred plays submitted by playwrights from all over the world, to open the Shakespeare Memorial Theatre at Stratford-on-Avon. The award of this prize to an American undoubtedly had a highly stimulating effect upon the composition of plays in this country, and upon the respect with which American stage work was viewed abroad. "The Piper" was produced at the Shakespeare Memorial Theatre by F. R. Benson in 1910 and at St. James Theatre in London, 1911. It was played at the New Theatre in New York, January, 1911, Edith Wynne Matthison having the rôle of the Piper.

During a productive period of about twenty years Josephine Preston Peabody wrote several volumes of verse, among them being "The Wayfarers" (1898); "Fortune and Men's Eyes" (1900); "The Book of the Little Past" (1908); "The Singing Man" (1911). She published five plays, "Marlowe"

(1901); "The Wings" (1905); "The Piper" (1910); "The Wolf of Gubbio" (1913); "The Chameleon" (1917). Of these the first four were in verse; the last in prose. All these are marked by a pure lyrical gift, an easy though not fecund fancy, a pervading note of charm and sentiment. Mrs. Marks (she married Professor Lionel S. Marks in 1906) had excellent control of sympathetic emotion and a style that flowed in graceful speech. The best qualities of her work are revealed in "The Piper," the play to which she owes her broader reputation in the theater.

The story of the Pied Piper of Hamelin, which has been frequently treated in literature, is not, strictly speaking, material for dramatic treatment. It is an appealing little fabric of old legend which derives its interest from no weaving of a pattern of human motives, but from its pictorial or sentimental value. The Piper was indeed said to have been urged by a desire for revenge against the older people of the village, but the mind does not linger upon his motive so much as upon the strange power of attraction he had whereby he could draw after him at will both the mice and the children. And as there was no real interest in the motive, there was little interest in the denouement. The Piper played and the children followed. That is all that remains of the story.

Manifestly there is not in this thin fable much material for a play. The author had to create a situation outside the legend by which the consequences of

her action could be sketched out, and a happy outcome could be maneuvered. In so doing the author
was perfectly right in keeping her invented action
simple and in adapting it to her own particular
genius of expression. She might have magnified the
contest between the Piper and villagers, in so doing
objectifying the theme and multiplying her episodes.
If she had done so she would have made the play
more vigorously dramatic. But she resists this
temptation. She centers the whole contest, in so far
as there is a contest, in the mind of the Piper. In
order to motivate this contest she creates the character of The Lonely Man, which is not only an effigy
of Our Lord, but is in addition the personification of
a loving, hungry, lonely strain in the Piper himself.
Pleas to the Piper for the return of the children, the
author does provide for. But the chief plea comes
from the Piper's own heart.

To the purposes of such an appeal the moving
verbal and poetic gift of the poet is well adapted.
The situation would be impossible—indeed, the play
would be impossible—without the unbroken poetic
power of the passages of emotional appeal. As
drama, the play would fall to the ground at any
moment that the author's verbal imagination failed.
The action floats poised in the language, it realizes
itself through the lips of the characters. The treatment of the character of the Piper demands the elim-
ination of many strains by which the Pied Piper in
legend obtains his vitality. The author lost a beau-

tiful Pagan when she made the Piper so good a Christian. The play is not without its vagueness of intruded symbolism. The episode of Barbara and the Sword-Swallower lies outside the main field of action. The Piper's refusal to give the children up to their parents, because their parents love gold, is an impertinence committed in order to strengthen in the play motives which are never very strong at best.

On account of its history "The Piper" must be considered one of the most important plays in the new movement of the American theater. But the author never was able to transfer to the stage the sure artistry of her poetry. A greater poet, and by this token a man who was better able to apply to the art of the theater the tenets of his poetry, was William Vaughn Moody. Moody carried poetry in the theater to the point of annihilation. So true was he as poet that he recognized that the requirements of verse were in mortal combat with the inner necessities of the playwright.

William Vaughn Moody had that rich complexity of attribute that gives the lie to the summary doctrines of the schools of criticism. Fine flower of a classical genius he had his roots in the prairies of the middle west; patriot and singer of his country's glories, there burned in his heart also the fires of revolt; a cloistered poet, he discarded poetry in order to reveal to his time the secret dramas that he saw fought out in the hearts of everyday people. William Vaughn Moody was born in Spencer, Indiana, July

8, 1869, the son of a steamboat captain. He was brought up in New Albany, Indiana, entered Harvard and was graduated in 1893. The following year he took his Master's Degree. After a year spent in Europe he returned to become instructor in English in the University of Chicago. He remained with the University until 1904. Meanwhile he had become known as one of the leading poets of the country. His "Ode in a Time of Hesitation" and "The Daguerreotype" had in them a mastery of moral forces as well as of the forces of beauty. From the beginning there was in him a forthright quality, usual among the greater poets, uncommon among those of lesser breed, of coming to grips with the spirit of the age and expressing his message with force and pure beauty. There was a quality of uncompromising patriotism in him—"my country to make it right"—that is heartening in days when patriotism seems to be a crime. In him, too, the spirit of revolt was strong, but it was a spirit that was hidden deep down in the necessities of his being and was brother to the spirit of affirmation. Moody did not raise his voice in a scream against every new manifestation of policy. Revolt was not to him a professional attitude of mind. It was a fundamental adjustment of himself to the deepest principles of living. It was a fashion of being continually on guard. It was another phase of that disgust that in the artist is so closely allied to rapture.

More than any plays written up to his time in

America, Moody's plays came out of moral conviction and mental necessity. He did not write as the
entertainers had done, to please the crowd, nor as
the reformers were doing, to elevate the stage. He
wrote because he had something to say that appeared
to him to be of moment. His message was relevant
to man in his human and divine relations. Therefore, it called for dramatic form. In his first plays
his themes were the generalized philosophical themes
that called for a wide symbolism in structure. As
he went on, his themes precipitated themselves into
the hearts of men. They were no less wide and significant, but their form of expression brought them
nearer home.

Moody wrote two verse plays, "The Fire Bringer"
and "The Masque of Judgment," one verse play left
incomplete at his death, "The Death of Eve," and
two prose plays, "The Great Divide" and "The
Faith Healer." Though the verse plays were conceived in a severely classic form, the author did not
put from his mind the idea that they might be produced. No extended review of these plays is called
for, as they do not fall into the current of practical
stage production. Moody had long had in mind the
idea of writing a prose play, and was making notes
on the play which eventually became "The Faith
Healer," when, on one of his trips to the southwest,
the underlying situation of a more dramatic play
came to his mind. The play in its first form was
quickly written. Entitled "The Sabine Women" it

was promptly submitted to Miss Margaret Anglin and was by her as promptly accepted for a trial performance in Chicago. The opening night of this production at Chicago in March, 1906, offered a drama behind the scenes, and out of sight of the audience, no less thrilling than the play that was being enacted upon the stage. After the sensational first act the curtain was held while arrangements for a contract were made among representatives of various interests. When these understandings were reached the play proceeded.

The germ of the play, as it had first come to Moody, had consisted of little more than a highly melodramatic situation. It was the kind of situation that of itself makes the fortune of a play. This situation concerned a young woman left alone in the great plains, who is come upon by a group of drunken ruffians. As a means of escape from the awful designs of the men she offers herself to the best of the pack if he will protect her from the others. The situation is one of great power, and on account of its daring nature became the nine days' wonder of the stage. The strength of the situation was a test of the author's powers as artist. As first produced the play was little more than good melodrama. It was in order to find an effective outworking of this fundamental situation in a higher order of drama that, after the signing of the contract, the play was turned back to the author for revision.

In this revision the author revealed his caliber.

Taking a sensationally melodramatic plot, Moody so raised its value by magnifying the moral and spiritual strains of the plot as to give the whole a wide and impressive significance that overshadowed the brutality of the central theme. Under the title "The Great Divide" the play was produced October 3, 1906, at the Princess Theater, New York, with Margaret Anglin as Ruth Jordan and Henry Miller as Stephen Ghent. It was produced at the Adelphi Theater, London, September 25, 1909, Miss Edith Wynne Matthison playing the part of Ruth Jordan. The difference between the earlier and later forms of the play is indicated by the two titles. In the final form the moral factors of the plot had been isolated and developed. In Moody himself there was the heritage of the Puritan. He knew as if it were a part of the experience of his own life, the struggle that lies at the heart of the Puritan conscience. The rigor of the Puritan sense of sin is the index of the Puritan experience of sin. The Puritan crucifies the flesh because the flesh is strong. Only superficially does the Puritan give the sense of quiet and peace. War is the key to his nature. Literature had falsified the Puritan because it had made the Puritan's standard of appearances the rule of its expression rather than the warfare in the Puritan's soul. Hawthorne alone of his generation opened the veil to the truth behind the repressions and denials of Puritanism and the impression he gave was elevated by a pellucid style into a region of lifeless concept. In this play Moody, Puritan himself, showed the war that is waged between the outer and the inner man. There is in fact a "great divide" between the code and the practice, between the demands of the flesh and the ideals of the spirit. On this "divide" are found the dilemmas of choice, the hypocrisies, the tergiversations of the Puritan nature. Here is the explanation of the lip service, the broken compacts of the impossible ideal. Moody began his play with Stephen Ghent as villain. He ended it with Ruth Jordan as villain. Stephen had at any rate kept the faith. He had acted always as his free ranging spirit dictated. She had kept the faith neither with herself nor with him. She had compromised her judgments, saved her body at the expense of her soul, acted always by quick reversals of policy instead of by sovereign principle.

In this play the "great divide" has another symbolism. The author objectifies the inner contest in the heart of the Puritan by showing that in different parts of the country, under different conditions of life, men govern their lives by different principles. While character itself does not essentially change from place to place, its manner of manifestation changes. The pressures of the older civilizations are such as to make character dig in. This in itself is one of the problems of the playwright. It provides the reason why the expansive methods of the drama of the past no longer serve the purposes of a society the chief work of which is to encrust, to invert, or to confuse the strains of personality and character. In great sections and groups of our Anglo-Saxon heritage character has dug in, the natures of men have been pinched, repressed, and made reflective. In other sections, particularly among those given to action, and among those whose checks have been released by life outdoors, life is free and expressive. Men act by impulse, in general they trust impulse; they are not given to contemplation and reflection. They have a morality, but it is not a reflective morality. It is a general belief in the square deal, in the rightness of appetite and passion. Between these two there is also a great divide. They do not speak the same language, they do not understand each other or as a rule respect each other. It would be a mistake to suppose that one section or one group is identified entirely with the one conception, and the other section or group with the other. And yet for the purposes of his story and the purposes of his interpretation of the American scene Moody was justified in making his divide a geographical one.

Such, then, is the theme of the play. It is a study of the "natural" versus the "repressive" doctrine of life as exemplified in the two leading characters, and incidentally by the secondary characters. Stephen is true to his codes and he comes through clean. Even in the first scene of attempted violence we see little to his discredit. He is there and he is following his leads as he sees them. But when she presents him other leads he is quick to seize and follow them. When she appeals to the better nature in him he responds immediately. This better nature is near the surface. The thing that makes him pay for her and save her is something more than passion. It is a native squareness in the man. When he pays he pays fairly by taking square chances in a pistol fight. And he gives her the chance to shoot him. When she lacks the nerve to do so—this failure of nerve is a shrewd index to something tortured and indirect in her nature—he holds her to her bargain. This too is a flash of truth in him. When the compact is fulfilled and he has married her and made her rich his morality remains fine and sure. He knows the hurt to her spirit involved in what he has done and he is willing to pay. He pays in various ways, in ways so subtle and intuitive that they should have evened up the score. Even then he knows when he is right and she is wrong, but because he had hurt her he is willing to serve her even while she is wrong, thinking that his own patience and honesty will lead her to see with open eyes.

Stephen Ghent is a simple character. Not so Ruth. Before she had met him she had tortured herself as later she tortured him. "I think I shall be punished for being so happy," she says, and Polly, her friend, remarks, "If Massachusetts and Arizona ever get in a mix-up in there" (indicating Ruth's heart) "woe be!" In words, at least, Polly is a free spirit. Polly expresses her idea in this way: "Happiness is its own justification, and it's the sacreder the more unreasonable it is. It comes or it doesn't. That's all you can say about it. And when it comes one has the sense to grasp it or one hasn't." Ruth hasn't either the sense or the power to grasp her happiness. And so in the face of his kindness she still hugs her torture to her bosom. He had bought her with a handful of nuggets. These nuggets weigh more than all his kindness. He serves her like a kindly man, but she breaks upon him with an anguished cry, remembering "the human beast, that goes to its horrible pleasure as not even a wild animal will go—*in pack, in pack!* I have tried—oh, you don't know how I have tried to save myself from these thoughts!" Again she says, "Every time you give me anything, or talk about the mine and what it is going to do, there rings in my ears that dreadful sneer, 'A dirt-eating Mojave would pay more than that for his squaw!'"

It must be clear that Ruth is a sick woman. He, knowing that she is sick, permits her to leave him. Separation from him, the memory of the wide truth and simplicity of the man compared with the tortuous beings around her, and the birth of her child all combine to cure her. When he takes her in his arms again, happy as he is to be joined with her more closely than before, he still cannot tell a lie. He stands by his guns. He is glad for everything that has brought her to his arms. And she at last understanding herself as well as him says, "You have taken the good of our life and grown strong. I have taken the evil and grown weak, weak unto death. Teach me to live as you do!" In this manner a true poet elevates a melodramatic theme to a universal significance.

In the measure that "The Faith Healer" has a larger abstract conception than "The Great Divide," it fails both of dramatic emphasis and of a real contribution to human knowledge. Again the scene is laid in the great Southwest. This play had been started before "The Great Divide" and Moody never completely satisfied himself in the form of this work. There are in existence two published forms, one in three acts and one in four acts. The play was produced in St. Louis in March, 1909, and in New York, 1910, in neither case with success. It appears clear that Moody had never thought through his great theme. This is not surprising, for it was not a theme that could be expressed within the limits of a three- or four-act naturalistic play. A naturalistic play may rise to the skies and compass all knowledge, given only that its earthly manifestations are within themselves consistent with human experience. When the playwright trenches human experience and ventures into regions which can be acceptable to the audience only by the creation of a superrational compact of common faith, he must at the same time surrender the closely knit surface of naturalistic action. In the case of "The Faith Healer" the author was careful to show that nothing that the healer did necessarily ran beyond human powers. An explanation or an alibi was provided for every supernatural event. And yet, as far as Michaelis was concerned, whether the powers he evoked were divine or not, the burdens he had to carry were such as to imply that his powers were veritably divine. It is only by such an interpretation that the drama of Michaelis is significant at all. To Michaelis it must have appeared that he was endowed with great powers, for he was called upon to pay the price of such powers. The author was apparently willing to show him paying this price, while he was not willing to ask us to believe that these powers are veritable. He dramatizes the agony of the faith healer with telling skill, but he is never able to give his work the final stamp of moral authority. As it concerns Michaelis, the play is a drama of sacred and profane love, with a new inclination away from the Oriental to the Occidental view of the soul's powers. On the side of the secondary characters it is of a much lower order, being given up to the study of the growth of a legend in a sparsely settled community, a community in which were to be found all degrees of faith and faithlessness, credibility and doubt. In the attempt to be detached and scientific at the same time that he is exploring the deeps of a soul's agony and creating a new conception of the dynamics of spiritual power, the author achieves an effect of vagueness and inconclusiveness.

III

THE "LITTLE MAN" AS DRAMATIC HERO: GEORGE ADE, GEORGE M. COHAN

It was, as I believe, the chief contribution of the poet to our drama that he taught the playwright that he, no less than other artists, could "follow through" to the ultimate values of his theme. The playwright has too often permitted himself to be waylaid before he has reached his end; he has been peculiarly subject to the seductions that lie along the way of the imagination. All art implies selection; selection implies underlying enthusiasms and disgusts. What more natural than that the poet, faced by the tinsel shows, the false controls of the old theater, should repudiate these with contempt? But there was in the American character another strain that turned no less imperatively against the falsehoods in the theater. This was that something canny and shrewd, humorous and self-knowing that is found in American character. The American is quick to accept but even quicker to discard. His gullibility is strong, but his disgusts are stronger. Taught by experience that everything may be tried, he is ready in test and ready in judgment. These qualities have their place in the everyday walks of life. Strangely enough they are closely associated with the qualities of the artist. When the tale is told it will be found that art was applied to the products of the American theater, not primarily by the practitioner of a subtle craft. The artistic method came from those men and women whose native reason taught them that art is the only way to truth.

America has made one contribution to the art of the world. This is a method of observation applied to the materials of experience by which these materials are preserved in "cold pack." This method is as far as possible from the self-conscious, doctrine-laden naturalisms and realisms of the Old World. These are systems, varying but slightly the one from the other, of doing life up in sirup. The American system is to catch and perpetuate our materials in the forms of life, selectively, of course, but in a cold, transparent liquid. The source of this technique is not literature at all. It is found in journalism. When the method of journalism first began to establish itself as a technique of art it had much to contend against. Perhaps the worst of its enemies was the falsehood and vulgarity that a "literary" realism had passed off as truth. Nothing better evidences the worm of falsehood that was eating the heart of "mere" literature, than the supercilious parodies on everything American that were passed off as realistic American observation. True observation did not exist. Instead, there was a false foreign pre-conception. When American characters were introduced they were burlesqued in the way that London burlesqued the colonial. For a conception of our own characters we went to the superficial and often

insulting caricatures of American life seen on the
Continental stage.   The American theme did not
exist on the American stage.   We adopted as our
own the colors that had been applied to American
life by a brush held in a hand four thousand miles
away.   For years our stage was busily engaged in
misrepresenting American life to the American people.   This fealty to an alien principle, particularly
among the superior and the apologetic, persists to
this day.   We borrowed the tricks and conventions
of the romantic play.   When Europe created the
problem play, we borrowed the problems of the Old
World and wrote heavy plays about problems which
were not essentially our own.   And when the craftsmen in color and design on the other side became
weary of a theater that choked the creative imagination and began to call for the destruction of the old
theater, our enthusiasts on this side of the Atlantic
joined the chorus and proceeded to plot the destruction of an institution that had never yet been born,
that had for us no real existence.   The American
theater and American literature had to be made, not
re-made.

Fortunately, not every American artist packs his
grip and goes to Europe every summer for inspiration.   There are even men and women of creative
gifts who do not subscribe to the revolutionary maga-
zines of the continent or get their ideas from the
bizarre drawings of the insurgent schools.   For the
beginnings of American drama I am disposed to go

to those men and women who first had eyes to see the American scene and to report it. They were not recognized as artists because it was not conceived that the materials they treated, materials so simple and lifelike, could be products of art. But they were artists, nevertheless. To them observation was enough. Every walk into the open air was a journey of discovery. Such observation as this was a kind of creation. It called forth a creative energy so absorbing that no force was left for further flights. Here then we have the reason why the first American plays to present the American scene with fidelity are almost worthless by any larger interpretation of the art of the theater. Character goes beyond theme. Few of them make any attempt to comprehend the potentialities behind the surfaces of events. "In the country of the blind, the one-eyed man is king." Literature and the stage were controlled by blind men who looked inward for truth and for want of knowledge made myths. Suddenly appeared men with sight. And merely to see was enough.

Of all the playwrights of yesterday, James A. Herne stands head and shoulders above the others for a native honesty of observation, combined with the power to construct an edifice of the imagination. Under a skill in the handling of pure artifice second to none in the history of our stage, Clyde Fitch possessed a real knowledge of the fundamentals of character. His treatment of feminine character was not alone the legerdemain of "the man who knows women." This mastery of character never eventuated into a play worthy of the insight displayed in its details. Fitch's failures in plot merely indicate the limits of his creative conception. These must not blind us to his real contributions to our stage, the flesh and blood and nerves of the gentlemen and gentlewomen next door. And in his last play, "The City," produced posthumously December 21, 1909, he breaks out of his accustomed rôle of facile entertainer and writes one of the strongest American plays. The very heaviness of hand of Augustus Thomas is in his early plays a mark in his favor, for it is a quality of his sincerity. No man of his time had less of the theater in his works, more of native observation of life. He was always held back from the utmost of the theatrical by a native genuineness and forth-rightness. In reviewing the work of Augustus Thomas it is well to remember the early "state" plays, "Arizona," "Alabama," "In Mizzoura," to which there adheres some of the native soil of the countryside rather than his heavy-handed society plays and plays of pseudo-intellectualism.

None of these men had that reporter's facility of observation combined with a cynical detachment of sympathy that has had so large a part in setting the standards of the American art of the theater. Thirty years ago George Ade began the composition of those "Fables in Slang" that for insight into character and pungency of expression take their place with the best work of the "character writers" of the past. I am not now interested in the slang in which these fables were couched, though this is an essential feature of their quality. Behind the slang of these fables there is a mine of knowledge of human character. The best of it is that this knowledge is unspoiled by the formulas of a conventional literature, art, or morality. George Ade was both an index and an influence. His popularity with the people is not to be despised; coteries to the contrary notwithstanding. The people are by no means always wrong. But more important than this is the fact that George Ade was a corrective and stimulative to the imaginative writer of America. Had he done nothing else than to supply a de-bunking test for American writing and psychology, his place would be secure.

Our interest in George Ade as a corrective influence in American writing is enhanced by the fact that he definitely turned his hand to the stage. No one of his plays requires or would permit revival to-day; nevertheless, they were milestones in the history of our native drama. His importance lies not so much in the musical plays (though of these "The Sultan of Sulu" had a satiric quality that gave point to its lighter graces) as in his comedies. In "The College Widow," "The County Chairman," "Father and the Boys," we have, among a number of Hick types from the yokel drama of the time, an assortment of characters that were new to the American stage. College students, the president of the Fresh-water college, the political figures of a small middle-western community, the "college widow" who buries one every commencement, the athletic hero, the new capitalist, the state's attorney, the store porch orator, the members of the fife and drum corps, the subscription book agent—these characters have to-day receded far into the past, but they have not receded from memory.   They were hand-picked from the streets on which Ade walked as a young man.   The actions in which they engaged, the caucuses, political campaigns, football contests, gossiping matches at the railroad depot and in the store, were the material of the life he and his neighbors had lived.   Let it be granted that these characters and materials were treated with a sportive levity, that the fable of the play was never of the slightest significance.   It remains that the author had brought observation to the theater.   George Ade was a humorist.   Like the best of humorists his humor consisted in having a good eye.   As this was a rare endowment in the theater of his time, he occupies in my opinion a higher position in the history of our stage than the themes of his plays would seem to indicate.   Urged by a self-judgment as sure as his observation was keen, Ade laid down his pen at the height of his success.   His had been a pungent, corrective wit.   He set many on the right way.

A recent writer has said, "Great drama cannot be written of little souls."   With this dogma I thoroughly disagree.   The world is filled with little souls.

What is the measure of a soul, after all? When is a soul great and when small? To require that the drama treat only the great souls is to require that the drama live in the world of legend after the era of legend is past. Rather than agree that no great play can be written about a little man, I should hold that the little man is peculiarly the subject for a great play. In so far as a play magnifies a man it places him above the values that are common to the experience of all men, those values that acquire force from the pressures of social life. Nothing is so puerile, so futile, as man's poor magnitudes. Take a play in which man is shown to be master of his fate and you have a little play. The stage has lived so long under the myth-making convention that even when it presents little men it tends to show them magnified beyond their station by a greater dignity or under a greater ridicule. It has not yet learned to treat the little man—that is, the average member of society—in his relative magnitudes as compared with other men. Until it does learn to do so the stage will not be true to life.

I should be far from suggesting that those men who have done the most to introduce the little man to the stage have been aware of any deep purpose, or that they have had an artistic intent. They have carefully eschewed artistic intent. Many of their plays have been in the last degree crude; they have been directed particularly to pleasing and drawing the crowd. But as I am concerned in tracing out the

strains of an incipient art of the American Theater,
I must take these strains where I find them. I can
no more ignore a man because he makes no extravagant claims to merit than I can accept without question the judgment of the man who calls himself an
artist.

The great successor of George Ade is George M.
Cohan. Gifted with much of Ade's humor and clear
vision, there is in Cohan a much larger endowment
of hocum than in Ade. Few can equal Cohan for
ability to see through the follies of another. Few
can equal him in the brazen effrontery with which
he himself employs cheap devices to win the applause
of the crowd. For this there is but one apology.
He knows, and he knows that the audience knows.
There is, then, between him and the audience an
engaging comradeship of understanding. Cohan is
Ade stagified. He adds to some of the wisdom of
Ade an efficient theater sense. He subtracts from
Ade that resolute self-judgment and discretion that
scorns to be on the wrong side with two or with a
million. To the extent that Cohan goes beyond Ade
in theatrical success he falls behind him as observer
and artist. Cohan never achieved himself for one
reason. He became so much a master of what "they"
wanted that he never wanted anything overwhelm-
ingly for himself.

In 1914 Cohan and George Jean Nathan worked
out and published a system of "mechanics of emotion" which is an amazingly successful summary of

the tricks of popular appeal in the theater. Developing the theory that theatrical emotions are largely mechanical, that we all laugh and cry at the same things, they catalogued the emotion germs under three classes: (1) tears, (2) laughs, (3) thrills, and named some hundred tried and trustworthy theatrical expedients by which these germs could be cultivated. Skillful as is this summary as a dissertation on the theater, it is even more valuable as a dissertation on the little man who makes up the audience at a play. To this little man Cohan appeals. And yet, because he knows the little man and can place him bodily on the stage, Cohan has a place in our drama from which he will not be dislodged. He has never yet written a play that is worthy of his skill and of his knowledge of commonplace life. He has approached the summit of his skill only in such works of adaptation and collaboration as "Seven Keys to Baldpate" and "The Tavern." And yet to ignore that strain of commonplace insight that is found in Cohan would be to neglect a creative strain in the theater of our day. Now and again in the midst of his theater tricks something true breaks through. You feel that Cohan would have avoided this if he could. He would rather have the applause of the "fellers" than the prizes of the schoolmaster. In the very *mauvaise honte* of his attitude there is something appealing and honest. Walter Prichard Eaton calls attention to the fact that Cohan doesn't want to be taken seriously. He does and he doesn't. If only he could put over something serious without being caught at it! There is in him the shyness of the man who has never learned to dance with the girls and therefore hangs around the door of the dance-hall jeering with the gang at the fellers inside. More than any one writing, he knows both Broadway and the country beyond. He recognizes that Americans are in essence small-town men, that the boy who presses the pavements of New York is a villager. There is the sense of the back-country in his work. There is the sense, too, of the great distances a boy may travel in a few jumps.

With Cohan the play of the little man became established. And before long its own particular technique had been created. The cynical sense of the audience required that credibility should not be stretched; the self-consciousness of all of us demanded that deeper emotions should not be touched; a youthful optimism and a belief in good fairies demanded that he who walked the gutter to-day should ride in his limousine to-morrow. The master of this type of composition is Winchell Smith, closely followed by others too numerous to mention. Such plays as "The Fortune Hunter," "It Pays to Advertise," "Turn to the Right," "Fair and Warmer," have in them a superficial truth; careful regard to the mechanism of emotion has brought this to the verge of falsehood. It is the same type of truth that caused a nine months' amazement following the publication of "Main Street" and "Babbitt." It is the truth as it presents itself to the mind of a precocious boy after he has learned something about the tricks and secrets of life; more important as a personal discovery than as a code of thinking. And yet it stands for thinking with many of us. In the text of "The Fortune Hunter," as stated by one of the characters, can be found a whole volume of American philosophy. "All you have to do is to select some small country town, far enough away from the city, where you can content yourself to settle down to the simple life for a while and make yourself solid in the community by your exemplary habits, combined with good clothes and polite manners." In this case the reward is to be marriage to an heiress; in any case the reward is to be a fortune. These attempts to bring the little American to the stage are crude enough and the eternal tendency to falsify newly discovered truth is evident in them. And yet they will serve. In such plays as "Too Many Cooks" and "The First Year" there are hints now and then of permanent values. In the freshness of humor, in the domestic emotions, in the faithful adherence of theatrical motive to the motive of life, and of stage fate to the teachings of experience, these plays command some admiration. They are not great art, but they are not lies. The stage must come down to the sidewalks and floors on which we live. The stage has no other subjects with which to deal than little men caught in the trap of circumstance. It can treat these men in many ways, but these are its materials. Great groups of the human family had formerly not existed for the theater, because they had been without free will. Now that they are free they come to have meaning for the theater. It is something new for ordinary people to have any interest in their own affairs. Now that they have obtained control, their own affairs become their only interest. The stage is crowded with plays which to a Martian or to a person one generation removed would be of an incredible dullness because the matters discussed are so unimportant. But to their contemporaries the action is illumined. The rocks and bowlders in the back lot behind the house have become acres of diamonds.

IV

EUGENE WALTER—EDWARD SHELDON

Nothing that has been said so far should imply that because the theater has come to treat little men imagination has abdicated the theater; quite the contrary. Imagination is in fact finding the only field that has not yet been exhausted. Here, in the motives and passions of the commonplace man, newly endowed with responsibilities the like of which he had never known before, caught in the mesh of social action and inter-action, there are opportunities for the theater richer far than the stories of lonely kings. This new drama can not be written by taking a superficial view. More than ever the admonition of

the critic—"See life steadily and see it whole!"—
takes upon itself meaning. Writes Storm Jameson,
from whose stimulating pages I have quoted before
in this book: "The difference between good and bad
artists becomes a question whether the artist has
given of a superabundant vitality to re-create life,
or whether he has merely taken the facts of life to
manufacture his work. The first is a sign of
strength; the latter, a sign of weakness." Simply
because the stage is coming to deal with the life
lived by every man in the terms of that life, it is
demanding of the playwright that he dig down under
the surfaces of life.

Two men appeared on the horizon of the American
Theater at about the same time. They had different
sources and their histories were quite unlike. Eugene
Walter had gone to school to the world. He had
been reporter, circus follower, and roustabout. He
came to the stage, so they say, by way of the park
bench. He was thirty when he won his first success.
Edward Sheldon was a Harvard man. He learned
the stage from reading, and under the tuition of the
first of the university courses in drama. He came to
his first success when little more than a school boy.
And yet after they began to write, the work of these
two displayed striking points of similarity. Both
attacked their materials with an extraordinary intensity. They believed in the power concept of art.
Walter never got over feeling that he could break
through to reality if he could only buck the line hard

enough. And there is something to be said for the idea. In a time when a facile trickery seems all that is necessary to secure a vogue in the arts of the novel, the short story and the theater, something must be said for the man who grapples reality rather than merely negotiates with its appearances. After all, art is not organization, and truth is not reached through schemes of promotion. The easy measures of the mobilizer of forces go haltingly in art creation. On the other hand, the man who would break through must be endowed with something besides force. Much of life opens itself to the interpretations of the motor or the kinetic values. Much of the best does not so open itself at all. Of the two, Sheldon was the first to learn that one does not make matches with a sledge-hammer. With all his skill Walter continued to treat playwriting as if it were a strong-arm act.

At the time when other playwrights were tossing about bright-colored balls or debating sententiously on the problems of life, these men proceeded to raise chunks of reality over their heads by their own muscles. Both men broke under the strain. The stage has not yet supplied a man who can, like Balzac, carry bricks and mortar in a city of the imagination for unceasing years. Balzac broke at sixty. On the stage they break earlier or they change to lighter stuff.

After "Sergeant James" in 1901 and "The Undertow" in 1907, Eugene Walter came to his stride in 1907 with "Paid in Full." Thereafter he wrote about a dozen acknowledged plays, only three of which (if we omit his dramatization of "The Trail of the Lonesome Pine") deserve serious consideration. Walter's reputation rests on "Paid in Full," "The Easiest Way," and "Fine Feathers."

Walter is a positivist. He subscribes to the doctrine more common a half century ago than to-day, "Character is fate." The entire action of his plays develops from the characters themselves. This type of playwriting implies a definite and rather restricted conception of human values. Character to Walter was represented by the moral forces of stamina, steadfastness, and fidelity. He has no interest in, he is not aware of, the romances of character that lie outside of these attributes. As this was his interest in the character, it followed then that this was his interest in the play. His plays were studies of the moral stresses between characters.

Because Walter is so much interested in character, and rests his play upon character, he is extraordinarily careful in building up a conception of the character in the minds of the audience before the real action begins. There is something implacably logical in his insistence that all the elements of the denouement should be found in the characters, that no room be left for chance. And he never permits his forces to run at loose ends, or, commits the sentimental crime of blaming the sins of the individual on society.

To guide his own thinking in the composition of his play, Walter worked out a complete scenario of the life of the characters before the opening of the play. This outline for "The Easiest Way" has been printed. The character of Laura Murdock as outlined in this Description of Characters is of such a nature as to stipulate the catastrophe of the play. Such a character could not escape.

"A woman of intense superficial emotions, her imagination was without any enduring depths, but for the passing time she could place herself in an attitude of great affection and devotion. Sensually, the woman had marked characteristics, and with the flattery that surrounded her she soon became a favorite in the select circles who made such places as 'The Poodle Dog' and 'Zinkland's' famous. In general dissipation she was always careful not in any way to indulge in excesses which would jeopardize her physical attractiveness or for one moment diminish her sense of keen worldly calculation.

"In time she married. It was, of course, a failure. Her vacillating nature was such that she could not be absolutely true to the man to whom she had given her life, and, after several bitter experiences, she had the horror of seeing him kill himself in front of her. There was a momentary spasm of grief, a tidal wave of remorse, and then the peculiar recuperation of spirits, beauty and attractiveness that so marks this type of woman. She was deceived by other men in many various ways and finally came to that stage of life that is known in theatrical circles as being 'wised up.'

"At nineteen, the attention of a prominent theatrical manager being called to her, she took an important part in a New York production and immediately gained considerable reputation. The fact that before reaching the age of womanhood she had had more escapades than most women have in their entire lives was not generally known in New York, nor was there a mark upon her face or a single coarse mannerism to betray it. She was soft-voiced, very pretty, very girlish. Her keen sense of worldly calculation led her to believe that in order to progress in her theatrical career she must have some influence outside of her art and dramatic accomplishment, so she attempted with no little success to infatuate a hard-headed, blunt and supposedly invincible theatrical manager, who, in his cold, stolid way, gave her what love there was in him. This, however, not satisfying her, she played two ends against the middle, and finding a young man of wealth and position who could give her, in his youth, the exuberance and joy utterly apart from the character of the theatrical manager, she adopted him and for a while lived with him. Exhausting his money she cast him aside, always spending a certain part of the time with the theatrical manager. The young man became crazed, and at a restaurant tried to murder all of them.

"From that time up to the opening of the play

her career was a succession of brilliant coups in gaining the confidence and love, not to say the money, of men of all ages and all walks in life."

Not only does Walter give this attention to a leading character. Effie St. Clair is of only secondary importance in the play, but her past history is presented with the same hardness of outline:

"Effie St. Clair is a type of a Tenderloin grafter in New York, who, after all, has been more sinned against than sinning; who, having been imposed upon, deceived, ill-treated and bulldozed by the type of men who prey on women in New York, has turned the tables, and with her charm and her beauty has gone out to make the same slaughter of the other sex as she suffered with many of her sisters.

"She is a woman without a moral conscience, whose entire life is dictated by a small mental operation. Coming to New York as a beautiful girl she entered the chorus. She became famous for her beauty. On every hand were the stage-door vultures ready to give her anything that a woman's heart could desire, from clothes to horses, carriages, money and whatnot; but with a girl-like instinct, she fell in love with a man connected with the company, and during all the time that she might have profited and become a rich woman by the attentions of these outsiders, she remained true to her love until finally her fame as the beauty of the city had waned. The years told on her to a certain extent, and there were others coming, as young as she had been and as good to look at;

and where the automobile of the millionaire had once been waiting for her she found that through her faithfulness to her lover it was now there for some one else. Yet she was content with her joys until finally the man deliberately jilted her and left her alone.

"What had gone of her beauty had been replaced by a keen knowledge of human nature and of men, so she determined to give herself up entirely to a life of gain."

These descriptions, long as they are, are necessary as showing the care with which Walter builds up the characters of his plays. Given this conception of character and of the imprint of character on circumstance, it follows that these plays possess certain qualities of strength along with no less striking limitations. The action of all of Walter's plays operates within narrow restrictions. As a critic and exponent of life as a whole he is not to be trusted. He must either love or hate. His characters are "all of a piece"; he judges them summarily. He has no interest in the internal struggle, the contest of dividing forces in the individual. There is in his attitude toward people much of the all-wise cynicism of the newspaper man. Never rising to irony, his attitude is that of gruffness, of the sneer. He particularly despises the weaker brother or sister, the welcher, the four-flusher. For such an one Walter's scorn is scathing. His cruelty in judging ideas, standards, pretensions, has drawn to him credit for the possession of an uncompromising passion for truth. For my part I should trust his truth more if it were less simple, if his judgments were more kindly. In his pursuit of the brutal truth I suspect that he has come to over-emphasize the brutal, to underrate the truth. There are times when truth is stark, when it sears the soul, burns through surplus tissue. There are times, too, when truth is tender. The more art is true the more it excuses. Walter excuses nothing; his sense of blame is strong. He has but one moral law. It is "Withstand!" All his plays are variations of this. In "Paid in Full" Joe Brooks is not enough of a man; he cannot stand the simplest tests of manhood. So the author puts him through his three hours of torture and shows him up for the craven he is. This play was produced February 25, 1908. Without doubt it is one of the outstanding plays of the period on account of the moral intensity the author applied to his theatrical judgment. Laura Murdock, of "The Easiest Way," does not love enough, is not strong enough. The author has shown by his meticulous analysis of her career of what stuff she was made, but his scorn is no less biting when she is shown up to be what indeed she is and always has been. Walter shows his moral predilections when in a letter to Montrose J. Moses (published in "Representative Plays by American Dramatists") he writes "Incidentally I do not think much of it (the play). To my mind a good play must have a tremendous uplift in thought and pupose. 'The Easiest Way' has none of this. There is not a character in the play really worth while with the exception of the old agent." To the present writer he once compared the play unfavorably with "Paid in Full" and "Fine Feathers," because while these latter treated the commonplace bread-and-butter temptations of life, "The Easiest Way" dealt only with sex passion as expressed in weak men and women. With Walter's requirement of uplift for a play I venture to disagree. Such a requirement places an unnecessary burden upon the dramatist. Walter's desire to make his every action morally significant is the greatest blemish to his art. It places a harness upon his observation and binds his action within a narrow round.

After writing several plays of pure melodrama, of force from which even morality had been lost, Walter came back in "Fine Feathers" (produced January 7, 1913) to the censure of the frivolity of a vain woman and the weakness of a too complaisant husband. In "Just a Woman" (1916) he gives again a picture of a faithful woman who withstands. In spite of his ability to judge women harshly, Walter belongs to the chivalrous school of writers. Woman is the weaker vessel. Her strength is the strength of the spirit. She has not had the discipline of responsibility that man has had. All the more honor then to her when she proves herself at once fine and firm. Walter had learned to go beyond the reporter in applying a creative intensity to his work. But he never learned in what deep mines true morality lies hidden. His plays derive a theatrical force from the lack of discrimination with which they are conceived. Even at their best they never achieve the finality of human documents.

Few American playwrights have shown as wide a diversity of style as Edward Sheldon and as wide a difference of quality. He has written three plays in as many different fashions, which stand among the best plays of the period. On the other hand, he can and does on occasion produce complete failures, plays that have excellence neither of conception nor of execution. Edward Sheldon was born in Chicago February 4, 1886. He took his Bachelor's Degree at Harvard in 1907 and his Master's in 1908. The same year he submitted to Harrison Grey Fiske for the use of Mrs. Fiske, the play "Salvation Nell." As submitted, the play was far too long and it presented no evidence that the author knew anything about the stage of a theater or the ways of the profession. Nevertheless, it showed such a graphic power of observation and such an unspoiled sense of dramatic values that its qualities were immediately recognized. Much cut and drawn together, the play was produced at Providence, Rhode Island, November 12, 1908, and in New York, November 17.

Edward Sheldon owed a great debt of gratitude to Mr. and Mrs. Fiske for recognizing the qualities of his play in a crude manuscript and for realizing these qualities in the production. The play as produced was appreciably the result of the loving and expert collaboration on the part of the producer and the star. It was a case in which a budding talent had the benefit of a sympathetic coöperation at its inception. Years passed before Sheldon turned out a play that equaled this first play either for interest or for the successful execution of his plan. And he never again did a work with the close observation and the emotional urgency of this first play. It would be difficult to magnify the promise held out by "Salvation Nell" upon its first production. The gift that Sheldon first brought to the stage was the ability to see reality free from the convention of the theater and to distil drama from this untheatrical reality. The play takes in the American theater something of the place occupied by "The Selicke Family" in the history of German dramatic realism. Had Sheldon followed his original flair he might have been known as the playwright of commonplace life. Instead, he becomes the highly competent, sometimes inspired playwright of theatrical emotion. "Salvation Nell" shows in their incipiency qualities that other playwrights toil years to attain. The play is particularly significant in what it avoids and in what it discards. It might have been written as a dramatic romance after the fashion of the plays of Henry Arthur Jones. The author chose to treat it as a hard-gnarled bit of reality unrelieved by beauty or fine writing. "Salvation Nell" is a story of stunted emotions and conceptions. Nell is a bar-room scrubwoman, who lives with a man not her husband. In an access of fury at a lout who insults her, her man kills the fellow and is sent to the Pen. When he comes back he is the same as ever, ignorant, very much disposed to trust his own way and to suspect any way other than his own. But while he has been in prison a change has come over her through the influence of the Salvation Army. She does not understand all that the officers of the Army tell her, but—always within her limits—she accepts it as true. She is confused, inarticulate, but she is through with the old life. And she is determined to bring him around to her view. She stands by her position with a stolid faith even under threat of death. And in the end she wins; her stupid fidelity has won him to her side.

After "Salvation Nell" Sheldon has written about ten plays and has had a hand as adapter and collaborator in others. Among these plays are "The Nigger" (1909); "The Boss" (1911); "Princess Zim-Zim" (1911); "Egypt" (1912); "The High Road" (1912); "Romance" (1913); and "The Garden of Paradise" (1913). In my opinion none of these requires serious consideration except "Romance" and "The Garden of Paradise." "The Nigger" was chosen by the directors of the New Theater as the fourth play on the repertory of its first season. It was produced December 4, 1909. In spite of a vein of high seriousness, this play is nothing more than a race melodrama with arranged situations.

The play makes no pretense to uncover the qualities of the chief characters concerned, nor does the situation ever rise to high significance or thrilling appeal. A governor-elect about to be inaugurated and to be married learns that he has negro blood in his veins. He resigns his office and gives up the woman he loves. Practically the entire fabric of the play lies in this field of external action. "The Boss" is a business play, the tensions of which lie in wide palpable emotions, motives for the uplift of the slums, the working man, and business morality. An Irish grain dealer aspires to handle all the grain in the country and to marry the daughter of his rival. Not only will this marriage save a father's honor and fortune, but also it will serve the interests of the poor who are dear to the young woman. A fight develops between her brother and The Boss; the brother uses his influence to call a strike of Union men. There is a contest of "titanic" forces, but in the end Boss Regan wins her love. Out of such materials as this the "strong" play of yesterday was made. "The High Road," produced November 19, 1912, by Mrs. Fiske, represents the thoroughfare of an ambitious woman's career. The play had novelty in that it employed the chronicle form. Each of the five acts is an episode in the career of a woman from the rural seclusion of her girlhood to the home of her protector and finally to a place as the wife of the governor of the state. Thrice she makes fateful decisions, first when she leaves her home to pursue her dream, next when she decides to give up her protector, and last when as the wife of the candidate she is threatened with exposure; she does not cringe, but makes a clean breast of her life and wins by audacity. In the midst of much that is old, amid a mixture of political and industrial interests and banal high sentiments, one element of originality stands out. This is the introduction of the Nietzschean doctrine of the "sinner devouring his sin". In "The Song of Songs," produced 1914, Sheldon employs some of the material of Sudermann's novel for dramatic use. The story does not lend itself to an American setting and the play was unsuccessful.

It is not until we reach "Romance" and "The Garden of Paradise" that we come again to works that require serious consideration. Excellent as each of these is within its class, neither returns to the form and method of "Salvation Nell." This play had been free from all smell of the theater. Its successors were essentially theater pieces with every theatrical artifice employed to the extreme limit. Not only has the author given up his pursuit of reality; he is no longer interested in truth. It is enough for him now if he can magnify an emotion or create an illusion of beauty. Both these plays are among the most skillful of American plays in sheer theatrical craftsmanship. Both are remarkable for sustained power of emotional expression. Neither one can be considered a great creative work of the theater.

"Romance" was fortunate in having a star who played the leading rôle as if she had been born to it. But the play would have made its appeal with any capable actress. Every possible use was made of the appeals of theatrical sentiment, even to the employment of a containing action in which the emotional mood of the entire play is established. The "dream" form of play, that flashes back to reveal the substance of a man's thoughts or of his experience, has become common on the stage in the last ten years. The form was not so common a decade ago. The story was sure of sympathy if only it was well told. Sheldon saw to it that his story was well told. The tales of "dear dead women," of loves past and done for, of the lingering regrets of past renunciations, never fail to draw their tear. How much more appealing are they if they deal with an altogether fascinating actress, an altogether lovable minister, and if the actress speaks a broken jargon and her career gives hints of forbidden intrigues. The author has not failed to use every expedient to heighten the allure of his play. No hard injection of meaning intrudes. It is a story of romantic yesterday in a New York that was simpler than now, and more loving. The play is "Romance" and nothing more. It is romance compounded with a truly remarkable sense of what the audience will accept and what reject. For let it be remembered that our audiences are suspicious of romance in these days, are ready to spew out of their mouths a concoction that is not spiced nicely to taste.

"The Garden of Paradise" resembles "Romance" in the imaginative energy with which, once having established his theme, the author develops all its possibilities. The play is a very much bigger piece of work than "Romance," though before the people it was rather a sad failure. The failure of "The Garden of Paradise" is not to be charged up to the play, except to the extent that the play went beyond the imaginative powers of the audience and the producer. "Romance" had succeeded largely because the stage possessed facilities for its adequate production. "The Garden of Paradise" failed because the stage did not at the time possess facilities for its production, or these facilities, if existent, were not employed. Neither in acting, stage setting nor direction did the production approach the demands of the play.

"The Garden of Paradise" must have been a labor of love; certainly it was a labor of imaginative courage. It is based on "The Little Mermaid" by Hans Christian Andersen, and tells the story of Swanhild, the mermaid daughter of the Emperor of Under Sea, who dreamed of the great world of men and of the happy ones who lived above the sea. She has heard of little human beings who run about on beautiful white legs and has determined to go among them. The characters of the fable are of two classes, Sea Folk and Land Folk. The scenes are Under the

Sea, the Open Sea, the Shore by the Convent, the Cave of the Sea Witch, the Kingdom of the Blue Mountain, the Queen's Bower, the Queen's Garden, and the Bridal Ship. The language employed in telling the story is simple and unaffected, a little Gilbertian, perhaps, with whimsical jests, and here and there a laughing allusion to the sea, and to fishes and under-sea folk and their ways.

On their fifteenth birthday the under-sea children rise to the surface of the sea. The three mermaids, Lona, Thorna, and Swanhild, rise above the sea and Swanhild sees the king. She sees men dancing and notices that creatures cannot be graceful on legs. There is something of Miranda's exaltation in her question, "Is that a man who is so—so white and glorious?" She races the ship; lightning strikes it. The ship breaks up and sinks. The King is lying in Swanhild's arms. "Are you Death?" he asks her. "I am only a little mermaid who did not understand . . . I love you. . . . Will you give me half your soul?" she answers. She lays him · on the ground and disappears.

In the next scene convent bells are ringing. Girls' voices chant:

> A voice in the wind that blows
>   From the land beyond the Sea
> Has sung to every rose
>   The song it sings to me—
> To the white rose on my breast,
>   To the butterflies and bees,

To the little birds that nest
Among the apple trees.

The King awakens; a dark beauty gazes down on him. Long ago this retreat had not been a convent, but a temple to a heathen goddess who had risen from the sea. Now the King loves the dark girl whom he sees in his waking vision. He and she are fated to carry each other in memory for long months. The scene shifts to the Cave of the Sea Witch; reminders are here of Hauptmann's "The Sunken Bell." Swanhild swims to the Witch's Cave, daring the great tree that stands at the door of the cave to trap the foolhardy. She demands that the Witch give her a human form that she may be near the King. "Has age a greater joy than guiding home the love-ships of the young?" the Witch asks, and grants Swanhild her boon, demanding only her promise that at sunrise on the morning after his marriage with another Swanhild shall come and lose her human form and serve the Witch as a slave forever after. Swanhild promises and goes. She has her dream of love.

The King on his part cherishes the vision of the girl who had leaned over him on the island. "Are you not well, sire?" Lord Otho asks. And the king answers: "Well enough, my lord; unless it be a sickness of the mind to sit alone here in my chair and wish for all the things that cannot be.

"*Lord Otho:* What things, sire?

"*The King:* (Smiling as he points to the sea) To

turn these waters into purple wine—to dredge the
heavens with a net of stars—who knows?—Perhaps
to be a sailor boy and not the King. Dreams, my
lord—but lovely dreams!"

The galleons are departing on an embassy to the
young Queen of the South. The King is to be married by his father's dying wish. Swanhild appears
at the palace stairs; she drinks the Witch's charm,
"White bird, is it you?" calls the king. Her sisters
call from the Sea:

> Mermaid, mermaid, come with me,
> Night has fallen, you are free!

She goes with the King, serving him as his page,
and is happy loving him, he dreaming forever of his
day in Paradise. He is to sail to-morrow to meet
the bride whom he has never seen. On her island the
Queen is dreaming of the shipwrecked vagabond with
broad shoulders and strong, white arms who had
been thrown up on shore and had rested on her
bosom and then had gone away. She does not wish
to wed the King. She would run away except that
she must feed her gold fish. Then Swanhild comes
and knows that the Queen is the King's maiden of
dreams. Being a faithful page she delivers the message that is to break her own heart and to deliver
her to the Witch. The Queen, too, makes her a confidant, tells that she cannot marry the King because
she loves another. But Swanhild knows all and contrives to bring the King and Queen together and as

the two meet and recognize each other Swanhild, who stands above the kneeling couple, "turns and smiles at the distant sea." Swanhild goes with them even on the bridal ship. But her thoughts are in terror of the things lying hidden in caves of the sea. She dances for them, "a sea gull skimming through the storm," hearing always the tolling of a bell under the sea and mermaid voices calling her. With fear and mad delight Swanhild answers her sisters. They are on the gunwale beside her, their cheeks cold, their kisses salt. If she is to be a mermaid again, if she is to escape the Witch's doom, the cave, the bones, the snakes, the hungry tree, she must kill the King. He lies before her. But she cannot kill the King. She throws the knife into the sea. Far away is heard the triumphant laughter of the Witch. But the Witch loses her, for the sky and sea fade and in their place appear the golden stairs leading to the Throne and at the foot of them Swanhild, dressed in woman's shining robes. Laughing and weeping she mounts and the curtains close.

V

CHARLES RANN KENNEDY, GEORGE MIDDLETON, RACHEL CROTHERS

George Jean Nathan once expressed a platitude with the force of a paradox when he said, "A play is never finer than the man who creates it." We may extend this truism to read, "The philosophy of a play is never deeper than the philosophy of the man who writes the play." We are developing in these days a form of dramatic construction fashioned out of pure observation in which the completed product stands for itself alone without any extraneous meaning or implication. Of such a work we are accustomed to say that it "throws no shadow." All parts of this work are under an equal light and the work is to be judged as an arrangement of factors, a presentative composition of the elements of dramatic construction. There is no question that such a form as this represents a high aspiration in artistic values. The possibilities of this type of "etched" realism have hardly yet been conceived. Probably the best example of this style of composition is "What Price Glory," by Maxwell Anderson and Laurence Stallings, presented in 1924.

Whatever may be the value of this style of composition judged by absolute standards, it remains that the average playwright expects to create, and the average spectator desires to witness, a play that "throws a shadow." Here we have to consider, not technique alone, but the author's outlook. The play depends not alone upon the author's hand and eye, but upon the formed conceptions of a brain that has occupied itself with the problems of living. In this field there is, of course, the widest divergence of gifts. There is a school of playwrights, excellent craftsmen as a rule, who seek to enhance the value of their observation of life by a censure of life and its institutions.   The stage is a platform; *ergo*, the stage becomes didactic.   The situation involves some strange paradoxes.   Men who are not in the least innovators, who are as conventional as the multiplication table, begin chastising society for its sins. In seeking to justify their work by something outside itself capable playwrights become incapable reformers.   Social zeal encroaches upon and edges out artistic discernment.   Of all the faults of the contemporary drama in America this is the most prevalent.

Charles Rann Kennedy's "The Servant in the House" was produced in 1908.   The play was one of the events of the season and maintains its importance as an outstanding exemplar of a certain style of playwriting to this day.   Charles Rann Kennedy was an Englishman who had transplanted his activities to America.   He had been associated with the more advanced movements of the insurgent playwrights of England; he was married to Edith Wynne Matthison, one of the leading exponents of classical technique in acting in the English-speaking world; he has consistently employed his influence and his resources in behalf of the better traditions of the theater.

"The Servant in the House" belongs to that type of play in which moral forces are not merely implied in the action; moral forces supply the action.   The action of the play develops from the clash of moral abstractions.   The play is therefore closely related to allegory. "The Servant in the House" is, in fact, a morality, but a modern morality. To a remarkable degree the author accepted the implications of the morality. As his characters were moral abstractions, they lacked those more indeterminate qualities of personality that create shadow zones in the action of most plays. There were no shadow zones in this play. The entire action was definite, categorical, and explicit. In form the play is as diagrammatic as a syllogism, which indeed it is. It is worked out like a demonstration in logic. The author permits himself no word, gesture, or action that does not serve definitely the purpose of his conclusion. Nor does he permit his action to be halted. Once it is started it moves without a break to the conclusion. While the curtain falls in order to give the audience time for momentary mental relaxation, the action of the characters is held over the entr'acts in such a way as to be continuous. The American stage has not elsewhere seen as perfect an example of adaptation of dramatic form to didactic purpose.

In "The Servant in the House" Kennedy set a standard for the modern morality. He has created a form of play in which an analysis of the moral content of the age, and a moral commentary upon the age are explicit. The form justified itself by its success. After the composition of this play Kennedy has written several others including "The Winterfeast" (1908); "The Terrible Meek" (1911); "The Necessary Evil" (1913); "The Idol Breaker"

(1914); "The Rib of Man" (1916); "The Army with Banners" (1917); "The Fool from the Hills" (1919); "The Christening" (1922), and "Christopher Columbus" (1924). In addition, Kennedy adapted with Louis Laloy the Chinese drama, "The Flower of the Palace of Han."

These plays are of varied types. Many of them are short. All are marked by a high moral, even a sacred purpose. The author is willing to admit his function as priest to his age. The plays are like "The Servant in the House" in identifying moral purpose with their characters and action. But they do not do so in a manner that is as thoroughly self-justifying as was the manner of the earlier play. In this the allegory was explicit, clear, and categorical; in the later plays the moral motive is implicit. Its trend is not always clear; it often leads to vagueness and mysticism. Often, indeed, the abstraction is not a moral force at all, but a sentiment. As a result the later plays are fabrics of mood; they cannot escape the charge of affectation and attitude, and they cannot claim to satisfy the clearest rational tests. They are little more than beautiful works, excellently fashioned, that leave upon us a sense of discontent.

George Middleton played his part in popularizing the reading play and in giving the stamp of serious intent to the practice of American playwriting. In considering Middleton's work it is well not to under-estimate the craft with which he made his little dissertations on the new morality. On the other hand, it is well to recognize that as contributions to thought they were quite without significance. Middleton used the play form as a means of getting a group of characters to talking about their problems and their souls. These characters were wraiths, without form, substance, or antecedents. They spoke a melancholy and allusive dialogue, their speeches filled with reminiscent phrases from advanced reading and "deep" thinking. No claim can be made that these plays take high place in the art records of our theater. And yet they served their purpose. And Middleton himself must be granted respect beyond that paid to anything he has done, for the reason that he had the vision of a serious play appealing to the minds of serious men and women and clung to this vision until it gained currency. His short plays are published in various collections entitled "Tradition," "Possession," "Masks," "Embers." "Nowadays," and "The Road Together" are long plays.

Of all the playwrights of the recent American theater Rachel Crothers is distinguished by the possession of a well nigh infallible formula for success. Rachel Crothers has had her failures in plenty, but few of her plays have failed to reach a standard of availability in production. Now and then a play may not register heavily, but it always acts. A gift such as this is as a rule bought at the price of heavy payments to conformity. Rachel Crothers pays her price, but the wonder is that she has kept her payments so low, that along with a sure-fire method she should have managed to retain so much of individuality and freshness of outlook.

Rachel Crothers was born in Bloomington, Illinois, and was graduated in the State Normal School at that place. Her stage experience was gained as an actress and in a dramatic conservatory. Her first play, "The Rector," in one act, was produced in 1902. Following this she has written a long series of plays of which the most important are: "A Man's World" (1910); "He and She" (1912 and 1920); "Young Wisdom" (1914); "The Heart of Paddy Whack" (1914); "Old Lady 31" (1916); "A Little Journey" (1918); "39 East" (1919); "Nice People" (1921); and "Expressing Willie" (1923).

Rachel Crothers has followed her course consistently. She advanced from a mastery of the resources of the everyday stage (she is no innovator) to a growing interest in the life that lies behind the stage. It is this growing interest in life, this desire to express something significant about life, that accounts for such croppers as she has come in her career. She is light in the saddle; she easily recovers herself; she rides gracefully, but she must be "significant." It occurs that she is a first-rate technician and a second-rate commentator on the world. Her ability in her craft has made some triteness seem smart; even her skill has not been able to pass off her profundity. Some of her idea plays were still-born. Her stage craftsmanship, sure as it is, has not been purified of artifice. But she is an indefatigable student of her craft and she has in herself a watchful and zealous teacher.

Miss Crothers' first play, "The Three of Us," is a thoroughly capable piece of stage-writing without an atom of pose or serious intention in it. It is a conventional enough plot of western mining claims and chicane, elevated by real characters and a healthy plot to something approaching distinction. In its vigorous, straightforward movement there is masculine method. And Rhy is that unusual thing, a thoroughly sympathetic girl character. I am not sure that in this play and in her other character and situation plays the author does not do her best work. Such plays are "A Little Journey," in which the author dramatizes with skill the chance happenings and acquaintances of a long railroad journey, and "Old Lady 31" which, although a dramatization, is in its play form a product of Miss Crothers' own skill. These plays are my favorites because more than any others of Miss Crothers' work they seek to appear to be no more than they are.

But such matters as these do not satisfy our playwright. Miss Crothers' interest in the problems of the time centered first on the problem of emancipated woman. In "A Man's World" and "He and She" she discusses the relations of a working woman with her masculine mate. "A Man's World" sounds very old-fashioned at this date, as indeed it was when it was written. Everything the author says about the life of her woman novelist and its relation with Gaskell seems now trite not because it is fifteen years old but because it is thousands of years old. The test the author contrives for Gaskell is machine-made. The whole play starts with arbitrary situations in part dictated by a wish to be daring, in part by a desire to be deep.

"He and She" better withstands analysis, though the situation is mechanical. This play was tried out under this title in 1911; the title was then changed to "The Herfords," under which name it was produced in 1912. In 1920 it was played again under the first title. Here the author considers the problem of marriage for artists. Tom Herford is a sculptor. Ann also is a sculptor who has led him into an "equality and companionship, man-and-woman, hand-and-hand-in-the-workshop-together" relationship. They have a daughter to whom they are devoted. Tom is working against lowered imaginative vitality on a frieze which is to be submitted in a competition. Ann works out an idea which she offers to him, but he repudiates it condescendingly. Submitting the plan herself, she wins the prize and then gives it up in order to protect her daughter whom she has been neglecting. The play is equipped with a *raisonneur* who expresses thoughts on love and marriage and duty, but the play contributes nothing to our understanding of life.

Millicent, the daughter in "He and She," for whom Ann makes the sacrifice of her career, is the first sketch of a favorite figure in Miss Crothers' plays, that of the emancipated young girl. "Nice People" is a play of the younger generation. Now children and adolescents we have always with us, but the young folks of the period of this play assumed an importance beyond their years because the older generation had shoved them into an important place. By the war and the war aftermath there had been withdrawn the disciplines which had kept the human machine on the track. What wonder that Teddy and her companions of both sexes, cocktail-drinking, motor-mad, joy-thrilled children, should take their lead? What wonder that their elders should become alarmed not only for youth but for the coming order? The author makes clear that all will come out right. Speaking through one of her characters, she says: "The vital things of character don't belong to anybody's day—they're eternal and fundamental." And so, after trials that are not too severe for the tastes of the audience, Teddy shows the stuff that is in her, takes her destiny in her own hands, and by cutting loose from the company of her elders and returning to the soil with the man she loves, wins through to poise and character. Again it is a machine-made conclusion, but it will serve.

Like Teddy in "Nice People," "Mary the Third" is interested in trying life's values for herself. In this play the author is careful to show in a succession of Marys that the generations do not change much, after all. The story is again the story of "nice people." Again youth revolts, but the revolt is not carried far enough to be distressing. Again the cocktail-drinking crowd of youngsters is shown to be sound at heart. Mary the Third runs away with the boy of her fancy with the stated desire that they shall know each other before they marry. She comes home in time to learn that while all may be well with Mary the Third, the same cannot be said for Mary the Second. At the end it is the younger Mary who has the stamina to pull the family through a nasty situation.

When Rachel Crothers turned from the serious and always "nice" treatment of vital topics to their handling under the convention of comedy, she made a great advance in her art. "Expressing Willie" is as serious as any play that Rachel Crothers has written. It is the only play among her serious studies that has the power to catch at the throat. The medium employed by the author in this play is her final warranty as an artist. The play is not perfect comedy. There is too much mental horseplay; there are too many bids for a raucous laugh; at times it approaches farce of the crudest and most episodic type. And yet the underlying conception is one of depth and beauty. The character of Minnie is one of the most genuine in the recent gallery of the theater. Moreover, the characters are all admirably chosen as factors in the working out of the central theme. The play is a real marvel of light and adroit, yet firm, handling of gossamer strands.

The double motives of "self-expression;" the devastating light thrown upon its crude egoisms; the genuine, soul-lifting aspiration to be done with fear, are well blended. It was a dangerous experiment to place the genuine manifestation against the false show and, while playing them on different moods, compel them to serve each other and the author's conception. Only a playwright who was master of her craft could have overcome the technical obstacles. Rachel Crothers triumphs and, for the first time in her career, blends her conception with her form in such a way that the two cannot be conceived apart.

VI

THE DRAMA OF SECTIONS

Nothing better indicates the general health of American drama today than the diffusion of its creative impulse to all parts of the country. The material organization and resources of the theater still belong to the city, but its creative imagination is seeking out the untrodden ways. There is an artistic justice in this. The imagination flees too heavy and monotonous a fare. The life within reach of the major theatrical organizations of the country had been raked over and over until all its themes and passions were conventionalized. It is by no means the case that the crowded life of New York has less drama in it than the "great open spaces." But its dramatic values have been more nearly realized if they have not been exhausted. He who would create about the life of the great city a work of outstanding force must bring an increased application and skill to his task. In the matter of regional drama it is important that we should not claim too much. Truth does not vary at national lines nor do the great fundamentals of human nature change from locality to locality. And yet it must always be remembered that drama is the art in which the ultimate truth is manifested through the near symbol. We can arrive at the ultimate only by gripping the proximate.

Recent activities for the development of a new American drama cannot be dissociated from local origins. When we note geographical divisions as marking differences in substance of our American plays we are not applying a great importance to these divisions themselves. These divisions are important only for what they suggest of uniformity of theme and substance of the plays, of accumulated legend and folk history and race qualities that lie behind them, and in a lesser degree, of customs based upon climate and habits of living of the people.

Study of the substance of plays written on American themes shows that they fall into four groups: (1) Plays of urban life, as a rule dealing with New York City and its surroundings; (2) Provincial plays, including plays on the life of rural New England, New York and the Middle West; (3) Plays of the Great West and the open spaces; (4) Plays of the New South.

Plays of Urban Life

Of these four sections only the first is adequately supplied with the complex machinery of the theater. At least half of the serious plays produced in metropolitan theaters deal with the life of the city. But while the great body of plays produced in the city deal with city themes, it does not follow that the majority of significant plays are city plays. Among the memorable plays of any season a surprisingly small number are city plays. These plays tend to a standardization of fashion. The field of metropolitan life has been cultivated so intensively that it fails longer to bring forth fruit. This is particularly the case with realism, the powers of which for the imaginative depiction of city life appear to be exhausted. For the adequate treatment of the life of the city, playwrights are turning away from the serious methods of direct attack and are employing comedy, irony and the freer expressive forms.

It would be impossible to mention all those who have dealt interestingly with the life of New York City. As this essay makes no claim to be a comprehensive history of the theater of our time, but is primarily a survey of vital forces, we shall not pretend to do so. We shall merely mention the work of a few men who appear to show decided powers:

At the time of its appearance in 1911 Charles Kenyon's "Kindling" was recognized as a play of more than average importance. It was one of the first plays to attract the organized support of a group of discerning critics. In view of the powers displayed in this play it is unfortunate that the author has not continued to write for the stage. "Kindling" tells the story of a sincere and lovable woman, the wife of a common laborer, who finds herself caught in the sordid life of the tenements. The study of "how the other half lives" appears rather old-fashioned now. It offers many class conscious appeals, and indulges in some theatrical clap trap. But at heart the story is very true and very moving. When Maggie finds that she is going to have a child she connives in a theft from a wealthy patron in order that her child may be born and reared in the country far from the dangers of the city. In texture the play is closely knit and, except for some over-elaboration, is realistic and veracious.

Gilbert Emery violates the usual rule that he who would capture the stage must engage it in youth. A graduate of Amherst, he won his spurs as poet, writer of stories and editor. He lived long abroad and knew Europe, and made himself as true a cosmopolite as the American drama shows. After serving in the army he returned to America and in 1921 produced his first play, "The Hero."

This play is of some interest both as a study of a particular type of character and as an interpretation of after-war psychology. The ability to be of service in war, Emery shows, is not connected with what is conventionally called morality in peace. Oswald Lane, who returns home from the war with medals duly earned, to bring havoc into the family of his brother, a plodding citizen with nothing heroic in his nature, is not less a hero because he violates the laws of decency and sportsmanship. The author is careful to emphasize this by showing that Oswald, even after he has deserted his seduced victim, robbed his brother and humiliated his sister-in-law, is still ready to do a heroic act and to die in the doing of it. He is not without his code, but his code is not the peace-time code. What shall we do with those of adventurous spirit? The very physical courage in them ill equips them for the ways of civilization. Now and then when civilization has need of them to save civilization, they are of use. Occasionally they make up the wanderers, explorers, pioneers. As such there seems to be a social place for them. But as nature offers fewer open opportunities of conquest, will they not more and more take their place among the gangmen, the bandits, the criminals who prey upon a society they are too rigorous to join?

Two years after the production of "The Hero," Emery produced "Tarnish," a play of a more popular theater quality but of less significance. "Tar-

nish" reveals excellently the shabby surface of souls
that do not wear well. The characters are well
observed, the action is theater-made. In early 1925
a later play of slighter texture was produced, entitled "Episode."

Arthur Richman had his first production in a
costume play of yesterday in New York entitled
"Not So Very Long Ago." In "Ambush" he revealed creative qualities of a higher order. He
shows a middle class family caught in the "ambush"
of temptations of the world of easy success. In
the characters of the young girl who follows step by
step the "easy" way, and of her father who fights
insidious powers until he, too, is enmeshed, we have
dramatic material of the first class. But Richman
has not yet learned to "think through." His plays
are based upon the morality of the theater and
not upon an absolute search for moral values.
Headed in the right direction his conceptions always
get "ambushed" in a manager's office. He has the
skill to write plays of first order, and he is still
young.

A metropolitan theme that has not yet been exhausted is the theme of "the stranger within the
gates," variously treated as "the unassimilated" or
as "the melting pot." In New York City this
theme is concerned as a rule with the Jewish immigrant from eastern and northeastern Europe.
Zangwill had introduced this theme to the stage
romantically in his "The Melting Pot." The dis-

position has been, as a rule, to treat the theme realistically. To this class belong among others Rita Wellman's "The Gentile Wife" and Fannie Hurst's "Humoresque." The German speaking and Yiddish theatres have introduced to the stage playwrights of Russian or German-Polish extraction who have treated the problems and traditions of a large group of our new citizenry. Of these Jacob Gordin in "The Kreutzer Sonata" and other plays created the most pregnant studies of the life of the immigrant in his new surroundings. Others including Sholom Asche and Ossip Dymov have lived for a shorter or longer period in America and have given pictures of life either among the immigrants in this country or in the ancestral homes of these races in Europe. These men are American dramatists only by adoption, but their work has not been without influence on the current of American drama.

Plays of the Great West

Of all the parts of the country, the West is the section which one would expect to have the greatest allure for the dramatist. And yet, as far as dramatic art of the more significant order is concerned, the West is practically unplowed land. On account of its breadth and diversity, and because the average playwright either hails from the East or early journeys thither, the West is still in the age of dramatic fable. The themes are still the generalized themes of the pioneer, the cowboy and the Indian. Such themes as these lend themselves to romantic treatment, demand it, indeed. To the average dramatist the West represents the region to which, after a devastating struggle between inimical forces, a man escapes to lose or to find himself. It need not be said that in sending a character out West the playwright gets not only his character out of trouble. He gets himself out of trouble by dispatching him. As the Greek dramatist employed the gods for powers beyond human understanding the American dramatist employs the West to solve situations which are otherwise beyond solution. In general it may be said that the West has not been treated in drama because the field is too great. Not until it is shredded into its parts will the West bring forth great plays, and these plays will not concern the great West as such, but New Mexico, California, the mountains or the plains. The plays of Moody were of the Southwest. In "Wild Birds" Dan Totheroh has written a singularly intense tragedy with some of the power of Masefield's "Nan." Mary Austin in "Fire" and "The Arrow-Maker" (produced at the New Theatre February 27, 1911) has written plays of the Indian, not realistically indeed, yet with a definite philosophy. When Miss Austin says, "The greatest difficulty to be met with in the writing of an Indian play is the extensive misinformation about Indians," she is both right and —perhaps—wrong. She is right in stating that

there is misinformation about Indians, wrong in
implying that this misinformation is any limitation
upon the playwright. It is always the duty of
the playwright to meet the audience on the basis
of their common knowledge. Those factors of his
knowledge which are wrong the playwright may be
able to correct. Mrs. Austin throws a light on
primitive drama when she opposes the idea of
"great primitive passions," saying, "What distinguishes the passion of the tribesmen from our own
is their greater liability to the pacific influences of
Nature and their greater freedom from the stimulus
of the imagination. . . . When the critics are
heard talking of 'drama of great primitive passions'
what they mean is great barbaric passions, passions
far enough along in the process of socialization to
be subject to the inter-actions of wealth, caste and
established religion, but still free of the obligation
of politeness." Neither in the case of "Fire" nor
"The Arrow-Maker" does Mrs. Austin's execution
equal in value the doctrine by which it is motivated.
Both are good reading plays; they do not succeed
in production. In "Glory of the Morning" and
"Red Bird" William Ellery Leonard has written two
plays of the Indians in a romantic temper.

One of the most promising figures in the new
drama of the West is Martin Flavin. Martin Flavin
has been industriously writing plays for some years.
His plays display a truly remarkable command of
the craft of the playwright. They are thoroughly

finished products when they appear in manuscript, and this in spite of the fact that the materials with which they deal lie off the main traveled road of the playwriting of the time. Only one of Flavin's plays, "Children of the Moon," has at this writing found professional production. This is an admirably developed study of the persistence of a pathological taint in a family, and the employment of this taint for her purposes of domination by a merciless and selfish woman. It is difficult to tell which to admire the more, the author's exposition through the lips of his characters of the underlying situation of the play, the characterization of the domineering mother, or the tragic interlocking of a love motif with the strain of hallucination and fear. The play is thoroughly hard, restrained and beautiful. "The Road to the City," unproduced but already fairly well known in a growing circle, is a free dramatization of the life of a man. In "Lady of the Rose" and in certain shorter pieces and lighter plays the author leaves the locale with which he has identified himself, and to his disadvantage.

Plays of the New South

Like the West the South has long been the sentimental happy hunting-ground of the theater. Southern playwrights are changing all that. In recent years there has been a disposition to apply the Southern play to actual conditions. Of these actual conditions the most important have to do with the race problem. The adjustment of races is by way of becoming the characteristic American theme. In New York it concerns the recent immigrants. In the Great West it concerns the Indian and the White. In the South it concerns the Negro and the White. Too commonly these subjects have been treated merely as the material of emotional situation plays. Babes of different race have been exchanged in the cradle, or a long-hidden taint is revealed at a peculiarly inopportune time. But playwrights are now going deeper than this. Where before they played on the strings of the "lost cause" or of race prejudice, they are now studying the social anxieties of the new industrial order that is replacing the old feudal order. In the changes of alignment the Negro still occupies the position of critical importance. Sometimes the dramatist treats the shifting industrial condition of the Negro and the effects of this on the life of the Whites. Sometimes the problem is a psychological one and refers to the aspirations of the black or yellow man to attain to higher levels of human association and of spiritual development. There is a sudden flowering of plays that deal alone with Negro life and character. Eugene O'Neill's "The Dreamy Kid," Ridgely Torrence's "Granny Maumee," E. H. Culbertson's "Goat Alley," Mary Hoyt Wiborg's "Taboo," Ann Bagby Stephens' "Roseanne," and the appearance of Negro revues, indicate the entrance into our drama of new and rich strains that had long ago entered our music, poetry and dance. The relation of the Negro with the White is even a richer and more poignant theme of dramatic art, a theme that too often has been treated with a careless and condescending hand. The potentialities of this theme we have already pointed out in the discussion of O'Neill's "All God's Chillun Got Wings."

The race problem of the South is by no means limited to the Negro. There has lately been uncovered in the mountains the drama of the mountaineer. Percy MacKaye in "This Fine Pretty World," Hatcher Hughes in "Hell Bent fer Heaven" and Lulu Vollmer in "Sun Up" and "The Shame Woman" have made themselves exponents of this tradition. It is difficult to exaggerate the possibilities for our art of the theater of the isolated groups in the mountains. In the treatment of these people the authors have all the resources in contemporary form for digging into the roots of native American character.

Plays of Provincial Life

"It is a better preparation for the career of a dramatist," writes Ludwig Lewisohn, "to have watched the actions of a few villagers and to have brooded over these actions to that spiritual core where criticism and creation are one than to have read all the manuals of playwriting and stagecraft in the world and be an expert in lighting and decoration." Lewisohn was emphasizing the necessity to the dramatist of an intense application to the facts of human character at the point at which character is most significant and most revealing. This point is usually found where character is under the greatest pressure. If that pressure be self-applied, if it represent a traditional or atavistic self-discipline or self-repression, then the character so controlled is all the more rich material for drama. In considering the drama of New England it is well to remember that New England is not a geographical district. It is a state of mind. It is a high pressure area on the moral barometer. New England covers not only the Northeastern States but all those areas throughout the country which have been populated by the descendants of the Puritan forefathers or have adopted their regimen as the rule of their lives. Under this interpretation New England covers a large portion of the United States north of the old Mason and Dixon's line and east of the Rocky Mountains, excluding the large cities. The New England character is found in the small towns of New York, Ohio, Indiana, and as far west as the prosperous agricultural states. A drama composed of these materials must set truth as its guiding principle; if the dramatist be not driven by a passion for truth, if the uncovering of a hidden principle be not his object, then he will not choose this material at all. For the life of this psychological area offers few allurements to the playwright other than that of intense search. The day is past when even the most frivolous stage shyster could take satisfaction either in caricaturing or idealizing his neighbor. "Know thyself" is the watchword of the drama to-day.

The formulas and situations of the drama vary widely. In essence the subject is always the same, the reaction of the individual to his environment, the power or the weakness of the individual in creating his destiny out of the events that crowd upon him and hem him in. For this kind of drama, what we are pleased to call the society of the provinces provides excellent material. Here the various types of social complication and pressure offer themselves in their most apprehensible form. In the large cities of the provinces (not in the leviathan of the metropolis) the interests are the impacts of economic forces on the individual, the quick changes in status, the insecurities in codes of manners and morals, the clash of adjustments between class and class, the perplexities of arrangements among diverse opinions, tastes and prejudices. In the more sparsely settled districts these interests are simplified and intensified to deal with the pressures on the individual of tradition and fixed circumstance, the tedium of monotony and the unchanging order, the force generated by repression, the clash of spirits too much akin. These things seem different; they are different only superficially. Both deal with the individual trying to find the key to his destiny and contending with powers outside and within.

No story is more interesting than that of Owen Davis. In the seventeen years before 1911 Owen Davis had written one hundred and fifty plays, including such works as "Nellie, the Beautiful Cloak Model," "The Opium Smugglers of Frisco," "On Trial for His Life," "Her Marriage Vow," "Broadway After Dark," "The Power of Money," "The Gambler's Daughter," "The Sewing Machine Girl," "The Lighthouse by the Sea," "The Queen of Poverty Flats," "The Burglar's Daughter." He tells us in a good-natured and cynical confession that he had reduced the writing of melodramas to a formula. There was required only a good title, which carried one-fifth of the success of the play, a painfully virtuous leading man, a leading woman in love with him, a faithful friend of the hero who was funny, a worthy soubrette, a villain who was wicked for no reason but pure cussedness, and a heavy woman who was in love but always unhappily. With these characters the play was written on the following formula: Act One starts the trouble; in Act Two things look bad; in Act Three the stage carpenter gets busy and saves the leading woman, and in Act Four the lovers are united and the villain is punished. Out of this kind of play Owen Davis had made a competency. And then things began to happen around him and within him. The motion picture knocked the support from under melodrama, and Davis suddenly found that he could not write these plays without laughing. He proceeded to experiment with other forms of writing. He dramatized "Robin Hood" and "The Arabian Nights" and wrote some problem plays, but not until he went back home to the provincial town in which he had grown up did he find that he could write plays that were not altogether divorced from truth. Let this be understood. Owen Davis of the later manifestations is not held up as a paragon of truth and of impeccable method. He was too much impregnated with hocum in his dramatic upbringing to be able to divest himself entirely of the taint. But he was so thoroughly the master of all stage tricks that he could, upon occasion, and if he would, employ tricks in the name of a faithful transcript of life. When he does so he is not guided by any hot passion for reality, but he does know a good thing when he sees it and now and then the appearance of reality is a good thing. Davis knows what he is doing, is moved by no ambition to elevate the stage; his periodic essays in the drama of sincerity are a tribute to his own wisdom and the rising standards of the age.

In "The Detour" Davis set himself consciously to reproduce the life of ordinary people caught in a backwater of the world. The plot centers around a family of market gardeners on a plot of poor land not far from the great estates of wealth and opportunity. But they are on a "detour." Each has his hunger or his ambition. Father wants more land; daughter wants a career; mother, who has missed a career for herself, prays that her daughter may be more happy, Tom prays for success in his garage. The episodes of the story, the means by which the plot develops, are in the last degree mechanical and forced, but the characters are true to life and the mass impression of the play is satisfying. The following dialogue sets the tone of the play and identifies two of the characters. The mother says, "I get so tired of sayin' nothin' but just exactly what's so and listenin' to folks that don't ever mean the least mite more'n they say, or the least mite less. What's the use of your imagination?" Tom answers, "Mine? I ain't got any, have I?" And Helen proceeds, "Oh, I guess so—but it's like a muscle; it gets awful puny if you don't use it."

Tom: I'd rather have one real dollar than dream I was a millionaire!

Helen: I suppose so—I'd rather have one real dream than be a millionaire!"

Throughout the play no voice is raised, no comedy is sought for, and the effects are gained by a telling under-emphasis.

In "Icebound," produced February 10, 1923, and given the Pulitzer prize, Davis turns to his own Maine people. In a heavily manipulated plot, with situations made to order, with sympathetic vice drawing favor away from unsympathetic virtue, with a *dea ex machina* wielding power from the other side of the grave, with a patient Grizzel heroine who draws a questionable prize at the end of the play, the author has raised the entire structure above the value of its parts. The play lingers in the mind as a study of a society. The characters are "icebound." Writing of the people from whom he had drawn his characters, Davis says: "In my memory of them is little of the 'Rube' caricature of the conventional theater; they are neither buffoons nor sentimentalists, and at least neither their faults nor their virtues are borrowed from the melting pot but are the direct result of their own heritage and environment."

Owen Davis writes of the repressions of New England. Zona Gale speaks for the little frustrate man and woman everywhere, but usually this character has the dust of Wisconsin roads on his shoes. Zona Gale is one of the first proponents of the "little man" in our literature and on the stage. How better could the futile, inconsequential qualities of a minuscule be suggested than in such names as "Miss Lulu Bett" and "Mr. Pitt"? Miss Gale plays second to no one in her knowledge of the inwardness of her characters. No one writing to-day has a better understanding of that trait that according to Browning can affright even a tyrant, "sheer minuteness in effect." In this understanding there is no sign of conventionality; it is all first sight. And in her later novels she has formulated a method that is as reticent and sure as her insight is infallible. As much cannot be said of her playwriting. Miss Gale has not yet reached the point at which she takes playwriting seriously as an art of construction rather than verbal composition. Around a central character who is admirably true she groups a set of automatons spouting "lines" for the presumable ecstasy of the mob. But it happens that the mob does not care for lines that drop from the tin lips of manikins. It demands speech that is the evocation of character. Miss Gale's characters live only while they speak and only in their speech; they are drawn to life by strings tied to the author's fingers. In its original form "Miss Lulu Bett" is one of the exploits of pungent condensation of recent years; "Birth" is one of the most deeply searching stories of the time. The plays taken from these works are but effigies of the originals.

In a series of one-acters ("The Clod," "Love Among the Lions," "Brothers") and later in several long plays ("The Square Peg," "The Goose Hangs High") Lewis Beach studied the characters of common people under the whip or the rein of the virtues and vices of everyday experience. By all means the most important of Beach's plays is "The Square Peg" (1923), which tells the story of the economies, intrusions, misplaced duties of a futile family that is dominated by a "capable" mother. "The Goose Hangs High," also a family story, is of a distinctly lighter vein. To something of the same class belongs Leon Cunningham's "Hospitality," which is also a story of a masterful woman. In this case the author contrives to show that the mother was right. Walter Elwood, whose plays "Blight" and "Tradition" are still unproduced, treats family conditions in the rural districts of the Mohawk Mountains. George Cram Cook's symbolical play, "The Spring," was based on the arresting idea that there exists a spring buried deep underground which, if found, can be the source of concord to those who are divided by misunderstanding and prejudice. The plays of Jane Dransfield, "Joe, A Hudson Valley Play," "Blood of Kings"; and David Liebovitz's "John Hawthorne" and "The Marriage of Tony" deal with provincial life not far from the great city.

In the plays we have mentioned we have by no means covered the works of those playwrights who bury their roots in the soil of a locality. No prophecies are made regarding the development of a provincial drama in America. This hangs upon the will of playwrights; it also hangs upon conditions that are beyond their will. If the playwrights of the provinces are to write plays of the homeland, they must find production for their work. Already, in several localities, such production is offered. In Professor Baker's workshop at Cambridge, now transferred to Yale (Workshop Publications); in Professor F. H. Koch's organizations in North Dakota and in North Carolina (Carolina Folk Plays); in Chicago, Indiana, Missouri, California, Ohio, Wisconsin and Texas, groups of playwrights have been encouraged by the existence of local producing societies to undertake the dramatization of the life near at hand.

VII

SUSAN GLASPELL AND ZOË AKINS

We have now briefly to study the work of two women who in their respective fields have shown high promise. As between Susan Glaspell and Zoë Akins the former has come nearer to absolute achievement. The two are by no means alike except in this that both are endowed with powers of the first order, and in both these high powers are upon occasion nullified or frustrated by a confusion of values or a failure in artistic discipline. More than any American playwright Susan Glaspell bases her art upon psychic as distinguished from physical reality. She began as a writer of one act plays. Her "Suppressed Desires" won wide popularity as an early playful dramatization of the jargon of psychoanalysis. In "The People" we have a serious study of the wider implications of the journalist's profession. Her other short plays are invariably interesting and significant. But there was in her art an urge that compelled a wider canvas. This is not because her plots developed in external magnitude. With one exception, "The Inheritors," all her plays have been developed out of a conception so minute and fine that it might appear to lie outside of the dramatic entirely. If in her handling of these her craftsmanship now and then spins a little fine there is small cause for wonder.

I imagine it may be said that her play "Bernice," published in the Theatre Arts Magazine in 1919 but not to my knowledge produced, is the study of the soul of a woman. The action of the play takes place after the death of Bernice but everything she has touched speaks of her with a clear and beautiful precision. Of Bernice's house in the country the author writes, "You feel yourself in the house of a woman you would like to know, a woman of sure and beautiful instincts, who lives simply." This is the case with all of Susan Glaspell's characters. They live simply and they live deeply. You would be proud to know them but they would not open themselves to you at the first meeting. They have intense secret lives and the force of the author's imagination is such as to give to these lives a full and rounded contour and even something of the warmth of coursing blood. Though Bernice has died before the rise of the first curtain the author is careful to show us that even in her death she is just as she was in life, withdrawn but not absent. I shall not try to outline the plot. It is profound and intense, and poised on decisions that are too delicate to follow save by the most sensitive of intuitions.

"Inheritors," performed by the Provincetown Players in 1921, covers a far wider canvas. Opening in 1879 on the prairies that roll back from the Mississippi it contrasts the visions and spiritual realities of the pioneer days with the realized facts of a later time. Here we see the generations stepping on each other's heels, each with its warm new and yet old enthusiasms, faiths and martyrdoms. With a wide pioneer vision of education in a new land old Morton establishes a college. In this he is aided by an exiled revolutionist, Fevejary, from Hungary. Later the granddaughter of the two men is called upon to test out in the same institution the principles of the founders as these apply to later days. The situation is a striking one; unfortunately it is marred by something that looks like special pleading.

In "The Verge" published in 1922 but not as yet produced, we have Miss Glaspell's best play and, in my opinion, one of the best plays of the time in English. It has been, as we have seen, always Miss Glaspell's urge to push her plays to the ultimate line of speculation on psychic experience. This urge provides the theme of "The Verge." Her heroine, Claire, is seeking to force life to new forms even through the destruction of the forms that are. Her passion to break beyond the verge is symbolized by her attempt to create new forms of plant life. But she is even more interested in breaking through with her own soul. In this quest she is of course impeded by the common sense humor and practicality of her husband, and the moral conformity of her family. But the final frustration comes from those nearer and dearer spirits who can indeed accompany her to the

verge but cannot break through with her. Expressing her aspiration she says, "I want to give fragrance to Breath of Life—the flower I've created
that is outside what flowers have been. What has
gone out should bring fragrance from what it has
left. But no definite fragrance, no limiting enclos-
ing thing. I call the fragrance I am trying to create
Reminiscence."

Turning from her plants to the soul itself she asks
how one can make a soul beyond any soul that has
ever been. Her answer is that we must break
through form. We must take a "sporting chance—
go mad." "If it were all in pieces we'd be shocked
to aliveness." Men must explode their species, make
the big leap. We need not deny that Claire's search
leaves the normal and goes over into the byways of
perversion. The language in which Miss Glaspell
has written this play is more richly allusive than
that of any other play written in America. In the
passages of greatest intensity it rises to a psalm
quality or to dithyrambic. And yet it is always
human speech; it is dramatic in the truest sense.
"Beauty," she says, "is the humility breathed from
the shame of succeeding."

Susan Glaspell is a very significant person indeed.
Her structure and her dialogues are sculptured
out of quiet. She can give the sense of deep mental
experience. Her characters live in their minds and
feel in their minds. Always indoctrinated, her work
carries the conviction that her characters themselves

are living through the deeps of decision. Along with these qualities, Susan Glaspell has others that are not so good. Her characters have opinions and convictions, but she has motives and purpose. To some of her plays there is added an element of intent that constitutes an incubus on the play. If playwrights knew, in fashioning the works of their brain, how temporal some of their enthusiasms for quick reform are, they would never add these to their more imaginative conceptions. In Susan Glaspell's plays there are some factors that are worthy of a long life; unfortunately these are confused with others which quickly pass into air.

In an engagingly personal confession Zoë Akins tells us that after a series of annoying mischances in the production or non-production of her early plays she had torn up her manuscripts and had returned home to write what she pleased to write. Here we have the explanation of the whole work and career of this woman who, still young in years, deserves the epithet of "young" in a double sense. After twenty years' writing for the stage she still has the nervous energy of beginning youth. Zoë Akins has had no outstanding successes before the public, but her career has been a success. She has written what she wanted to write. If she had had a point of view as significant as her temper is courageous and individual, she would be one of our greatest playwrights. As it is, she is one of the most interesting.

Zoë Akins was born in 1886 in the Ozark Mountains of Missouri. She is thus a Midlander of the Midlands. In early youth she moved to St. Louis. She joined a stock company at seventeen; wrote verse and plays as soon as she could hold a pen. And well before she was twenty she had written a poetic play on Isolde, a play called "The Meddlers" for Mrs. Fiske, and another play called "The Learned Ladies." All of these came perilously near to production but escaped. After she had started to write to please her own fancy she wrote "Papa, an Amorality," half a dozen short plays, including "The Magical City," in which she sought to give a sordid tragedy an unreal, illusive quality by means of verse and new settings. After these plays had secured her the inquisitive interest of the public, she proceeded to write for the professional stage, "Déclassée," "Daddy's Gone a-Hunting" and "Greatness," sometimes called "The Texas Nightingale," and others.

In an essay on the writing of plays Zoë Akins says, "Playwriting is a divine pastime." In this she speaks by the book for manifestly she has enjoyed her playwriting. She is an omnivorous snapper-up of random influences. Among the infatuations of her youth were the Castle Square Grand Opera Company, Ibsen, Shaw, Julia Marlowe, Shakespeare and William Marion Reedy. But to Zoë Akins influences do not so much constitute indebtedness as points of departure or stimuli to original

flights. Her reactions are quick and productive.
She has a strong feeling for line and sound, and an
equally strong revulsion from anything that offends
her. Above everything she hates to be bored; as a
result—she dreads boring any one else.

Of all her plays "Papa" is the most original. It
must be confessed that part of this originality is
bought by achieving anarchy. This play was written under a strong sense of repulsion against the
discipline she had been subjected to in seeking
to write for production; in part, also, against the
sham morality that dominates the stage. She seeks
to break away from all the formalities of the theater
and fly in the face of prejudices and taboos. She
says, "I set out to write a play that was penetrating
and sophisticated, but neither flippant nor cynical."
This play, which was produced unsuccessfully in
1919, reminds one somewhat of the playful sophistication of Schnitzler. A large part of the inspiration
of this play lies in turning topsy-turvy the hoary
clichés of the theater. Papa is a worthless old
exquisite. The plot plays upon the outworn themes
of forbidden babies, elopements, sacrifice marriages
to save paternal fortune and other such fashions of
the theater of yesterday. It is all playfully and
gracefully done, with no pretense of sequence or even
of theme. The emotions are purposely unreal, the
climaxes are arranged, there are forced changes of
feeling. Instead of the child being the object of
solicitude, Father is the spoiled darling. The play

is a piece of Dresden China among comedies. The characters act by good breeding and without morality. Now and then it breaks into burlesque, or would if there were any meaning to it all. Miss Akins has written no other such lawless piece as this. A playwright cannot buy her pleasure at such a price.

"Déclassée," produced October 6, 1919, is Zoë Akins' most successful work before the public, but by no means her best. "Technique," she says, "is what enables the playwright to work out in cold blood what he has conceived in hot." In this respect the play is an achievement. As a fabric of experience, or commentary on life, it is without value. The dialogue is forceful, distinguished, colorful, aristocratic beyond that of any other of our playwrights. But it is dialogue that continually falls into reminiscent strains, dialogue that is inspired by the love of words and of their sounds. And the attitudes are as artificial—and as graceful—as the words.

Speaking of a déclassée one character says, "One is always seeing them about, and sometimes one meets them like this. They are always living in hotels, always apparently on the wing; always good-looking; always beautifully dressed; their friends are always people they've just met; they're agreeable enough, frequently they're amusing; they never have such things as husbands or relatives or children; and they emerge from obscurity, as detached from any background whatever as silhouettes cut from black paper and pasted on a blank page." Undoubtedly the author meant this speech to set the key for her chief character. But the means by which Lady Helen Haden achieves ostracism for herself are in the extreme tortuous and perverse. The author could not have forced the issue more, played more arbitrary tricks, if she had been satirizing the whole school of drama of "vague regrets." But she is satirizing nothing. Her cynical reason is dethroned. She is enjoying every minute of it just as Lady Helen enjoys her outcast state, because it permits her to use with such telling effect the organ tones of her voice. Of course, the author knew what she was doing when she played upon this chord of melo-theater. How, otherwise, could she permit the repeated refrain of "The Mad Varicks"? It is all very adroit, very effective and thoroughly false. Lady Helen has a fantastic love of gesture. Very good. Why, then, make her die in the midst of her gestures? Is not this a gesture on the part of the author? The other characters, Thayer, Solomon, Alice Vance, are no more consistent than Lady Helen. They are shifted from purpose to purpose as the necessities of the action demand. None of them has enough character to make any demands for himself. They are all the instruments of the author's love of a graceful pose. One might almost believe that the author had started out to make an "arrangement in hypocrisy." If we could only once catch the author's eye while she is making her puppet's posture! If we could only once see her smile! "Life has been from the start one of those mistakes that sometimes happen," says Lady Helen. Are we to weep at that or to smile, Zoë Akins?

"Daddy's Gone a-Hunting" is a tragedy of art life, of wandering fancies and of a woman who pitifully tries to understand. The only way she can understand is to try for herself. She subjects her husband to a test, and he does not meet the test to her satisfaction. The play dares greatly in introducing again into a play of marital cross-purposes a child who dies.

"Greatness" or "The Texas Nightingale" (1922) is the most consistent and objective of the author's works. It is, indeed, the best essay on the artistic temperament in our theater. It is a study of a strong, ruthless, creative character who devours her husband and anyone else she needs, and rides "a magnificent thundercloud driving an invisible chariot" over scenes that would distract a lesser mortal. The story is negligible; again the episodes are forced and arbitrary, but the play is adorned with some of the most brilliant dialogue in the recent theater.

Zoë Akins began her career on a note of precocity. She has continued on this note. The danger is that as she lives longer this air will sit less gracefully upon her than it did at first. There is on her still a mental awareness that goes beyond experience, a sense of the theater as something artificial and separate from life. Though she loves the theater, she can never quite respect it. The best of her work consists in individual snatches of insight that are too often isolated and even inconsistent with each other. She has not yet learned to gather up her art into a synthesis. She has not yet learned to discriminate between the inspirations she gets from life and those she gets from art, from books and plays, and from the attitudes of friends. She has the soul of an artist. She handles her pigment richly; her brush with courageous strokes. She is not timid before her craft. She has it in her to do something better than she has done.

CHAPTER IV

ON OUR AMERICAN COMEDY

I

REMARKS ON VALUES IN COMEDY

"WE are all going to the play or coming home from it," wrote Charles Dickens. And the mood in which we best love to go and come is that of laughter. Is there behind this popular desire to be amused, this irrepressible tendency to treat everything with levity, a deeper principle? Does this demand on the part of the audience correspond to a need on the part of the creator? To both of these questions I give an affirmative answer. Aside from pure beauty, a rare thing in the theater, comedy is the greatest specific of values, the best test of the medium of art. It is an almost indispensable instrument in the hands of the creator of art. Some dramatists have achieved greatness without a sense of comedy; none of them but would have been better for its possession.

A sense of comedy is of particular value in the treatment of themes that lie outside the domains of comedy. It forbids overplus, it applies discretion; it fastens the soaring fancy to the ground.

219

For comedy is always concrete. Whether we take comedy to be derived from "sudden glory" or from the "play instinct" its inspiration and its expression are always found in the here and now. Comedy does not concern itself with phantoms or myths or gods; it cares nothing for symbols or allegories; at its advance mysteries disappear.

In the world of art, comedy has saved much; by what then can it be saved? For comedy, too, has its dangers. As presentative art tends always to lose itself upward in metaphysics, the art of comedy tends always to degrade itself to burlesque or caricature, or to formalize itself into a shell. While the passions of the serious theater need, so to speak, to be "held down," the motives of laughter need always to be "keyed up." Comedy of itself is not enough. Comedy has no existence, save as a spirit, a method of attack. The comic spirit is a method of judgment applied to the substance of life. But comedy does not supply that substance. The danger of comedy is that a formula of treatment comes to be elevated to the dignity of the substance of life, or that laughter which should be the sign of mental recognition becomes only an automatic cackle. Comedy formalized, stereotyped, is less than nothing. Comedy in the true sense exists only as it applies itself to a vital issue which it isolates, identifies and illuminates.

If these things be true, then it must appear that much that goes under the name of comedy is not comedy at all. We in America have had much that roughly passed for comedy, little that supplied illumination of the comic spirit to vital issues. The American stage, like American life, has not wanted for laughter. We have been willing to subject all the holies to satire. We even enjoy fun, or did until recently. And yet we have not attained that sure discrimination of values by which only can the discriminations of laughter be validated. There are many reasons for this. Chief among them is the fact that our technique of comedy has not been derived from a study of our own issues. A fairly self-critical people, we have not erected our criticism into a native code of judgment. In writing our comedies we have borrowed the formulas which were created in other lands and for other times. Our sense of the comic continually wars against our practice of comedy. We have tried to impose upon our comic sense a set of standards that are themselves the proper materials for comedy, so widely separated are they from the right reason. High comedy, so called, remains a synthesis of the attitudes of the past. It is a mere effigy of judgment. In pointing a finger it points to the dead. And its laughter is that most cruel and pointless of all, a laughter that satirizes only our memories.

Certainly what we need to do is to elevate our sense of comedy into a technique of comedy. This is not to be done easily or quickly. Everywhere throughout the world there has been an undermining of the values upon which the practice of comedy has been postulated. The old comedy passed away with the old fundamentals by which men lived. Not until we have achieved again an authority of taste, a workable hypothesis of truth, can we create a style of comedy that is everywhere acceptable and everywhere recognizable. Our judgments to-day are too much involved with personal predilection to permit a universal standard of laughter. Comedy is the product of detachment rather than of participation. Comedy can neither be written nor enjoyed by one who cares deeply or is charged with the responsibility of choice. Until we are able to achieve a recognizable and acceptable standard, comedy will continue to be as at present, either an imitation of old forms of judgment or it will be a tentative and individual assay of values. There is no doubt that of the two the latter more nearly approaches the heart of the comic muse.

The composition of high comedy in America has been so thankless a task that few have been willing or able to undertake it. The composition of this style of play demands the assumption on the part of the author of standards that he must support alone. These standards are those of taste and grace of manner as based upon differentiations in class. In his respect for these standards the author can presume upon the sympathy of only a small minority of the audience, and this is too often the sympathy not of experience but of tradition. The game of manners provided the finest sport in the world. And it was of the essence of the game that the rules should be applied to oneself. As long as this game was played by men and women who were born to it, it was of the very essence of comedy. But Americans are not born to the game of manners. Comedy based upon such a code is more than an anachronism. It is untrue to the fundamentals of our life. The conditions which created the comedy of manners ceased in Europe a century ago, except as touching an ever lessening group. Except for isolated districts here and there these conditions have never had any place in this country. The man who tries to use this form for the treatment of contemporary interests is like the modern musician who plays upon a clavicord. He may bring forth sweet sounds, but he is sadly restricted by his medium.

II

Langdon Mitchell and Jesse Lynch Williams

The only American writers who have handled the comedy of manners with aristocratic pen are Langdon Mitchell and Jesse Lynch Williams. The former is altogether true to type; the latter, while maintaining his aristocratic poise, diversifies his form in such a way as to make his play a fabric of intellectual conceptions. Both men play rigorously within the limits of good breeding. The tasks they have undertaken are of great weight. They have accomplished them effectively. But they have been pulling against the tides and the sun. For the treatment of the interests of a busy practical day they have chosen a single track medium which moves forward only through speech. Their themes are, as always, marriage or the relations of men and women outside marriage. For the development of these themes the authors permit themselves only the precise speech of convention-bound men and women. The life we are shown never transgresses the bounds of a witty, allusive, graceful talk. This life has no other dimension, no other expression, no other form, than that created for it by the conversation in well chosen syllables of highly articulate men and women. By an insistent convention it is understood that everything relevant must somewhere be said. That which is not spoken does not exist. The plays of Langdon Mitchell and of Jesse Lynch Williams are rare achievements, made all the more noteworthy by the fact that the authors caged themselves within the formulas of yesterday.

It was at the Fifth Avenue Theater on September 12, 1899, that Mrs. Fiske produced "Becky Sharp," a dramatization by Langdon Mitchell of episodes in Thackeray's novel, "Vanity Fair." For the purposes of this re-creation of the life of the past as related in Thackeray's pages Mitchell's form was admirably chosen. "Thackeray on the stage — Thackeray, the charming cynic, Thackeray the lachrymose sentimentalist, Thackeray, the inimitable humorist, Thackeray, the great literary artist! How in the name of Apollo are all these precious essences to be tasted on the large, empty plate of the theater?" asks Huneker. The fact is that Mitchell succeeded where others had failed. He did not put all of Thackeray on the stage. What he did transfer was acclaimed even by the Thackeray lovers as no desecration.

It was in "The New York Idea," produced by Mrs. Fiske at the Lyric Theater, November 19, 1906, that Langdon Mitchell came before the American theater public with a comedy of his own contriving. The occasion was in every way a notable one. The cast was distinguished, including Mrs. Fiske, John Mason, William B. Mack, George Arliss, Ida Vernon and Emily Stevens. Nine years later, on September 28, 1915, the play was revived by Grace George.

For weight, for craftsmanship, for raciness of line, for lusty conception, this play takes its place with the best comedies of its order written in our times, and is beyond comparison with any other play of its type written in America. There cannot be the slightest doubt that the play will last in our drama, for though we have gone beyond the particular conditions outlined, this fact only emphasizes the universality of the "idea." From the notes published in connection with Montrose Moses' edition of this play in "Representative Plays by American Dramatists" I quote the author's own confession: "When

I was writing the play I had really no idea of satirizing divorce or a law or anything specially temperamental or local. What I wanted to satirize was a certain extreme frivolity in the American spirit and in our American life—frivolity in the deep sense—not just a girl's frivolity, but that profound, sterile, amazing frivolity which one observes and meets in our churches, in our political life, in literature, in music. . . . Our frivolity is, I feel, on the edge of the tragic. Indeed, I think it is entirely tragic, and there are lines, comedy lines, in 'The New York Idea' that indicate this aspect of the thing."

It was therefore essentially as a serious undertaking that Mitchell attacked the composition of this play. He has himself elsewhere notably expressed the ideals that he would have govern an American art:

> Oh, I would have you look
> With judgment on your life, and not to brook
> The less in art, as not in truth;—forgive
> Much in you now I can, never that you less live!
> I may put by whatever choice of themes,
> But not this air of being by rich dreams
> Roofed over, and floored under, and walled in.
>
> *To a Writer of the Day.*

This seriousness of motive is manifest not only in the moral structure of the play—few plays are so thoroughly bulwarked in moral principle; it shows also in the action plot. In a sense the plot of the play is highly mechanical. The meetings and exchanges on the part of persons who would be presumed not to meet are partly an expression of the New York "idea," they are partly an expression also of the author's necessity. Such a whipping and marshaling of the characters by authorial fiat would hardly be forgiven were it not that we recognize that what the characters do is unimportant beside what they represent. In other words, the meaning is the thing. This being the case, what the author had to do was to express his meaning in an unflaggingly interesting manner. The vitality of the theme depended upon the vitality of the characters, and this depended upon the vitality of line and dialogue. It is surprising how little of the interest of the play depends upon situation and how much depends upon the revelations of truth and character contained in the lines. The characters were keyed to their highest tension of self-revelation. The character himself is of less importance than is the vitality with which he is realized. The motives of society are indeed stripped bare,—its selfishness, its show, its false honesty and false virtue, the eternal willingness to think the worst, the grudging disposition to think well of another. The unpardonable sin is to marry for love. Social necessity will force any convention, even the convention of meeting and being friends with the discarded mate. But while ugly facts can be accepted, they must always be cloaked in the mantel of fine, laconic phrase. Happily this gives rich opportunity to the author's powers of epigram. "At what hour did you say the alimony commences?" Sudley asks. Another character speaks of the "halcyon calm of second choice." Philip and John discuss the second marriage of the wife of one to the other under cover of a discussion of horses. "She's a dangerous mare . . . as delicate and changeable as a girl. I'd hate to leave her in your charge." And elsewhere the trainer complains, "Ah, madam, when husband and wife splits, it's the horses that suffers."

As has been said, the story is of the slightest. The exchange of wives is too condensed a formula to represent the true inwardness of the change that is taking place in the relations between men and women. But this true inwardness has in this play another expression. It is found in the complex character of the play, in the mood which is involved of different motifs, the surface motifs all cynicism, the sub-surface and the submerged tending to, and sometimes breaking over into, tragedy. "I know not where to look for a speech of profounder ironic implication," says William Archer of one of the passages. I would go further and say that I know not where in American drama we are to find speech of such ironic implication. The play has been well recognized abroad, although when produced in London it was played as farce! England and the Continent are determined not to accept our art at its best valuation. They roar over our snappy "success" comedies, but they cannot believe that "The New York Idea" is as good

in its order as the best done in England in its time;
and Eugene O'Neill is too "intense" for their taste.
The play was done by Reinhardt at the Kammer-
spiel Theater, Berlin, October 7, 1916. It has been
translated into Danish, Swedish, Hungarian, and
half a dozen other languages. Mitchell has only
once again taken up his pen, in dramatizing "Pen-
dennis" for John Drew in 1917.

Mitchell succeeded as well as any man living could
succeed in writing a Congreve play for the nineteenth Century. He succeeded, that is, in forcing
the substance through the lips and actions of a group
of unwilling characters. In compelling his characters to play the game of a poised nicety of decorum
he was creating a beautiful imitation of a Restora-
tion piece of furniture, he was giving a dynamic personal reaction toward life. He was not—quite—creating a work of art with the stamp of the age. "The
New York Idea" stands out as a lovely monument.
Throughout the play the author lacked one aid that
the author of a play ought to possess. He lacked the
sense of urgency in his characters that would force
an action even outside of the author's will. This lack
is shown in the speech of the characters. When
Etheredge and Wycherly and Congreve wrote their
comedies, speech was a joy. The human tongue had
but lately been released from the gyves of blank
verse, the heroic couplet, and an affected prose. Now
the toes of language first touched the ground and
began to dance a graceful measure. When Oscar

Wilde and Langdon Mitchell performed their feats of revival, language had become weary. It danced only at the whip. The tongues of characters spoke indeed, but only at the expense of much prompting on the part of the author. One can almost imagine these characters saying to the author what so many heroines of the drama of revolt have said: "I want to live." They must have been tired of being locked in the prison of words. They must have wished to break out of the leash of manner, free their impulses to action, and break the scheme of the play to pieces.

When Jesse Lynch Williams started to write comedy, he undertook a task somewhat similar to that of Mitchell, but he based it upon a slightly different convention. With Mitchell the convention had been "manner." Any conception that was realized had to be "put over" the barriers of an artificial and largely arbitrary standard of decorum. These characters were not interested in their own fates, in their characters or predicaments. They were bored, and they covered their boredom with epigrams. Jesse Lynch Williams created a new and more timely convention. His characters were interested in themselves as specimens. Their destiny was in their hands, and while they were going to pursue their destiny with a certain regard for appearances, they were honestly concerned in getting down to the truth of the dilemmas in which they found themselves caught, in talking them over and coming to conclusions. Manifestly this form of comedy, while closely related to the former, is much more in accord with the canons of responsibility and free will.

Williams does not provide a new style of comedy. He only provides a new motive power for the old comedy. Like the personages of Mitchell's play, his characters have only one outlet of escape, and this is through a trickle of words. But he has done much in supplying these words a new energy. While in Mitchell speech had been at best a game, and like all games a bore, in Williams speech became an adjunct to "straight thinking." Within the narrow limits set up by their understandings, these characters are determined to think through. They are determined, also, to express their thoughts without fear or too much self-consciousness. They live in a time that is very much concerned with its own processes, that tells itself that it is re-valuing values. All of this is a great aid to an author who must bring his play to pass on the tongues of his characters and must in so doing maintain a level of niceness and grave good humor.

Jesse Lynch Williams was born in Stirling, Illinois, August 17, 1871. He was graduated from Princeton in 1892. He has written comparatively little, but what he has written has been marked by standards of elevated taste and a transparent honesty of conception. He first attracted attention with his short stories, and published two collections entitled "Princeton Stories" (1895), and "The Stolen Story" (1899). An interest akin to that of Meredith in the more delicate features of the relations between men and women culminated in the long novel, "The Married Life of the Frederick Carrolls" (1910). His comedy, "Why Marry?" on the same general theme was begun as fiction but was developed into a stage play, first entitled, "And So They Were Married." First produced at the American Academy of Dramatic Arts, this play after its subsequent professional production in 1917 ran for two years.

If comedy means the arrangement of the lines of human motives in graceful and arbitrary contours in order to reflect a coherent criticism of life, Jesse Lynch Williams is undoubtedly the first writer of comedy in America. While he is keenly regardful of the design of his composition, the source of his comedy is always an inner essence and not an artificial agglomeration of laugh lines and sure-fire situations. In many respects Williams is like Meredith. He is a comedian of fine flavors. But there is an important difference which refers more to his environment than to his own method. He was reared in a country in which the quiet, almost unsmiling comedy of the deeper essence is practically unknown. Whatever poise he has achieved has been at the expense of tremendously hard work. His plays are the products of frequent re-writings, each one representing a deeper stage in his understanding of his characters and their situations. He has not been able entirely to clear his plays of the evidences of

hard work.   Angularities and forced postures appear
here and there.   Like Meredith, Williams is not content to permit his works simply to develop a situation
and there rest.   He seeks outside the work and beyond it a conceptual value.   He is more interested
in what his play implies than in what it displays.
More than this, he seeks by the careful choosing of
his characters and the arrangement of his action to
cover all aspects of the theme.   He is very anxious
not to be charged with special pleading, nor with
disregarding anything important to the understanding of the problem.   Nor can he be so charged.   But
his plays pay the price of his detachment and his
catholicity.   They appear to be scaled to a sympo-
sium rather than to the action of a play.   Revealed
truth becomes more important than the revelation
of truth.

"Why Marry" is a comedy of such clean-cut and
diagrammatic situation as to approach in structural
respects to farce.   It is, in fact, a higher type of
farce in which the ends are not momentary laughter
but deep understanding.   Farce calls for the moving
of men and women as puppets across the stage to get
effects of laughter and surprise.   This play calls for
the moving of men and women as puppets across the
stage to get effects of sympathy and insight.   In
spite of everything that can be said for Williams'
characters, I insist that they are puppets.   The
ordinary good play takes upon itself meaning by the
humanity of its characters.   These characters take

upon themselves humanity by their meanings. The author is interested first of all in presenting a picture of marriage as an institution, not any particular marriage, but marriage in general. And the picture the author presents is sufficiently devastating. The cross currents of opposition to marriage are all represented. Legalized prostitution, boredom, frustration of will, the dominance of the weak over the strong—all the charges against marriage are faced. No problem play has presented a more terrifying view of marriage than does the author of this play. He literally says not one word for the institution. All the couples represent some phase of fundamental discontent. The author spares no pains, and softens no blow. And his courage is well advised. After saying and implying everything that can be charged against marriage, there comes the final question: What then? What have we to offer instead of marriage? Everything that can be said against marriage can be said against life. Yet few of us choose not to live. The greatest castigators of marriage, of woman, have been the much-married men like Strindberg. Is there comedy in that? There is unless you wish to take it tragically. Williams chooses to take it in a spirit of comedy. He shows at the end of the play all the couples who have been in one way or another tugging at the leash safely united in dis-union. He shows them married because he can think of nothing better for them to do, and he can think of nothing better because man in all the ages has thought of nothing better. Rex does not want to get married because he wants to go on with his affairs, but marries nevertheless; Jean loves another, but lacking him, marries anyway; Lucy is weary to death of a husband with a mind of the Pleiocene age, but cannot leave him because neither of them has "sinned"; Uncle Everett believes in divorce in theory but has become used to his wife and cannot give up his bad habits; the clergyman brother reconciles himself and his wife to their hard lot by reference to the sacredness of sacrifice in marriage; Helen and Ernest want above all things to work together without intrusions of sex, but they are not allowed to do so and so they are married. For all of these marriage is the only outlet, the only "practicable" thing.

I think such a play as this cannot be judged by the ordinary standards of comedy. The situations are forced into line. The characters are abstractions. No one could seriously claim that such an imbroglio as this could realize itself in the talk of any group of people, however sophisticated. John, who is in many respects the key character—for he it is who starts the action moving and keeps it going by his dictatorial pig-headedness—is unbelievable either in himself or in relation to the other characters of the play. No character is so all-of-a-piece as John, so consistent in his attitudes. He represents the hidden spring of everything wrong that the author sees in marriage or in human institutions. Any man acting as he acts would be thrown out of doors on his head by some one before the end of the first act. As we cannot accept the play on the score of verisimilitude, we must find some score upon which it can be accepted. For it must be accepted. It is a drama of abstract forces identified with personalities, so arranged and thought through that the impact of the forces takes on a dramatic character. With Shaw and Barker, Williams is the exponent of the brilliant idea in drama. Less adroit than Barker in burying his theme deep under the action he is more entertaining than Barker. And he is more consistent in pointing a situation and seeing it through than Shaw. With a little of Shaw's brilliancy he has more ability to discard what does not belong to his theme; and unlike Shaw he has no disposition himself to come before the curtain and dance. "Why Marry" was awarded in 1917 the first Pulitzer Prize as the best American play of the year.

Williams' second play, "Why Not?" was made from a novelette, "Remating Time," which had been published in 1916. It was produced by Equity Players with success at the end of 1922. The play serves the same underlying philosophy of the earlier play with less force and originality. Mitchell and Williams are not alone in seeking to make comedy significant. Many authors have treated in a light and graceful way some one or another of the aspects of social relationship or individual character. Among the better comedies of

this order are Algernon Tassin's "The Craft of the
Tortoise," and Anne Crawford Flexner's "The Marriage Game." Expert in the handling of the craft of
the stage, Thompson Buchanan in "A Woman's
Way," A. E. Thomas in "Her Husband's Wife,"
"Just Suppose," "Only 38," and other plays; Louis
Evan Shipman in plays of a more romantic order,
including "The Fountain of Youth," and "Fools
Errant"; Lee Wilson Dodd in "The Changelings";
Arthur Richman in "The Awful Truth," have
treated manufactured stories with some regard to the
principles of human nature. And still under the convention of "manner" is one of the most trenchant
pieces of character analysis of recent years. Louis
K. Anspacher's "The Unchastened Woman" was produced in 1915 with Emily Stevens in the leading rôle.
The play is set in an action that is overloaded with
social motive and awkward in development. Nor is
it to be denied that the unchastened woman has her
ancestry in previous literature and drama, particularly in Hedda Gabler and in Becky Sharp. Nevertheless, the character of Caroline Knollys will live in
the theater.

III

MODERN DOMESTIC COMEDY:
JAMES FORBES; KAUFMAN AND CONNOLLY;
GEORGE KELLY

I have sufficiently indicated my belief that by the
circumstances of its structure and nature the comedy

of manners does not adapt itself to American conditions. An author can do something to force his theme into inappropriate molds. But the effort demanded will always leave its mark upon the finished play. The writer of comedy cannot be content until he has adapted his structure to the spirit of his materials. Large fields of American life cannot be drawn into the narrow confines of the comedy of manners. For this field there must be evolved other types of comedy based upon new and more intuitive discriminations. Some have been pleased to call these new forms of comedy the comedy of bad manners. I cannot accept this term. As manners are good or bad only by reference to a standard of good manners, and as the former codes of good manners are no longer serviceable, our comedy must be concerned rather with the testing of all manners than with ascriptions of "good" or "bad." Manners are in process of adaptation to new conditions. We cannot say that manners are either good or bad until we know what those conditions are. We are not then to inquire whether manners and customs are good, but whether they are serviceable and tend rationally to order.

It is only recently that writers have been able to turn upon the commonplace customs of American life and character the light of comic discriminations. This began about the time that playwrights began to treat on the stage the little man in his own magnitudes. I have already introduced "the little man" in another connection. He has an important place in comedy for the reason that comedy is the most concrete, the least illusioned of all forms of dramatic art. Comedy is the only form of dramatic art that shows man in his natural magnitudes. Too often the stage play treats the little man as a disguised great man. The pettiness of the hero is made to seem only external; as a mask of great virtues. And so the little man is made to suffer for a period, for two acts and a half, to be precise, the disadvantages of his littleness, and then for half an act he reaps the rewards of his greatness. Manifestly the author is not really interested in depicting a little man, and he certainly does not depict a great man. All that he indubitably does is to write a little play. When the time came that a character's littleness could be employed neither for him nor against him, but simply as a quality which he possesses in common with all his kind, a great step toward an American comedy had been reached.

In the comic treatment of "the little man" the stage is still behind the novel. The stage does not give the opportunity for the iterated depiction of little qualities that a novel offers. The tendency on the stage is always to sum up a quality in a symbol which is ever thereafter memorable as belonging to the character. Comedies from Ade and Cohan to Frank Craven and Winchell Smith represent American life in elementary symbols, which because they are so elementary are to this extent untrue.

These plays have all the tricks of surfaces; they are racy, sophisticated, facile. They are of a type which the Frenchman and the Englishman identifies as essentially American. And they are American. No purpose would be served by denying that they represent a large arc in our American life. And yet they are not all of America. And they are not comedy in the best sense because they do not get down to cases. There is nothing more insistent than comedy in getting beneath the surface to the underlying reality; there is nothing more cruel than true comedy. Our American playwrights of the popular school have lacked that cruel edge.

Perhaps it was the war with its magnified emotions, its formal and official dependence upon mass passion and gullibility that turned the stomachs even of those men who had been appealing to the crowd taste. This is to be noticed, that in so far as there has been a change of front respecting the fictions of crowd psychology, this change has taken place among the crowd artists and not among the more sensitive plants of the ateliers. The men and women who turned against crowd "bunk" were the men and women who had been handling the bunk. It is just as well that it was so. They knew the material they had been handling, knew how much less than a yard wide it was, and how much shoddy there was in it. And to turn against their own craft gave them a greater craft still. So strong had been the tendency to generalize character, to sentimentalize its motives, and elevate them above their worth, that among the keener playwrights there has developed a de-bunking school. Looking over society, and the plays and novels of society, they see them governed by illusions. They determine not to blow them up by a big wind, but simply to show them in their right magnitudes. Sinclair Lewis in "Main Street" and "Babbitt" performed a miracle in carrying home to the people a satire of the people and of his own and your and my standards. Others have done similar things in both the novel and the play.

I have already discussed Zona Gale, but I must mention her again here, because beginning with sentimental conceptions she has subjected her own method to the discipline of the comic spirit. Not only did she see life through the emotions, she saw it through conventionalized emotions of nice shadings and æsthetic values. The measure of her art is found in the rigorous discipline to which she has subjected her native gifts. Much of this discipline is a discipline of laughter turned against herself, a laughter in which there is little evidence of mirth. Few American writers to-day wield a harder instrument. While it cannot be claimed that Zona Gale has the command of the play that she has of the novel, her plays demand highly respectful consideration for what she has tried to do. In seeking to bring the corrective observation of comedy to the treatment of men and women, she is doing much to introduce to the stage men and women in their own magnitudes without the fairy cloak and seven-league boots of popular fiction.

Long before Zona Gale had turned to the stage, James Forbes had applied to the drama an observation trenchant and humorous. Forbes had the advantage, rare when he began to write, of seeing that the very best material of comedy is the material the author knows the best. Tragedy travels afar, but comedy lingers at home. James Forbes had the gift of seeing the salient feature in the thing near at hand and in the commonplace walk. He has been called "The snapper-up of unconsidered trifles." So he is, except that after he has set these in their place they are no longer unconsidered. "The Chorus Lady" is indeed an exaggerated piece of millinery for a star. But in "The Commuters" and "The Show-Shop" Forbes provides true comedies based upon the closest of observation of definite groups of human beings.

For the purposes of this book George S. Kaufman and Marc Connolly are one. Both these young men came to the stage by way of Pennsylvania and the newspaper "column." The first was born in Pittsburgh, the second in McKeesport. Both have been reporters and dramatic critics and have all the irreverence of their tribe. They also have the quick eye and the ready pen. Humor to them does not lie in caricature or exaggeration. It is a quick nudge and a pointing finger. If you get it, good! If you do not, no harm is done. Their plays do not abound in laughs; they do abound in smiles. They have the rare quality of discrimination without cruelty. They have taken the laughter of comedy out of the class of "sudden glory" and put it in the class of "benevolent recognition." The trick of alternating smiles and tears is an old one. Kaufman and Connolly blend them.

One would imagine that with such a method as this the plot might suffer. So it might if the authors sought to justify the plot for itself, but they do not. At their best they avoid the tiresome necessity of making plots for themselves by accepting a plot ready-made and developing this into two hours and a quarter of observation. Their first play, "Dulcy," was taken from the character gallery of a brother columnist, F. P. A. By F. P. A. the character of Dulcy had been established. There was nothing more to do with her or for her except to prevail upon her to go on the stage. This Kaufman and Connolly did with success. "Dulcy" opened at Indianapolis February 14, 1921. The same year it came to New York and played in New York and on tour. After this the authors produced "To the Ladies" (1922); "Merton of the Movies" from the novel of the same name by Harry Leon Wilson (1922); "Beggar on Horseback" (1923); "West of Pittsburgh," or "The Deep Tangled Wildwood" (1923); and "Minnick" (1924) from a story by Edna Ferber. Of these only "To the Ladies" and "The Deep Tangled Wildwood" were altogether original. The latter satirized rural comedy of the Winchell Smith school and was unsuccessful. "To the Ladies" remains their most considerable original achievement to date. The commonplace character of the scenes and persons of "To the Ladies" is indicated in the description of the two-family house in Nutley, New Jersey. It is, say the authors, "a decidedly livable place, and the reader is hereby encouraged to think of it as a room not as a stage." Leonard Beebe "is a middle-class youth of about twenty-five, and somewhere in the country there are ten million just like him." In the comedy-drama of this little home we have all the ingredients of middle-class American life, the absorption in success, the brash, rather pathetic sophistication of the go-getter world. There is the American fortune lying just around the corner. The difference between this and the "success" plays lies in the way in which the theme is treated. The authors at any rate are not deceived by appearances. Though the story deals without apology with the ever-present ideals of commercial success, the authors manage in the treatment to show how tawdry and just a little pathetic these ideals are. In "Dulcy" the authors had satirized a bungling woman. Here we take the story of "What Every Woman Knows" and apply it to suburban affairs. We would look long in our theater for a play with abundant human sympathy which still treats all characters with a clear-seeing disillusioned comprehension. Only men who are not afraid of the stage would dare to put bodily on the boards the fatuity and boredom of a series of after-dinner speeches. Kaufman and Connolly do this with success.

Kaufman and Connolly possess a perception of reality that is so clear as to amount to a comic judgment. Only one writer has this gift in greater measure and this is George Kelly. To his gift of observation Kelly adds a strenuous moral sense, a respect for the standards of his art, that are by no means concealed by the light and frivolous air that his work carries. Presented August 29, 1922, "The Torch-Bearers" soon had New York delighted. More than any one else the play pleased those who by their association with the insurgent movement in the American theater recognized in the characters of this play either themselves or, preferably, their dearest enemies. If only the little theater workers of the country could all see this play! Here is a new talent in the American theater. George Kelly is not a poet or a social philosopher. He is a young man with a busy eye and a note-book crowded with observations. Who then is he? All that it is important to know is that he hails from Philadelphia, entered the theater through the door of vaudeville, didn't take himself seriously at all but did take his work seriously. He learned to write plays in that hard school of the two-a-day, where the play must be a success during its first minute or it does not live to its tenth minute. In the dozen or more one-act comedies he has produced for Keith's and the Orpheum Circuit, he has learned that every word counts and that the surest way to please an audience is to tell them something they know already but do not know that they know. "The Torch-Bearers" has its extravagances and farcical features. With all these it is a cooling potion poured over the follies of the "new theater" movement. The events are less than negligible. But the characters are amazing. Like her sewing basket Paula is "fraught with meaningless bows and weird-looking knots." The stage is crowded with enthusiasts, pedants, pretenders, and—torch-bearers.

"The Torch-Bearers" was but a promise. "The Show-Off," produced at the Playhouse February 4, 1924, fulfilled the promise of the earlier play. Says Heywood Broun in his "Preface to the published play": " 'The Show-Off' is the best comedy which has yet been written by an American." We may agree with this or not and still admit that by all the standards of vital comedy there are few better. For no one can claim that this too does not enlarge one's views of life. Again the story is negligible and there are conventional features in it. As far as plot is concerned the play is another comedy of sudden riches. Certainly the author makes no effort to break new ground in his story. But this very conventionality of event is an advantage to the play in that it makes the characters of greater account than the plot. On this point Broun is again of help, for he calls attention to the fact that in the play "with a

big idea" the author must "scrunch and whittle his
characters now and then to make them get into his
plot scheme. He must bulldoze a little." But
fortunately here it is not the plot that is important.
It is that which lies behind the plot and gives the
plot significance. It is the conception of life as
illustrated by a character. For a conception of life
we want no manipulation of scenes of comic or dramatic effect, no arranged curtains. We want to see
a character in grip with his fate. His character and
fate are no less interesting because he happens to be
a fake and a pretender. Broun holds that Aubrey
Piper is an authentic character and that he is a
symbol of all mankind. His "personality endures
against the blows of circumstance. Aubrey is consistent in his faults. From Prometheus down mankind has chosen for its heroes men who stood pat."

Aubrey Piper is a liar, a braggart, a pretender,
who is raised to significance in drama because he is
consistently so. There is in him an irresistible fund
of good spirits. His lips drop stereotyped phrases:
"How is the little mother?" "Anything to please the
ladies!" "Sign on the dotted line." He fills the
room with boisterous laughter, he smites his sweet-
heart's father on the back. Aubrey's entrance to the
room is so depicted:

"Stay right where you are, folks, right where you
are." *(He moves to the mirror over the mantle-
piece.)* "Just a little social attention,—going right
out again on the next train." *(He surveys himself*

critically in the mirror, touching his tie and toupe gingerly, turns from the mirror and indicates his reflection with a wide gesture.) "There you are, Mother! Any woman's fancy, what do you say? Even to the little old carnation!" *(He gives the table a double tap with his knuckles, then laughs and moves up toward the kitchen door, and calls out to Amy.)* "Come on, Amy, step on the United Gas out there; customer in here waiting for the old aqua pura." *(Moving down to Mr. Fisher's right.)* "Man's got to have something to drink,—how about it, Pop?" *(He gives Mr. Fisher a slap on the right shoulder.)* "You'll stay with me on that, won't you?" *(Laughs and moves up to the mirror again. Old Man Fisher is very much annoyed.)* "Yes, sir." *(Coming forward again at the right.)* "I want to tell those of you who have ventured out this evening, that this is a very pretty little picture of domestic felicity," and he proceeds to administer another slap on Father's shoulder bone, saying, "What about it, Popcorn? Shake it up! Right or raving?"

Of course Aubrey marries Amy, and after marrying her proceeds to borrow from her brother-in-law. He talks about improving their way of living, but the income does not improve. A tragi-comedy of little stupid failures culminates in the death of Father Fisher at the moment that Aubrey, still pretending to riches he does not possess, gets into a collision with a traffic cop in a borrowed car. His magnificent effrontery never leaves him. "Don't let it get you, Honey. . . . The Kid from West Philly'll never go back on you,—you know that, don't you, Baby? . . . Don't cry, Honey, the old man's better off than we are—He knows all about it now." And then he goes into commentary, " 'Sic transit gloria mundi.' It's an old saying from the French meaning, 'We're here to-day and gone to-morrow.' " How Aubrey comes out doesn't matter. In the play he learns of an invention made by the young brother of his wife and by interfering stumbles into a good stroke of business. This will only make him worse thereafter. "God help *me*, from now on!" says Mrs. Fisher.

I cannot pretend to review every play that reflects the comedy of intense observation. In J. P. McEvoy's "The Potters," to mention only one, we have realism so insistent upon facts as to become funny. A derby hat, the stubbed toes and run-down heels of low-cut shoes, baggy trousers, a little cropped mustache—these are not funny in life. Place them with a certain care on the stage and they become not only funny but vastly expressive. "McEvoy has written a play not about a certain kind of character, or even a certain group of characters, but about a certain kind of life. . . . He hasn't shirked a single thing. Mr. Potter's home is ugly, and a little messy. He is crowded and jostled on the way to work. His work is without any vestige of dignity or importance," writes Heywood Broun. But while Mr. Potter's life is a joke, he has his dream. He, too, would go adventuring. What if his Odyssey is a gamble in oil? He fails and comes home a pathetic figure. Of course in the play the author contrives it in such a way that he does get a fortune after all. That is only an amiable falsehood. The Potters and the Easy Marks do not carry oil wells up their sleeves. It is from the little frustrate men, the little pretenders of democracy that this bourgeois school of American comedy comes.

IV

BIOGRAPHICAL COMEDY: PHILIP MOELLER; LAWRENCE LANGNER

If true comedy bears hard on the material and personal manifestation it is in order that through this manifestation the truth may be seen with greater clarity. There is no one symbol by which the deeper drama of the soul may be represented. The Great Dramatist employs all symbols and never is better pleased than when for a time He puts aside one symbol and takes up another that may have been despised. For long the convention of manners has been in control. We have seen how this is being put aside for a convention derived more closely from the facts of commonplace life. Everything in the drama of these days indicates the passing of the importance of plot, and the "social" factors of the play, and the enhancing of the importance of character and free imagination. The drama in the comedies treated in

this chapter has been almost entirely character
drama. The character would have been interesting
in isolation. We now know that the figure of the
man in the desert island without human contacts is
a fiction. Robinson Crusoe took the world with him
to his island, locked within his breast. Everything
that had gone before and everything that was, existed in him. If you would see the universe you no
longer need to see many men in clash and contact.
See one man and you have seen all.

This fact explains the new vogue of the biographical play. Written in the comic spirit, that is, in a
spirit of criticism of life, this play uses a single
individual as a microcosm. In the illumination of
the processes of this individual it is presumed that
human nature is illuminated. Frequently this individual is a historical personage about whom in the
course of time myths have gathered. The play then
undertakes to extract the true character from the
layers of romance and legend that surround him, or,
employing the life of the man as a focal point, the
play then develops a radical or destructive commentary on legend in general. The extreme types of
this order of play are on the one hand, Drinkwater's
"Abraham Lincoln," and on the other, Shaw's "Saint
Joan." It is not only in the theater that the new
critical temper in biography is manifest. In the
novel and in the informal biography the same tendencies are seen. The biographical play has not
become extremely common in America. Neverthe-

less, some highly significant work has been done in this order. "Queen Victoria," by David Carb and Walter Prichard Eaton, dramatizes the wise biography of Lytton Strachey in the same spirit in which Drinkwater had dramatized Lord Charnwood's "Lincoln."

The Americans who have done the most to apply a constructive criticism to the characters of history are Phillip Moeller and Lawrence Langner. Moeller had become known for some witty and sacrilegious short plays on historical and near-historical subjects, including "The Road House in Arden," "Two Blind Beggars and One Less Blind," "Helena's Husband," and others. The scene of the latter play is "that archæological mystery, a Greek interior." It might be said that all the interiors of Greece are a mystery. These have been treated with banal seriousness quite out of harmony with the spirit of the background. "Helena's Husband" burlesques this seriousness, the frayed glories of Menelaus. It gives an irreverent treatment to subjects that reverence has buried under a shell. In the play there is a conscious mixing of modern motives in ancient legend, the only purpose being to prick the bubble of dead mythology. In "The Little Supper" we have a comedy of Du Barry. "Sisters of Susannah" is a biblical farce and "The Road House in Arden" burlesques the speech and characters of the legendary Elizabethan era.

In "Madame Sand," produced by Mrs. Fiske

(1917) Moeller provides his first and best full length biographical study by the new method. The question before the author was, as Arthur Hopkins writes, how to bring historical characters to life "free from the odor of camphor and the rattle of moth balls." It is a daring group that includes George and Casimer Dudevant, Dr. Pagallo, Alfred and Paul de Musset, Heine, Liszt, and Chopin. As presented by Moeller, George Sand is a "creature of a thousand colors—Grande Dame and Bohemian—gamine and daughter of kings, soubrette and philosopher, pagan and religieuse, hausfrau and mad lover, every-day hard-worker and impassioned dreamer, simpleton and sage, poseuse and farm woman, tragedy queen and imp of mischief, Sibyl and 'big child' " (Mrs. Fiske). The author gives splendidly the impression of the divine confusion in the midst of which George spent her life. The world was all at ears about her; she was always calm. The play is rich with epigrams. Epigrams do not always serve their turn; in no other way could George be revealed. Madame de Musset is no match for George, "because she is a lady while George is a woman." Says Heine of her, "Pinnacles are her obsessions. But she'll come down. Bed's the great leveler." George is "never sentimental, never sententious, never conscious of her exuberance or her exaggerations; mistress of everything but her emotions which, though she thinks she masters, master her." When Buloz, the journalist, is asked how long

George's affair might last, he answers, "Does that matter if the copy is good?" And George says, "Though I write with my heart's blood, still I must write!" Of one it is said, "He is beginning to realize that virtue is its own disappointment." Alfred says of George, "She writes novels as a cow gives milk. All she has to do is to jerk at her mind." No purpose would be served by following the action of the play. It follows with sufficient fidelity the events of the flight to Venice, showing George with her successive lovers, writing always through scenes of violence. "Madame Sand" is a delight because of the humorous abandon with which the play moves. When Moeller turns from biographical levity to romance in "Molière" and tragedy in "Sophie" one loses interest.

In "Moses," by Lawrence Langner, we have one of the most significant of American biographical plays. "Moses" is far more than a drama of the great patriarch. It is the author's mocking bow to his own age, and, in view of the intrepidity of the author's deed, it is not too much to say that he has succeeded magnificently. Taking a leaf from the book of his master, G. B. S., Langner has fronted his comedy with a portico larger than the house itself. The author's foreword to "Moses" is one of the most solid pieces of constructive exposition of a social theorem I have seen in some time. With the courage and sweep of an aviator, Langner covers four thousand years in fifty pages, connecting Moses with the

Nineteenth Amendment with the ease with which other men go back to Rousseau.

In dealing with this play one cannot forbear treating it rather as idea than as play. The most real things in life to us are our gods. And yet these are the things of which we are most afraid, which we therefore permit most to befool and bedevil us. Quoting from a character in Andreyev's play, "He Who Gets Slapped," Langner says in his preface, "My friend . . . your speech was a sacrilege. Politics—all right! Manners as much as you please! But Providence—leave it in peace!" We are always controlled by the gods whom we have made. We are most free when we have many gods. Then we pursue adventure and beauty and build monuments. But those who have many gods are greatly at a disadvantage in this world beside those who have but one. Moses was a great lawgiver, organizer, and single track engineer. We call him a Jew but he might as well have been a Puritan. For the Puritan keeps Moses alive through the ages.

Such a biographical drama as this magnifies greatly the limits of drama. Moses is more than a man. He is decidedly not a myth. He is a social principle embodied in a man. In studying him we study the social principle. And the result is most decidedly a comedy. It would not be comedy if these social principles were treated in the form of the give and take between groups of people. This side of the baldest didacticism, the most flamboyant romance, the drama has no place for such serious stuff as this. But the drama has room for the incisive, satirical study of a man in whom are epitomized the qualities of a general idea. One cannot bring an indictment against a people, it is said. That is not so clear. We can bring an indictment against a people's ideas, principles, and gods. We can do this by identifying their ideas with the man who was their exponent and subjecting this man to the cruel light of comic judgment. Whether it is necessary to write a play in order to do so is another question. It is almost uncanny how completely the play of "Moses" brings out in action and dialogue the points made in the Preface. Whatever interest there is in the action is immensely illuminated by the Preface. Here is uncovered one danger in this kind of writing for the stage. The gloss tends to be more interesting than the text it interprets. Since the play gains so greatly by its Preface, why write the play at all? Why not be content with the Preface?

V

Clare Kummer, Booth Tarkington, Stuart Walker

In one of his letters to his son, Augustus St. Gaudens wrote, "I feel that the ambitions, artistic, monetary, or any old thing, the jealousies, generosities, are hopelessly mixed up with one another and are affected by *vanity. Everything is vanity,* com-

plicated with affairs of the heart." One who studies
the theater is impressed with the fact that playwrights are continually trying to apply simple motives to conditions and actions which are in fact the
results of a complication of motives. The will to see
all clearly sometimes develops into a will to kill all
that refuses to harmonize itself with a clear conception. The artist feels so strongly the obligation of
truth that he surrenders to the temptation of vivi-
section. In pursuing the ends of analysis the organic
is lost. Would it not be better to seek rather the
feel of life than an understanding of life? Does not
understanding lie beyond the artist's powers and
therefore beyond his province? Certainly it is true
that a play must be more than comedy or it is less
than comedy. After the author's full critique is
apprehended there must be a residuum of life that
goes beyond the critique. This probably means but
this, that the writer must bring not only his intelli-
gence and skill to his craft; he must bring his own
particular point of view. Quintilian's first law of
rhetoric was that the writer should be a good man.
This requirement applies to the playwright as well.

We have in our day come to look a little askance
upon a writer's injection of his own personality into
his work. And yet the writers who have most en-
deared themselves to their audience and readers have
been those who have been most free in giving themselves. If but the artist have a certain sign manual,
if we can recognize the timbre of his voice, we come

to love him and to value him for being himself. Inconsistencies of opinion are overlooked in the consistency of personal outlook.

Clare Kummer brings to market no heavy philosophy of life. Undoubtedly she has her own pet sophisms, but she does not introduce them into her work. She has not, as far as I know, expounded any principles as to the place of the theater in society. She has a thorough command of her craft. But her not inconsiderable hold upon the affections of the theater public arises from the fact that she has an individual outlook and she has been far-sighted enough to capitalize her own best gift. In a world in which almost everything, even in comedy, is significant, or impressive, it is refreshing to find a gayly playful spirit that is not too much overcome by anything she sees. Clare Kummer has a wide enough gallery of enthusiasm and sympathies. She chooses to dress these in a discreet and not too garish motley. There is in all her work a vein of delicate and inconsequent whimsy which, taken in connection with the fact that she knows well most of the people you and I meet in a week's journey, gives to her work a piquant and satisfying charm.

Clare Kummer had written many short plays for vaudeville and for amateur production before she brought out a longer work. Among these were "Bridges," "Chinese Love," "The Choir Rehearsal," "The Robbery." Then in 1916 Arthur Hopkins produced "Good Gracious Annabelle," with Roland

Young and Walter Hampden in leading rôles. The play was immediately recognized as a new thing in comedy. There was in it dexterity, truth of characterization, freedom from theatrical cant and convention and, above all, an atmosphere of refined living. In such a play as this, plot is of the least importance. The first requirement is that the characters shall take the reins of the action into their own hands and drive it whithersoever they will. It must be so because the characters are that kind of characters. They are to the last degree refined and irreproachable—this was the day before the super-sophisticated sub-deb—and they are to the last degree foot-loose and irresponsible. The world of indigent, happy-go-lucky artists meets up with a world of happy-go-lucky wealth. With the lightest heart in the world the play moves among situations that might have a taint of tarnish but there is never a suggestion of guile. Desperately put to it, Annabelle takes a position in the country-place of the one rich man who can save her and marry her. She takes her indigent friends with her. There are complications about various things, including two precious shares of stock. But she marries her millionaire.

In her ability to handle "fancies light as air" in the midst of the skyscrapers, elevators, hotels and detectives of a great city, Clare Kummer shows true genius. It would be too much to expect all her works to be of equal success. One of the successful whimsies is "A Successful Calamity." A tired and perfectly solvent gentleman in the forties desires a radical, intoxicating joy, a joy that the poor may have any day of their lives. He wants to spend an evening at home. So he gives his family to understand that he is ruined. Out of the situation there develop some episodes that are not convincing, to say the least. But the author had not intended them to be convincing. Enough that his wife did *not* run away with her handsome Italian, that by an indiscretion his partners are led to make unexpected millions, and that he gets one mad, ecstatic evening. "Be Calm, Camilla," produced 1918, is a study of the lonely woman in a large city, moving through scenes that would affright the most hardy. "The Rescuing Angel" is a comedy of a happy-go-lucky family and of Angela who succeeds in being of some account more by luck than by good sense. The play degenerates into farce and is not in the author's best mood. But in "Rollo's Wild Oat" we have Miss Kummer at her very best. Here the author indulges in a riot of pranks against the world of the bored rich and against the world of the theater. Rollo is rich and discontented. There is moving in him a mad passion which must break forth. He must sow just one wild oat. The oat he must sow is nothing more nor less than that he must produce Hamlet and act in it himself. What comes of this, the people he meets, the dire confusion of his real scandalized world with the mimic world of his dreams, cannot be suggested in a review. The play must be read, or better, seen, if its thoroughly cogent inconsequence is to be appreciated. The author by no means limits her playfulness to Rollo. There are scenes in this play that throw the same cruel light on the stage-struck that shines from "The Torch-Bearers." The respectable stupidity of Goldie, the actress' daughter who could not act, the pathetic collapse of the ambitions of Hewston, the butler, equal in satiric force the sudden withering of Rollo's lone oat.

Booth Tarkington has broken many pitchers going to the dramatic well. A playwright of great diversity in the forms and qualities of his plays, few of his dramatic works demand consideration among the lasting plays of the time. This is not the case with "Clarence," one of the most delightfully whimsical comedies of recent years. "Clarence" was produced at the Hudson Theatre, September 20, 1919. Excellent as the play is, it is not of uniformly good quality. Beginning upon a plane of pure inconsequence, the author's more reasoning and therefore worse judgment prevailed at the end, and in scenes of even toilsome particularity he clarified every issue and ended the play in the dust. But the matter-of-fact ending of the play should not blind us to the half-inspired dexterity and humor of the earlier acts. The opening of the play introduces us to a modern family that is, as far as family feeling is concerned, scattered to the four winds. Brother Bobby and Sister Cora are growing up into the modern world so fast as to strike terror to their parents. And Father and

Mother are powerless to be of use to them for they no longer see eye to eye. The less said of Mother's mental equipment the better. And then to complicate matters, there is a governess who is the innocent cause of much disturbance in various bosoms. To this family comes Clarence from the war, a perfect specimen of spectacled, long-armed ineptitude. How he found his way into the family does not matter. Before any one knew how it had happened, he was master and all others were his slaves. There is just a little satire on soldiers but not much. Mostly the author avoids satire entirely and contents himself with developing the character and charms of one of the most engaging young jackanapes in recent comedy. There is no doubt that Tarkington enjoyed the writing of the play. This is evidenced by the fact that many of the most laughable features of the play are quite extraneous to the plot and unnecessary to the understanding of the character. Before long, Clarence has won the confidence of Cora and of Bobby. The complications that threatened each of these adolescents are resolved by Clarence's casual hand. These two youngsters have formed the models of a long line of talkative young sophisticates. But Clarence is helpful not only to the children. At the moment that conditions are strained between Father and Mother, and Father is turning in desperation to Violet for sympathy, Clarence enters playing his saxophone. Throughout the play he is an inspired blunderer who, in spite of missteps, lands on his feet and pulls the world to order around him. The last two acts, which are devoted to telling who Clarence really is, awarding him a Ph.D. degree, a place in "Who's Who" and a wife, are not on the level of the inspired foolery of the first two acts. But the play as a whole is of a high order of comedy.

Stuart Walker is one of those who might have made his mark as a writer of the whimsically imaginative comedy of character had he not withdrawn from the study to spend his life producing the plays of other men, thus making himself a collaborator and interpreter rather than an original creator. The plays he has written are all short and are presumably composed for a children's theater. Though children love them, there is food in them for older people as well. There is in them a strain of Barrie combined with a strain of Dunsany, the tender intuition and playful vagaries of the one combining with the braver imagination of the other. Among his plays are "Six Who Pass While the Lentils Boil," "The Trimplet," "The Very Naked Boy," "Nevertheless" and the more ambitious "The Lady of the Weeping Willow Tree." Walker is not without credit for aiding Tarkington in bringing to the stage "Seventeen," that play that introduced the youth movement to the modern stage. No better indication of his temper is to be found than his Prologue to the Portmanteau Theatre.

"(*As the lights in the theater are lowered the voice of MEMORY is heard as she passes through the audience to the stage.*)

"*Memory:* Once upon a time, but not so very long ago, you very grown-ups believed in all true things. You believed until you met the Fourteen Daughters who were so positive in their unbelief that you weakly cast aside the things that made you happy for the hapless things that they were calling life. You were afraid and ashamed to persist in your old thoughts. . . . Here are your cities, your gardens and your April pools. Come through the portals of Once-upon-a-time, but not so very long ago—to-day—now!"

VI

"A Weathercock and a Mighty Twirling"

Nietzsche spent his life in "revaluing values." Measurably inspired by him the art of our time busies itself in house wrecking. Now and then temporary "codes of practice" are fabricated. Few of these last long. In literature, in the theater, judgment by standard is not at present in effect. Our only present standard is that we have no standard. We no longer maintain the pretense that stable values lie just around the corner. These have receded with our Utopias. To-day our artists say with Steeplejack: "And now when the Great Noon had come Steeplejack touched the top of the spire where instead of a cross he found a vane which swung as the wind listeth. Thereat he marveled and rejoiced. 'Behold!' he cried, 'Thou glowing symbol of the New Man. A weather-cock and a mighty twirling!' "

It would hardly be reasonable to speak of the comedy written under any such impulse as this as if it were a new and significant school of comedy. This would be like making a system out of chaos. And yet is not this what our modern art is doing? Art has no existence of itself. It is a reflection of, a reaction to, reality. We may well imagine that in a solar system in which the hop, step and the jump represented the rhythm of the stars, it would represent the rhythm of the seasons, of the steam engine, and of music as well. Art derives its movement from sources deeper than itself, dramatic art no less than others. We do not say that man moves in a great orbit around the sun. We say the earth moves, carrying man along. Man is even unaware of the rhythms, the harmonies, the wide circles of movement that are implicit in his life. It is only the artist that now guesses, now postulates, these hidden values. But the artist does not create these values nor is he responsible for them.

One result of the collapse of disciplines is to throw the practitioner of an ancient craft over into reversals and paradox. This is the more simple and more easily followed reaction. Our stage has seen many plays which derive their interest from the fact that they turn the back side of truth forward, advance what was retired and retire what was advanced. In its simplest form this process is so easy as to be trite. It is present in rudimentary form in almost all artistic activity. It is a recipe for discreet daring and for popular acclaim. While it gives the appearance of thought, it by no means follows that thought is involved, though thought is sometimes the by-product of the formula. The high priest of this style of writing is George Bernard Shaw. From handling paradox as a formula, or as a rule of practice, Shaw has advanced until he has made himself one of the chief stimulators of thought of his age. We have no American George Bernard Shaw, but we have many who have gone to his school. In this style of composition the simplest of all is that which burlesques the formulas of art. In this order of things George M. Cohan is a master. His chief claim to distinction lies in his possession of a "sincere" streak that leads him to make a large fortune by satirizing those stage formulas by the practice of which others make smaller fortunes. The occasional satires of romance, of the classical forms, and of the fervid problem play are examples of this kind of comedy. In so far as they resemble burlesque they belong not to our age alone but to all time.

Beyond the satire of the formula of art there is the satire of the formula of conduct. This provides a deeper order of play composition. Our drama is not rich in these kinds of comedy. They demand a sustained attention on the part of the author that our stage has not heretofore encouraged. Mark Twain, whose power came nearest to comprehending this order of comedy, reached its true values only infrequently in fiction and never in the drama. To be noted is the passing of the hero. By lighter blows the modern comedian is accomplishing the same destruction that Cervantes sought. "The Bad Man," by Porter Emerson Browne, takes the figure of the Southwestern bandit and desperado and by showing him observing the amenities toward the ladies makes of him an engaging figure, albeit one outside the law. The bad man is not the first popular desperado of the stage. "The Nervous Wreck," by Owen Davis, shows the figures of Western romance scared by pistol shots and outwitted by a neurasthenic. "The Egotist," by Ben Hecht, subjects the myth of the "marauding male" to a searching comic analysis.

The more significant result of the collapse of disciplines is to throw the authors over into complete levity or lawless experiment and innovation. In other arts this has resulted in the riots of futurisms, vorticisms, cubisms, imagisms and free art and free verse. These tendencies have been no less active in the theater than in other arts, though on account of the conservatism of the institution of the theater, a conservatism firmly bedded in its economic structure, they have been more repressed. In the next chapter I shall refer to the experiments toward new forms to express the tortured and insecure philosophies of this day. Here I shall consider only a few comedies which, in the face of a ridiculous world, break into levity.

H. L. Mencken and George Jean Nathan call their

as yet unproduced play, "Heliogabalus," a "buffoonery." Like many buffoons, "Heliogabalus" is cross-eyed. One eye looks toward classicisms, the other toward moralities. The whole world of the sacrosanct and academic is insulted with an abounding zest and good humor by bringing the figures of classical comedy into a lusty and obscene burlesque. And moralities are trounced by being run over, trodden under foot and generally ignored. The play is rich in ribald spirits and impudent lines.

Harry Wagstaff Gribble's "March Hares" was first produced in 1921 under the title of "The Temperamentalists" and was called a fantastic satire. By that the author meant, I imagine, that the satire was informal and scattered over things in general. The play deals in a spirit of delightful abandon with a thoroughly disjointed set of events. We have moved into a very crowded world and the crowding seems to be mental rather than physical. Instead of a kingdom the mind has become a prison; the servants are masters, and every one has his pet attitude or ism. In such a world the best one can do is to go through the mêlée with an air of aloof detachment. "Just keep your mind clear all the time and eliminate things," says Geoffrey. "Above all don't take things as they are. If you do you are lost. Take them with imagination." The play is an incomprehensible but fascinating piece of work.

Other comedies that have attracted some attention are W. J. Turner's "The Man Who Ate the Popomack," and Knowles Entrekin's "Julia Counts Three" and "The Small-Timers." It is a characteristic of this lawless comedy that no conclusions can be drawn from it, that it tends nowhere and is expressive only of a condition that must in the nature of things pass. Comedy has suffered too much under the tyranny of an assumed omniscience and clairvoyance. We have in comedy too many little patterns that reveal only the bad draftsmanship of the designer. It will do the muse of comedy no harm to kick up her heels for awhile. If she provokes resentments and scandal, we shall, at any rate, know by what spirit these resentments are urged.

CHAPTER V

THE MYSTERY OF FORM

I

The Short Play

With the passing of the last geographical frontier an end comes to the long era of exploration. There begins now in an intenser and more universal form than ever before the era of exploitation. The theater cannot be unaffected by this new ordering. The theater, too, is learning that there are no new things; that there are only new arrangements of things. It is learning that progress will henceforth be rather by an extension of use than by an extension of physical resource. In the multiplication of use, indeed, resource is multiplied. As interest in substance decreases, interest in form increases.

The theater has for a long time been going through a process which closely parallels the process of its origins. As the theater has been called upon to apply itself more closely to a world suddenly become small, there has been a testing of its values, a reorganization of its facilities. This tendency has been manifest not only in the theater as a producing institution; it has been particularly manifest in play construction. Within recent years there has been a revolution in the attitude of the playwright toward his work. A new code of responsibility has manifested itself in the psychology of the playwright toward the audience and particularly toward the materials out of which his play is made. The old rules and objectives no longer hold. New rules and objectives have to be created, tested, discarded or accepted. The drama has again to be referred back to the simplest principles of human conduct and motive. A structure has to be worked out that will employ in their simplest connotations these elementary principles. After these things have been done all the resources of the expressive art of the theater through the ages have to be put under tribute, all the untouched potentialities of science and discovery have to be imaginatively employed in order to make the theater of the new time an expressive agency of the new spirit. Form becomes the chief concern, even the obsession of the playwright. And when I say "form," I do not mean the stereotyped pattern handed down from earliest draughtsmen, but form electric, vital, aspiring, "beating its wings against the unknown."

Until twenty years ago the one-act play existed simply as a filler, an after-piece or fore-piece, for a long play. In form the one-act play was a little copy of the longer play, with the plot complication, progression and climaxes of the full length play.

The only difference between the short and the long play lay in the magnitude of the action presented. Little effort was made to employ the short play for the attainment of effects quite different from those of the long play. When one reduces the canvas in a painting one changes the quality and objective of the work. Not so with the play. Whether short or long, the play was adjusted to a set of conventions that had grown up through years and now had little relation either with common experience or common sense.

It was when the playwrights began to apply to their craft the tenets of art that the short play came into its modern vogue. The creative playwrights who sought in their work to satisfy a rigorous standard of individual judgment had to learn their art from the beginning. This was not so much a matter of policy as of necessity. While it had something to do with the fact that long plays of an experimental order could not hope to find production, that the amateur producing groups were the only productive outlet of the self-respecting artist, this cart-before-the-horse argument should not be driven too far. In this book we rest definitely on the doctrine that the playwright is the primary creator in the theater, that his work is a play once it is produced in the mind of its creator as truly as a symphony by Beethoven was a symphony before it was heard by any other than his inner ear. It was in pursuit of a new and honest art of the theater that the one-act play was developed by the playwrights. Producers and organizers, draughtsmen and scenery builders, coöperated to make the one-act play an important step in the progress toward a new theater art. But it was the playwright who learned most from the experiments.

The drama in one act has played a Protean rôle in the history of the American stage during the twentieth century. To writers of first rank, O'Neill, for instance, it has been a trying-ground of experiment and values. To writers of second rank, and the great body of rebuilders, renovators, and "torch-bearers" it has been the medium through which dramatic art has been definitely established in American life. The significance of this latter service can hardly be over-estimated. It applies rather to the theater as a social institution and as a land of promise for future imaginative creators than to the creative achievements of the present theater. In this book we are interested in the accomplishments of dramatic writers. For this reason we must leave the more general social function of the one-act play without further comment. Few of the thousands of one-act plays written in this country in the last twenty years attain the highest value as judged by rigorous dramatic standards. Among these the plays by Eugene O'Neill, published in the volume, "The Moon of the Caribbees," occupy first place.

When one compares the mass of these short plays with the general run of long plays produced in the

United States in the same period, the high quality of the short play is manifest. Almost all of these are characterized by honesty of intention,—not high praise indeed, but still not a disgraceful qualification in a time when sincerity has been at a premium on the commercial stage. The authors of a surprising number of these plays do seek to free themselves from the incubus of theatricality. Directness and simple motivation are the rule. In view of the tribute so frequently paid by "new" movements to preciosity and æsthetic fine shadings it is surprising how free the majority of these plays are from affectation and an over-reaching for adornment. If I should bring any indictment against these short plays it would be that they are dull. The imagination seldom reflects sudden ecstasy, deep feeling or an experience of life concretely realized. This is but another way of saying that we have applied our journeyman methods even to the fabrication of a free art. Our playwrights of little plays work by pattern, from stencils. The patterns are good of their kind; the stencils are well selected. But in the content of our lives, the comparative effortlessness of the daily round, there is little stimulus to the imagination to heat itself hot and break through the acceptable stencil into inspired creation.

This is one side of the medal. The other must also be shown. The art of America does not require, will not permit, the hunger stimulus that has presumably so often produced great works of art. The monuments of the past have been produced in a world that was niggard of material resources, lavish only in the spirit of man. It was not far from Athens to the marshes, from Rome to hovels in the swamps. The Paris of Molière, the London of Shakespeare were cesspools now flowering luxuriantly, now stricken by disease. I do not seek to discover all the reasons why Phidias carved his marbles and Shakespeare wrote his plays. I know that in these works they built themselves temples of beauty of the mind against a plentiful experience of bodily discomfort. I do not seek to compare the artists of our day to their advantage with the artists of other days any more than I would seek to show that social conditions are better in our day than in other days. Such speculations are footless, or to be of value require more knowledge than I can claim. I seek only to show that the stimulus to creation is different in our day from other days. I dare say that never before did the stimulus come to large numbers of people to create a world of the imagination because this world was *too* comfortable, too well equipped with the mechanical conveniences of living, too richly provided with material things. This is definitely the source of the creative urge among large numbers of our people. The impulse is to flee from reality, or to clear away the too obtrusive material presence and find the hidden essence underneath. Admittedly this impulse has not yet flowered in many great and enduring works. As an impulse it is, however, as defensible as any other, for it grows from the conditions of our life. And its manifestations are so various and cover so large an area of our society as to promise events of some interest in a future not too distant.

It is for these reasons that, while I do not take many of the short plays that have been written in this country seriously as works of art, I do take the recent and persistent vogue of the one-act play very seriously. As a rule, this type of play has appeared as a product of the work of local stage societies. There have been the "Plays of the Harvard Dramatic Club," the "Harvard Workshop Plays," "The Indiana Prize Plays," "Morningside Plays," "Dakota Playmakers' Plays," "Carolina Plays," "Provincetown Plays," "Wisconsin Plays," "Washington Square Plays," and groups of plays from many other movements. Many of the writers of plays have written for a particular audience or following. George Middleton wrote his one-act plays in the volumes entitled "Tradition," with the general reader and dramatic study groups in mind. The plays of Marion Craig Wentworth, Mary Louise MacMillan, Augusta Stevenson, have been written for school and club use. Percival Wilde's short plays have had hundreds of productions. Stuart Walker's plays were written originally for his Portmanteau Theatre; Mary Aldis's plays were written for her private theatre near Chicago. Alfred Kreymborg's many plays have been composed for a special kind of rhythmic or puppet production. The number of collections of one-act plays for various uses is very great. It would be a daring and thankless task to undertake to select from the thousands of short plays which have been written those of greatest merit or reputation. Without doubt such a list would include in addition to those mentioned above, Ridgely Torrence's three negro plays, "Granny Maumee," "The Rider of Dreams," "Simon, the Cyrenian"; Jeanette Marks' Welsh plays; the many plays of Thomas Wood Stevens, written either alone or in collaboration with Wallace Rice and Kenneth Sawyer Goodman; the plays of Kenneth Sawyer Goodman, written alone or in collaboration with Ben Hecht; the plays of Colin Campbell Clements, including "Four Who Were Blind"; "A Modern Harlequinade," "Yesterday," "Seven Plays of Old Japan," etc.; Louise Driscoll's "The Child of God"; Floyd Dell's "The Angel Intrudes"; Alice Gerstenberg's "Overtones"; Harry Kemp's "Judas"; Theresa Helburn's "Enter the Hero"; Witter Bynner's "Tiger" and "The Little King"; John G. Neihardt's "Two Mothers"; Edna St. Vincent Millay's "Aria da Capo"; Zoë Akins' "The Magical City"; Lawrence Langner's "Another Way Out"; Philip Moeller's "A Roadhouse in Arden" and "Helena's Husband"; Josephine Preston Peabody's "Wings"; Alice Brown's "Joint Owners in Spain"; Frank G. Tompkins' "Sham"; Susan Glaspell's "Suppressed Desires," "The People" and "Trifles";

Lewis Beach's "The Clod"; Zona Gale's "The Neighbors"; Booth Tarkington's "Beauty and the Jacobin"; Victor Mapes' "Flower of the Yeddo." This rough list might be indefinitely extended by any one who follows the output of the busy little theaters.

II

BREAKING INTO NEW FORMS: EDWARD KNOBLOCK AND OTHERS

The one-act play offers an opportunity for the development of a single unbroken action in tabloid form. Aside from this it represents the first step in the playwright's progress toward a better handling of the problems of dramatic structure. In the nature of the case the one-act form is limited to the simplest action. This form could be of no use for a theme that involved either a complication or a progression of action or both. The same logic that dictates the use of a single unbroken form for a simple coherent action dictates also that the structure of the longer play be diversified to reflect the organic divisions of the action. The practice of a forced condensation of an entire action, whatever might be its stages of natural progression, into three, four or five tight compartments had deadened the imagination of the playwright. Playwrights now began to diversify the close logic of the construction either by breaking the action up into many scenes or by breaking the time scheme through the use of "flash-backs." Of themselves these changes were of comparatively little importance. Mechanical expedients are by rights subsidiary always to the imagination that directs them. It is only when mechanics controls and stultifies the imagination that the change from one mechanical form to another more flexible form becomes important.

The breaking up of the act and scene scheme of the play into a more flexible form has become common on the commercial stage. No comment is now caused if the playwright employs from six to ten or more separate scenes to represent the movement of his action. There is a tyranny in the theater which, for want of a better term, we may call the tyranny of time. While the historic unities are no longer enforced, the demand that the action shall work out within a limited period of time has been of binding force. This requirement has made it impossible to present within the action of the play and before the eyes of the audience the effect of the lapse of years that is so large a factor in life. In the English play, "Milestones," Arnold Bennett and Edward Knoblock had so administered the action as to cover the events of three generations. In so doing they were not violating unity. They were retaining unity, for the unity they had in mind was that deeper unity that persists in a family and in human customs and outlooks. By spreading the action over fifty years the author had, in fact, given the effect of the unity of human striving and as well of human frailty and stubbornness.

Edward Sheldon had given the effect of the unity of life under its varying episodes in his play, "The Highroad"; and in 1922 Henry Myers gave a pointedly unified view of the long stretch of an unhappy marriage in "The First Fifty Years."

But the tyranny of time in the theatre does not operate alone in compressing the action within narrow limits. It demands as well that the various actions shall be in sequence. For providing the release from the tyranny of time sequence the legitimate stage has to thank the motion picture. The motion picture taught the writer of plays for the legitimate stage that some of the limitations of this latter form of dramatic art are inherent in the form. These limitations are to be accepted, then, with good grace. But there are other limitations that are not essential. There is no more reason why the play should enforce a chronological sequence of events than that the novel or the movie should do so. In either case there is demanded only that the reader or audience shall be aware of the relationships among the scenes. It lies as well within the power of the playwright to provide this understanding as of the novelist or continuity writer. The first play to put successfully into effect the theory of a broken time scheme was "On Trial" by Elmer Rice (Reizenstein), produced August 19, 1914. Of this play the author says, "It occurred to me that it would be an interesting experiment to write a play backward, just to see how it would work out—to make it analytic instead of synthetic, deductive instead of inductive—to make it break down instead of build up." In following out his plan the author eliminates explanatory scenes entirely. The retrospective action with which the usual play begins is cut out and in its stead are introduced visual scenes in which every phase of the plot is realized before the audience. The story is of itself of no importance. It deals with a trial for murder in which each one of the witnesses is compelled to live through in action before the audience the events upon which his testimony is given. The play is closely knit in structure and the action achieves clarity and carries conviction. Some years after the production of "On Trial" Zoë Akins gave another fillip to the idea of dramatic sequence when, in "The Varying Shore," she presented a play in which the action moved backward from the denouement to the early premises. The play was not successful in production, but one cannot be sure whether its failure lay in the idea itself or in the failure of the producer to realize the conception of the author.

The constraint of a hard logic upon the imagination of the playwright extends not alone to the mechanical features of the plot. It is even more serious when applied to the substance of the play, simplifying what is not simple, and subjecting to a cold regimen forces that are elusive and complex. The unities of whatever order have been under heavy fire in the theater of recent years. The idea that a human equation can be resolved with all the finality of mathematics has few adherents in the newer drama. A man may stand for many things, according to the light that is thrown upon him or the angle from which he is viewed. We no longer believe that one arbitrarily selected aspect can be employed to represent the man. Perhaps the man is better presented by a dualism of aspects. In the drama of life a man plays many parts. May he not do so in the drama of the stage as well? He is observer and observed, creator and created. He both gives and takes. The very prevalent custom of employing a containing action in which one or more characters are shown not alone as acting in the play, but as creating the action in their own minds is true to this fundamental conception of the unity in complexity of all human manifestation. In the same year, 1914, in which "On Trial" was produced, A. E. Thomas and Clayton Hamilton had produced "The Big Idea." This play employs the expedient of a play within a play to unusual effect. A young man and a young woman undertake to write a play to make up for a defalcation on the part of the young woman's father. But instead of writing the play the two proceed to live their own play before the audience. The dual situation is developed with much skill and humor. A play on a comparable plan is Biggers' and Cohan's "Seven Keys to Baldpate." In "Plots and Playwrights" by Edward Massey, produced by the Washington Square Players in 1916 we have another application of the system of the duality of action in a play. The idea of "Plots and Playwrights" is that any street, any house, will provide material for a play if only the writer can see it. Once this idea is developed in discussion between two men it remains only for one of them to put it to the test. Visiting successively three floors of a lodging house the author finds a drama on each floor. The play is a play of youth. All types of youth's disappointment and aspiration, from the vaudeville actors on the first floor to the frustrate student on the top floor are represented. The three playlets taken together and incorporated in the drama of the observer and his friend make up the larger play. Not only is this play an interesting illustration of the principle of which we speak. The play itself is a criticism of many common features in the drama of the time.

Beyond the dualism of the containing action or of double motivation in a single character, there lies fantasy. In fantasy the author throws away the claims of reason in behalf of a higher logic. The sequence and connections of the action are broken by an itinerant fancy which, playing upon all the manifestations of the theme, illumines those which best bring out its inner qualities. Eleanor Gates' "The Poor Little Rich Girl" had been written first as a novel. Produced in 1913 as a play by Arthur Hopkins it was the means of establishing his position as a producer. Of this fantasy George Jean Nathan said at the time, that it is "the best and most imaginative dramatic fantasy this country has given birth to." The play deals with a little rich girl who is surrounded by all the riches her heart can want but has no companions and is badly neglected by father and mother. So she proceeds to invent for herself a different world and to call to her all those kindred spirits who are denied to her. The play is sentimental and is not altogether successful in establishing a "cessation of disbelief." The neglected child goes into a delirium, and her dream is peopled with a rare combination of people. Needless to say, when she gets well she is promised by her remorse-stricken parents all those joys which before had been denied to the poor little rich girl.

More than any playwright of the time Edward Knoblock has made himself the exponent of the open technique in dramatic construction. Born in America, most of his writing has been done on the other side of the Atlantic. If there is any playwright who might be called "The Neglected American Playwright" it is Knoblock, for his work has greater value than the repute awarded it would imply. Early in his career Knoblock dedicated himself to the "story" in dramatic art. In the emphasis of various factors it appeared to him that the factor of the fable had been overlooked. To Knoblock "story" did not mean forced complication of plot. It meant an imaginative use of the vital factors of action and event that go to make up the content of life. Knoblock's insistence on story involved many things. It involved a far greater insistence upon color and movement. It demanded clearly cut and dramatic characters. And it demanded that the structure and all the factors of the play be subordinated to the fable. In another time Knoblock would be called a romanticist. He is not a romanticist. He is a man to whom the appeal of events is strong; a man who loves the color and odor of material things; a man who tends to see the ideal world in an arrangement of concrete events. There is in his work a fresh spirit of theatrical imagination. He makes no claims to great depth, but he is an accomplished artificer in the theater, and employs the theater always for the effects that please his own cultivated and unconventional taste.

Knoblock early appeared as a playwright with "The Shulamite" and "The Cottage in the Air." He next wrote "The Faun," in which, in 1911, Faversham appeared as the denizen of the woods who breaks into English society. The trick of bringing a faun on the stage was more striking fifteen years ago than it would be now and offered the author opportunities for satirical hits on our civilized ways. Needless to say, the forest visitor is at the end glad to return to his woods. "Kismet" was offered in vain to many American producers. Finally accepted in London, it was produced by Oscar Asche. It was then produced in New York by Harrison Grey Fiske and Klaw and Erlanger, in 1911. A

lavish stage spectacle, "Kismet" belonged more to
the order of the old sensation plays than to the more
recent types of play-writing. It must not be forgotten, moreover, that this was the first play to
dramatize for the American stage the rich and colorful life of the Orient. In "Discovering America"
(1912), Knoblock employs an episodic method to tell
a tale of two cities, Rome and New York. His "Milestones," in which he collaborated with Arnold Bennett, is well known. Probably the most original and
imaginative of Knoblock's plays is "My Lady's
Dress." This play is a series of short plays dealing
with episodes in many different countries, including
Italy, France, Holland, Siberia and England. These
plays are connected only by the fact that each deals
with one of the steps entering into the making of
a lady's dress. A wife and her husband have quar-
reled about an expensive dress. She then dreams a
series of scenes which reveal how the dress had come
into being. The somewhat sordid stories are softened
by the element of dreams. The discarded lover, the
dying husband, the tipsy weaver, the unwelcome
suitor, the crippled girl in Whitechapel, the trapper
who learns that his wife has been untrue to him and
sells the sable that was to go to his child, all have
their part in the making of the dress. "Marie Odile"
(1915) was one of the first and best of the war plays
written during the war. It is a tale of unhappy
Belgium symbolized by an innocent young girl
reared among the cloisters. Some of the most deli-

cate situations in contemporary drama are here handled with authority and beauty. "Paganini," "The Lullaby" and "Tiger Rose" are others of Knoblock's plays.

III

PLAYWRITING AND DESIGN

If we are to understand how the new dramatic forms have developed it may be well to review some of the movements of opinion of the last twenty years as these relate to forms. Every change in the fashions of the theater is accompanied by a great fanfare. The change is not always worth as much as the bruit would seem to indicate. Our own time has been particularly busy with the noisy patter of criticism. Some time ago men discovered that the theater is a world of conventions and illusions. Such the theater always is, but the discovery was a shock to many and they demanded at once that the conventions of the theater should be destroyed, that the old illusions should no longer illude. They ignored the fact that in destroying the old convention they were but setting up a new one which would come under attack in its time. All art is convention. All opinion is illusion. There is the dead convention that hangs like a millstone around the neck of the imagination. And there is fresh convention that is a medium of discovery, that is like a hand opening doors. When men demanded that the dead wood be removed from the old theater they were right. When they called for a theater without illusions they were talking nonsense.

It was when workers in the theater began to put into effect the ideas derived from these misconceptions that some serious errors were made. The theater as a whole had been identified with its own dead past. In revolt against dead formulas the call came to de-theatricalize the theater. In seeking to demolish the old theater with its false ideals, false morality, false and insincere values of beauty, a theater was built without ideals, without morality and without beauty. The theater of dead conventions became the theater of reason. Attitudes were exchanged for arguments. Thrills were exchanged for sermons. Another result followed: as the dynamic urge of dramatic imagination was lacking in our plays, men presumed that it had passed away from earth. And so they began to introduce into the theater other types of imagination, color, line, rhythm, lyric imagination, anything other than the dramatic. And as they had demanded the abdication of the theatrical from the theater they began to demand the abdication of literature and of personality. The theater was to take its place with the arts of design and music as an art of absolute composition of fixed and eternal symbols without the interposition of the uncertain and mysterious values of speech and human nature.

An extraordinary thing was happening in the

theater of the world. Finding the stage in the hands of the tailors and the efficiency experts; finding in the whole corps of busy workers no one who would not blush to be called an artist, the artists of other arts moved upon the stage *en masse* and proceeded to stake it as their own. There were musicians, and reformers with new ideas of production, and archæological zealots with old ideas of production; there were free verse poets, pantechnical iconoclasts, and above all there were the artists of design and mass and color. Overnight the stage was remade. It came to look like a cross between a carnival and a display in a futurist gallery. Rich with ideas, though not always well informed in the history of the theater, these men had a favorite theory that a new control had come into the theater, that all that was necessary was design, arrangement, made of the factors of color and mass and line. They said a dramatic production was a composition. Their ideas were innovating, stimulating and reconstructive. They accomplished a great deal of good. But they ignored the heart of the theater, which is passion.

What the stage needed was not to be de-theatricalized but re-theatricalized. By a series of pressures and expulsions extending over decades if not centuries, the true creative artist of the theater has been eliminated. One needs only to read the history of dramatic production in the 18th and 19th centuries to know that no free art could continue long to

exist under the conditions prescribed. As a free art
the drama did not exist. The only way in which it
could be made to exist was by freeing the playwright
to the use and the direction of the resources of the
theater. While the playwright was held as an adjunct to the glory of the manager, actor and scene
designer, these gentlemen were killing the art by
which they lived, of which their lives were but sub-
ordinate functions. The long-suffering playwright
had revenge in his hands. When the conditions of
composition became impossible he ceased to compose,
and the managers, actors and designers, with a
market on their hands and hard put to it for wares,
began to rake up the treasures of the past. When
the demand for these was exhausted they put up a
cry to the authors, "Come over into Macedonia and
help us!"

Nothing I have said should indicate that advantage has not come to the theater through the collaboration of the brother artists. Their contributions
came at precisely the moment to enrich the expressive
resources of the theater—given that there were creative artists to employ them. The drama can learn
much from the arts of design and of music, for a
play is as truly an "arrangement," a "study in
harmonies," as is a painting or a symphony. It has
a broader and more unruly orchestra of factors, but
the play can only benefit by the application to its
construction of the absolute standards of the sister
arts. We are now coming to apply these standards

and there is a consequent enrichment of the entire art of the theater. These standards must be applied by the dramatist as an expression of his creative vision. When the musician, the designer, work in the theater, they work as executants, not as creators. All this sounds trite enough when spoken. But it has been forgotten, nevertheless.

We are long past the time when a play can be embodied alone in words. Frequently in this book we have had occasion to refer to the limitations of words as expressive mediums. Not only do words supply a very thin channel through which to pour the water of life. The channel is crowded and clogged with memories of past meanings. And if words are becoming increasingly impotent, then verse is even more nearly valueless. When Arthur Symons says he does not see why people should break silence upon the stage except to speak poetry, he is revealing how little he knows of the stage, or he is employing the term "poetry" in a more inclusive sense than is common. The stage must, indeed, employ poetry but it is a poetry that is far more extra-literate than literate. It must be a poetry that is composed upon many dimensions and of a multitude of factors. In short, it must be a poetry unlike any that was ever written in a book. Language of speech and written verse has failed to be an instrument of those wide realms of experience and sensation that lie deeper than language. The playwright must create such instrumentalities and employ them with the command with which the versifier of yesterday spun his iambics.

Various attempts have been made by playwrights to approach the creative art of the theater through the pure medium either of design or of music. These have usually failed because they have been one-sided. But they have been worth the experiment. One of the most interesting attempts to apply the standards of design to dramatic composition is "The Grotesques," which is called by Cloyd Head, the author, a "decoration in black and white." This play represents a series of designs by Capulchard, a demi-urge or fate.

> I design a world for you in black and white,
> Woman and man; old age; youth and the sprite,
> Woman and man again in many forms
> And different episodes, each with its tang,
> And each a sign for the thing signified.

Then against a silhouette background a series of designs are projected which represent the patterns of life or of fate.

It is early discovered that design is not enough. Though the artists have introduced movement into their design, that design itself becomes dramatic, it still lacks that by which the flow and rhythm of time may be suggested. For this one must turn to music, and music, indeed, provides the qualities to which all arts, including the drama, tend. The supreme critic, such as Huneker, tends always to rest upon the sanctions of music, that art in which, as Pater says, it is impossible to distinguish the form from the substance. Any effort to apply these sanctions in the present state of dramatic production would of necessity be abortive. Nevertheless, very interesting experiments have been made. These experiments attack, as a rule, two features of the produced play; first, the tone value of the speech and vocal and instrumental sounds; second, the rhythm of the production. A man who has carried experiment in absolute design and rhythm over into dramatic composition has been Alfred Kreymborg. Unfortunately to this date no productions of Kreymborg's works have been made that adequately test and interpret the principles of his composition. At its heart the work of Kreymborg seems to demand an absolute standardization of the mediums of dramatic expression. He would standardize action by subjecting it to the formal controls of puppetry. He would standardize speech by giving it the rhythms of music and the dance. Kreymborg is a practical playwright who works with a playful fancy among new mediums. Of course it should not be thought that in standardizing his medium he restricts the imagination. It is his objective to liberate the imagination by eliminating the insignificant and the accidental.

IV

REFRESHING OF THEATRICAL RESOURCE

Outside the instrumentalities of pure design and music, the modern playwright has called to his aid many expedients from the theater of the past. These have the advantage that their symbolism has been fixed and that through their antiquity and associations they have a deep and direct appeal to use. They speak a rich and mysterious language. In many respects the dance lies half-way between the arts of design and of music. It is an expressive combination of both sound and line. And everything implied by the dance has come to be important in the new drama. Whether in physical posturing or in rhythmic movement the play cannot now ignore the qualities of the dance. But the dance possesses a deeper interest for the theater than either music or design, for it is in the dance that the folk elements first appear and are preserved. The dance is the living temple of tradition. The colors of myth and of fable are burned through it; they do not come out in the wash. The contributions of the masters of dance and folk lore, of Isadora Duncan, the highly colored ballet of Russia, the classical ballet of Italy, of the folk gymnastics and dances uncovered by Cecil Sharp and the hundreds of their fellows, have been of incalculable use in enriching the resources of the new drama. Others have pursued their researches into the theater of the Middle Ages, into puppet plays, folk farces, mysteries, moralities and interludes. The Commedia dell' arte and the Harlequinade have been a mine of information and suggestion. Pushing beyond these the more recondite of the artists of the new stage have inquired into the ways of the theater of Greece and Rome, beyond these into the ways of the classic drama of the Orient, into the theater of India and Persia, Japan and China, and still beyond into the secret rituals of the hidden cults of Asia.

Of all the contributions of archæological research to the modern art of theater, one of the richest is that of masques. Here is a factor that is derived both from the artist of pure design and from the research worker in old theatrical practice. The sources of masques are found in the early history of races and tribes. Their modern employment depends upon the adaptation of an ancient tool to new uses.

It would be too much to expect that all this material had been incorporated into the new drama. And yet interesting things have been done. One of the outstanding works of imagination of the American theater is "The Yellow Jacket" by George C. Hazelton and J. Harry Benrimo. By any standard this play is a work of genius; taking into account the conditions of the stage at the time the play was written, it is a miracle that it came into being at all. The relative share of each author has not been apportioned. There was glory enough for two. It is fair to believe that the knowledge of the Chinese theater and perhaps even the idea of the employment of the simple machinery of Chinese faith for telling a story in an Eastern manner for Western ears came from Benrimo. The creative genius that completed the work and made of a set of detached episodes a unit of imaginative power and beauty was Hazelton's. Certain it is that the play could not have come to pass without the collaboration of two men of widely different backgrounds and methods.

The story of the play is not to be sketched in outline. Here is one play in which form and substance are fused. Any attempt to isolate the substance from the form destroys both. The story is derived from the theater of China; it is developed through Chinese characters; it is instinct with the Chinese philosophy. If this were all it would be something, but the authors did more than tell a Chinese story. They employed the simple symbolism of the Eastern stage to release pure imagination in the Western world. They demolished at once the four walls, the unities, the single-track channels of the Western stage. Percy MacKaye expressed the truth of the authors' achievements when he wrote:

> To these you have restored their heritage:
> To humor—loveliness; to undefiled
> Passion—its splendor; to our native stage
> Enchantment and the rapture of a child.

Produced first by Henry B. Harris, and for many seasons by Mr. and Mrs. Coburn, the play has literally gone around the world.

Even more important than the Chinese theatre as a source of a pure and fresh symbolism is the Japanese stage, particularly as found in the Noh plays. These plays permit an unlimited flexibility in place, time and action. They appeal only to the inner mind. For this reason they offer alluring models for imitation or adaptation. In this order Colin Campbell Clements has done imaginative work. Deriving his material from various out-of-the-way sources, Thomas Wood Stevens has in plays and masques created modern shows of the materials of legend in "Cæsar's Gods," a Byzantine masque, in "The Daimio's Head" from Japan, and in "Masques of the East and West," composed with Wallace Rice. Stark Young, who constructs his plays of color and sensation and folk legend, derives his materials not alone from the past but from out-of-the-way places in which the color and the savor of life run more high than in our cold zones. To these materials he has in "At the Shrine," "Madretta," "The Saint," "The Colonnade" applied symbols reminiscent of the earlier and purer practice of the stage.

The number of modern plays written under the Harlequin convention is very great. Of some importance are Alfred Kreymborg's "Plays for Merry Andrews," "Plays for Poem Mimes," and "Puppet

Plays" among others. Many plays that appear at first view to be simply imitations of old romance are found to be better than this, in that they are or seek to be a vital recharging of an old mood or emotion. Sidney Howard's "Swords"; C. S. Brooks' "Luca Sarto" have in them an independent vitality that is not lost because the symbol is old. Among the many other plays demanding to be noted are Edna St. Vincent Millay's "Aria da Capo" and "Two Slatterns and a King," Wallace Stephen's "Three Travelers Watch a Sunrise," James Oppenheim's "The Book of Self," "The Pioneers," "The Prelude to Creation."

Aside from these works, all of which are written in words, there are other works from which the language factor has been eliminated. In the pantomime ballet I have here no interest; but in the ritual drama in pantomime I find a great deal of interest. Both the pantomime ballet and the ritual drama have been restricted by the fact that they demand a highly skilled company for their production. One cannot print a book of a pantomime or a ritual and permit it to rest on the shelf until recognition comes. Such a work exists only in production. For the reason that they have the best nucleus of a ballet company in this country, and because their own inclinations and gifts lead them to the purest types of stage production, the ritual dramas created by Misses Alice and Irene Lewisohn, of which "The Salut au Monde" and "The Arab

Fantasia" are examples, are the highest productions of this order in America.

The changing conceptions of stage management and structure do not come into the field of this book. Much attention has been paid to these matters in recent years. Important as they are, they do not so much represent the primary as the secondary conditions of stage art. A vital imagination in the playwright creates its own stage just as truly as it creates characters and story. Whether footlights shall be used or not, whether scenery shall be in perspective or solids, whether the stage shall lie behind a picture frame or shall be an extension of the world in which we live, are questions that go back in the last analysis to the playwright.

The new drama makes interesting and novel demands upon stage resources. The old limitations as to "what is a play" no longer hold. He would be a daring person or a stupid one who in these days attempted with any precision to define a play. The same may be said of the theater. The old specifications of a theater no longer hold. A theater is any place in which a dramatic action takes place. It may be a playhouse, a world, or the mind of a man. Formerly the play was a thin fabric of fancy rendered by the speech and action of players upon the boards. To-day the play tends to be a solid model of an event in action. It is speech and action and character and event and scene. There is a real difference between these two conceptions of a play.

The plays of yesterday had had a tremendous vitality, but they had lost it. Efforts were made to inject a vitality into an anæmic substance by giving it fever, fervor, passion, or by giving it meaning or uplift. These efforts did not succeed. Dramatists continued to construct their plays *about* life. Not until they learned to construct them *of* life did plays take on vigor again.

And when they learned to do so they were astounded by the riches of the dramatic material around them and by the sheer simplicity of their task. Playmaking ceased now to be writing. It came to be a species of modeling. True, this modeling involved materials of many different kinds, all of which had to be pieced together, unified and energized into a coherent whole, and it was a kind of modeling unlike any before known because it involved elements of motion and rhythm and sound.

There now followed a great simplification in the order of plays. When the playwright was seeking to speak for life he had continually to rake his mind to find something significant to say about it. And he seldom found anything significant to say, and so contented himself with repeating with ever greater emphasis the old truisms. When the playwright came to permit life to speak for itself, his work was simplified and, paradoxically enough, made more significant. He could now throw away the freight of ideas, banal commentary, frivolous jest and fanned-up passion. Not realism, but reality was his salva-

tion. Nothing has been less real than realism, not
fantasy, romance or melodrama. The playwrights
are recognizing that they are not called upon to tie
up their action into little packages or doctrine, that
if the action itself be but true, the doctrine will take
care of itself. It is out of this recognition that there
has come the great increase in freedom of form of
recent years, the return to story and character as
the central interest in dramatic art, the dictation of
form by substance.

Of all the plays that represent this new simplification and objectivity of outlook, "What Price Glory,"
by Maxwell Anderson and Laurence Stallings is the
most apposite example. There are those who profess
to see in this work a diatribe against war. The play
is no more a diatribe against war than against
peace. It is neither diatribe, polemic nor propaganda. It is an abnormally solid piece of modeling
by men who have the intuitions of artists. The
material with which they deal is war-making men.
To say that these men know their material by heart
is not to the point. It is, in fact, an insult to them
and to the stage, for it implies that playwrights
often treat material that they do not know. The
essential point is the treatment they give to the material, the solidity, balance, restraint and suggestive-
ness the completed product takes under their hands.
If it has the qualities of spiritual illumination
through the lens of base matter then it, too, is a work
of art, and all discussion of its meaning, lesson, is

beside the mark. "What Price Glory" has these qualities in an unusual degree. More than any recent work of stage art it responds to the tests of sculpture and music. The significance of its war theme lies not so much in the horrors of war and the passions of war-making men as in the weight and difficulty of the material the playwrights chose to handle. A play so modeled and disciplined could be written about an old man going in the evening to the post-office for the mail and meeting on the way a woman whom he had loved in youth and who had married another. In short, it is not the theme selected that gives a play importance, but the adequacy of the handling. In the case of this play the authors ran many dangers. Not the least of these was that very doctrine-making proclivity of people that causes them to see all reality through a haze of melancholy and ideas. They had to avoid this danger in their own artificering. They did avoid this and other dangers, and the fact that they did so is the measure of their success.

Another play produced during the season 1924-25 that borrows significance rather from its modelling than from its substance is Sidney Howard's "They Knew What They Wanted." Here is a play that deals with a very old theme that has for generations been sadly marred in the handling. Human motives and impulses have so long been prescribed within the theatrical as distinguished from the natural or instinctive convention that it is difficult to say

what is false and what is true. It is Howard's chief
service to this play that along with an effortless
craftsmanship and a sunny temper he brings a quick
and infallible eye for human values.

The contribution of a clear and corrective vision
to materials that have been badly confused is a rare
and valuable thing. It would perhaps appear that
a study of Don Marquis's play "The Dark Hours"
(1924) dealing with the last phase of the life of
Jesus should not find place in a discussion of form.
And yet the test of the treatment of the most sacred
legend of history lies rather in form than in any
other quality. The story is known by heart to millions. To tell it again in such a manner that all its
values stand out in the purity and dignity of first
discovery is a rare achievement indeed. This Don
Marquis has done, and in so doing has, in my opinion, provided one of the outstanding works of dramatic imagination of our time. The play has not
yet been produced. This is fortunate. It is not a
play to be rushed upon the stage in precipitate enthusiasm. That the play will find its production
there is no question. The production itself should be
as consecrated a work as was the composition.

"The Dark Hours" is variously distinguished. It
is distinguished by the limpid purity of its language.
The author does not seek to avoid the archaic by
recourse to the scientific or journalistic. He rather
employs the purity of form found in the various
early versions of the scriptures. It is distinguished

by the dramatic balance by means of which a fair judgment is given to all actors in the great drama. The author shows not only the sacred fire of Jesus. He is just to the rhapsody and fervor of those who keep the law and condemn him. He is just to the Sanhedrin and to Judas; to Peter and John and Pilate. It is distinguished by a command of the dramatic resources of a great theme. This is not alone the drama of a Man, even the King of Men, but a drama of Humanity at the moment when all the currents of history were conspiring in a mighty event. While the play is a tragedy of spiritual forces the author is not ashamed to realize these in an action that is always concrete, forceful and moving. The opportunities of staging are grasped; the difficulties are avoided with the ease of mastery.

The tendency of playwrights everywhere is to incorporate into the action of the play the characters, motives and action of the life they live. Needless to say, this lessens the importance of the proscenium arch and the curtain; it bridges the gap between audience and actor; it carries the stage down into auditorium and extends the auditorium on to the stage. Every day it is becoming more difficult to say where spectatorship ends and participation begins. The tendency is to make the entire audience participant. In physical pattern the stage develops slowly and surely toward the treatment of the theater as a unit. The carrying on of an action in certain parts of the audience, the entrance and exit of char-

acters through the audience are simple expressions of
this tendency. And in playmaking there is an
increasing disposition to develop the story through
the employment of a circus, a magician, or a play
within a play in the enjoyment of which audience
and players are presumed to unite.

But stage architecture still circumscribes the
playwright. In the more significant experiments
toward a wider stage of action we must leave the
theater play as at present composed and produced
and consider the pageant and the masque. Let it
be said at once that nothing in the world is new.
These forms go back to ancient sources, to the plays
of Sophocles, to the Progresses of Elizabeth and
James, to the Court Masques of Jonson and his
fellows. But the modern practice and principle are
new. These forms have to-day resources of light and
color through the use of electricity and of magnified
sound that did not exist in other times. And the
intent, too, is to-day different from that of the past.
The arts of the past, whether in Greece or in Elizabethan England, depended upon a differentiation of
classes. The arts demand to-day a fusing of classes.
The movement has begun to take the drama away
from the theater and back into the grove and into
the circular amphitheatre of its origins. No one
can say how far this movement will go. Few plays
have been written for this style of production. The
Grove Plays produced for many years by the
Bohemian Club in California have been written for

production in a setting of nature abetted by art. In such a play the best effects partake of the quality of accident. Now and then effects are created to be blown away by the wind, to disappear like star-dust. But the accidental quality of these plays, the uncontrollable elements of the production operate against a sure artistry.

The man who has done most to enlarge the physical equipment of the non-theatre stage is Percy MacKaye. If we are to understand what MacKaye has done we must remember that he discards entirely the differentiation between audience and actor. The audience is participant in the action. To accomplish this he must vary the location, shape and equipment of the stage with relation to the audience. Only a few illustrations of this widening of resource can be given, and these rather to indicate the greatly extended scope of the author's imaginative creation than as a discussion of scene construction. The action of "Caliban, by the Yellow Sands," takes place, symbolically, on three planes: "(1) In the cave of Setebos (before and after its transformation into the theatre of Prospero); (2) in the mind of Prospero (behind the cloudy curtain of the inner stage); and (3) on the ground circle of the Yellow Sands (the place of historic time)." The action of "The Evergreen Tree" takes place in four regions indicated by two stages and two aisles, the audience being located between the two stages. The stages represent places, the aisles represent pathways. The action of "Caliban" is realized through eight principal parts, speaking on a raised stage before sounding-boards, through mute presences, choral presences, pantomime groups and dancers. In "The Masque of St. Louis" MacKaye employs for the first time a great Puppet symbolizing a majestic presence greater than an individual man.

V

THE NEW SUBSTANCE BREAKS THROUGH

Like the theater as a whole, which is coming to occupy fields of our common life which had before been closed to it, or of which the existence had been hidden, the substance of our plays is breaking through the hitherto established forms. The new form of our plays is less an expression of æsthetic sense than of the sudden and unparalleled piling on of new substance and new values in our life. Experimental psychology, psychic research had been for years collecting data based upon close observation of the habits, hereditary and acquired, of man. As long as the drama remained locked in its old shell, while it was a mere verbal gloss on life, and not a concrete realization of it, these materials did not touch the theater at all. When the theater became the art of immediate reality these materials became the center of its interest.

Essentially, then, when we speak of the new form of the drama, we mean the new substance. Any effort to achieve novelty of form aside from the vital pressures that condition form and create it, is in effect dishonest and self-defeating. So judged, form is the final standard of excellence in the play, for it is the measure of the success with which all the elements have been mingled in it. There is no other standard than that of form. Neither popular appeal, nor moral import, nor simulation of reality, nor universal symbolism, nor laughter, nor tears, nor intellectual approval applies the final test of a play. In referring the play back to form we are admittedly placing its criteria beyond the reach of debate. On doctrines there may be dispute. But on taste there may be no dispute. Beyond debate also are the means by which this form is achieved. Almost without exception great work is done with comparative ease. And the qualities essential to the creation of form are among the mysteries of the creative spirit. They are not acquired by discipline or by study. There is in them something of fortuity. The love boat of "The Yellow Jacket," the rhythmic drum-beat of "The Emperor Jones," the successive inspirations that made up "The Hairy Ape" are products of powers that lie deep hidden under the surface of the author's technique. These powers come anew to each artist and the knowledge dies with him. He cannot pass it on to his disciples. It follows from this that there is in great art something like the lucky stroke, the inspired flash in the dark. There is in such work the sign manual of the artist, the indication that he alone has done it. It is not too nicely smoothed down, some of the crudities of construction hang to it, the mischances of adventure are acknowledged courageously. The artist is concerned with things deeper than form, of which form is a revealing attribute.

The most interesting works of recent playwrights are those works in which the adventure values higher than the cargo brought home. In 1913 Charles Frohman said in prophesying what the theater would be like in twenty-one years, that it would all sum up in "the outspeeding of speed. . . . From now on the universal ambition will be to increase speed by eliminating middle distances. . . . It is the desire to pack so much into life that the average human existence will gain in intensity what it may lose in length. I should not be at all surprised if twenty years from now managers will be selling plays in tablet form." This is of course exaggerated, and yet time has shown that Charles Frohman was right. We have grown to be contemptuous of our nicely turned toy dramas; distrustful of the dramatic *quod erat*. We demand of our plays that they take the platitude for granted and explore more into things that are not matters of common knowledge. Wide public interest in psychic research and in psycho-analysis has found its natural reflection in the stage. Speculation on the after-life remains, as far as the drama is concerned, simply speculation. No play has yet been written which in any degree throws a new light on this old question. Belasco's "The Return of Peter Grimm" is in every respect a situation play. Effective in its order it has nothing to say about the other world; it shows Peter back again on this side of the line of death. In "The Adding Machine," the other-worldly factors are colorless and secondary to the main motive of the play which is to show a human automaton. "The Happy Ending," by the MacPhersons, produced 1917 by Arthur Hopkins, was ambitious but sweetly sentimental. In short, no play has been written in America that draws one up with a quick rein before the after-life as do "Liliom" and "Outward Bound."

The American playwright may respond that he does not know about the after-life anyway. But what he thinks he writes. In treating the "confusion of worlds" uncovered by psycho-analysis, American playwrights are taking an advanced position. "Overtones," by Alice Gerstenberg, "Suppressed Desires," by Susan Glaspell, "Orthodoxy," by Nina Wilcox Putnam, were early and amusing dramatizations of the subconscious. Theodore Dreiser in the series of plays published in "Plays of the Natural and Supernatural" ("The Girl in the Coffin," "The Blue Sphere," "Laughing Gas," "The Light in the Window," etc.), draws his actions together on a plane of thought, but violates unity of place. His plays are interesting and convincing for reading, but are hardly adapted to production on the stage. They are plays for the stage of the mind.

The distrust of objective appearances objectively displayed is strong in many playwrights. They seek then to treat subjective reality as if it were objective, giving it speech and action, but always under the convention that what is spoken and done is to represent the inner and not the outer life. Several years ago John Howard Lawson, who had spent some years in studying the advanced stage in Europe, brought home the manuscript of "Roger Bloomer." Of this play one can say with John Dos Passos that it "is a raw, unlabeled attempt to use the emotional possibilities of the theater to their fullest extent for the expression of the commonest American theme—a boy running away from home to go to the big city." But it is more than this. It is the revelation of the inside soul of the boy, the untamed adolescent, in his feverish self-searchings and in his agonizing communions with others. It is a study of the adjustments and reactions of boy psychology to a world that is too crass and crude for it. The play may be considered in another way as an experiment toward the expression of the uncoördinated energy of American life, its complexities of appearance and substance and its spiritual blocs. In this respect the work is better done. Roger Bloomer was played by Equity Players in a production that did not serve well the author's conception. In a note in the published edition he insists that "Roger Bloomer *must* be played by an actor of sturdy virile appearance, giving the impression of an average American boy. . . . He is not neurasthenic, but rather the most normal person in the play." While the part as played was sympathetic, it was not virile, nor did the settings follow the author's idea. "The suggested division of the stage into sections, with the action taking place first at one side and then at the other as indicated in the text, does not mean that the movement of the players is confined to small cubby holes. . . . These divisions are rather used to suggest the background of the scene."

Even those who were most responsive to the author's purpose in the writing of this play had to admit that the execution was not worthy of the author's design. Great forces were released but were not sufficiently held in check. The vague, inchoate and undisciplined power which it was the purpose of the author to reveal in action broke through the channels of the author's dramaturgy. It is one thing to write a play about sophomores; another thing to write a sophomoric play about sophomores. While "Roger Bloomer" cannot wholly escape censure on this score Lawson's later play "Processional" produced in 1925 by the Theatre Guild rises well above any such criticism. With a considerably larger theme this play also has a discipline of sardonic good humor and awareness that holds in bounds the excesses of passion that are its necessary substance. The earlier play treated the subjective life of a boy. "Processional" treats the subjective life of America as a whole. Fortunately the production was entirely up to the demands of the composition. "Processional" is a work of great importance.

The employment of dreams and hallucinations to uncover for dramatic use subconscious and repressed states antedates the new psychology. And yet the new psychology has given this use sanction and wider currency. It is subject to a wide variety of use. Sometimes a solid texture of narrative is set between prologue and epilogue and explained as being a dream. Sometimes the play represents the broken, disjointed phantoms of mania. "Beggar on Horseback" (1924) by George S. Kaufman and Marc Connolly was suggested by "Hans Sonnenstresser's Hohlenfahrt," a German play of fifteen years ago, by Paul Apel. In its American form it is essentially an original work. Better than any recent work it reveals the undercurrent of discontent and disillusion that exists in American life. We have had radical and bad natured censures of our ideals in plenty. These accomplish little, for they stir up resentments that impede the search for truth. "Beggar on Horseback" is light, fanciful, sympathetic and terribly revealing. The play begins slowly and with even a pedestrian movement on the plane of commonplace fact. The authors doggedly insist upon the realities of the situation, the failure of the musician in his ideals as a composer, the success of the man in his impending marriage to an heiress. It is in accord with what psycho-analysis has told us of the subconscious that Neil McRae is shown to be conscious of no mental doubts. The system of American life owns him and he knows it. And then by a trick that the authors do not even seek to explain, the repressed subconscious begins to come to the fore. Through the movement of the play a rhythm begins to move. We advance, whether in dreams or in reality, into the marriage scene. The scene moves upon a rhythm which might be that of a galley slave's toil, or that of a jazz dance. It is both. From this the action delves deeper and deeper into the hidden consciousness of the composer. Now the universe is grotesquely at loose ends and events follow each other in wild inconsequence and without moral values. And then there breaks through the nightmare the pure loveliness of the fantasy, "A Kiss in Xanadu." It would be a mistake to seek for symbolism where the effort was to avoid symbolism. The play is a work of imagination of first order.

"Conscience" (1924) by Don Mulally, is interesting because the hard structure of remembered event is embedded in a mania of dreams and regrets. The portions of the play that deal with neurotic mental states are not of equal quality with the more closely observed realistic action.

"The Bronx Express," by Ossip Dymov, deals with the dream of a Jewish immigrant in the Bronx, a dream peopled with characters from the advertisements in the Subway.

In "The Crime in the Whistler Room," by Edmund Wilson, presented at the Provincetown Playhouse, September, 1924, we have a more complex structure. While the action of the dream is supposed to take place in the mind of one of the characters, the dream itself, as well as the entire play, has a widely symbolic significance. Into an exquisitely appointed room, the characters and furniture of which represent an old and refined order, there is invited a young woman from another world. Soon she has surrounded herself by people of her class, and by these in her mocking dreams the crime of the murder of her benefactors is committed. Between these two worlds the author keeps the needle poised. The dream features are developed with rich imaginative powers.

An early play on a supernatural motive was George Bronson Howard's "The Red Light of Mars." This had faint hints of Faust in it. Upton Sinclair's "Singing Jailbirds," effectively dramatizes the mental sufferings of a prisoner for opinion bound in an underground cell. Most of the action of the play takes place in the mind of the prisoner, which gradually breaks under the strain.

The modern playwright is not concerned alone with entering the dreams and the subconscious planes of his characters. He must play the part of the all-seeing eye, the ear that hears all things, the understanding that comprehends the secret thoughts of men. Supremely interested in men as individuals, the new playwright begins to see, or to think that he sees, man losing his individuality under the pressure of mighty forces that move him about at will in phalanxes, put uniforms on his back, rubber stamps in his hands, stereotyped phrases in his mouth, and an adding machine in his head. Under such a view as this man becomes not only a repository of unconscious memories, passions, and habits; he becomes a machine whose will is no longer important, whose pains and pleasures no longer shock him to deep feeling or ecstasy, who does not live when he lives and does not die when he is dead. In the depiction of such a figure as this, there is no place for the older motives of drama, for those were the motives of men. These individuals are pulled by external strings like puppets. The author of this book is not equipped to comment on the value or worthlessness of this idea as a social theory. As a dramatic concept it has an unquestioned force. This is made manifest in the reduction of the factor of free will in drama, and strangely enough in the reduction of the value of the actor. Never were the shortcomings of the actor more apparent than they are to-day. Are the stage designer and the author carrying the play beyond the powers of personality to reflect and interpret? Or will a new generation of actors arise equipped by training and skill to body forth the meaning of the composer? There are those who think that personality is becoming *de trop* in dramatic art, that the stage production of the future will minimize rather than enhance the appeals of personality and prestige. Be that as it may, the use of fixed symbols in the form of masques, puppets, or stylized make-up, does not necessarily mean a surrender of the deepest expressiveness. It may be a more direct and economical means of expressing truths that lie beyond representation.

The manikins on Fifth Avenue in "The Hairy Ape," the dummies in the club chairs in "Roger Bloomer," carried some meaning, no doubt. What that meaning was has been dramatized into a complete play by Elmer Rice in "The Adding Machine." Mr. Zero is a "lost soul" in the deepest and most tragic sense. When he lost his soul he became a machine. Nothing that happened after he had lost his soul mattered. Has a machine senses, instincts, feelings? Can a machine think? Is it morally responsible? The absolute deadness of Mr. Zero, the inconsequence of his worst as well as of his best acts are effectively brought home. Nothing that he does or thinks has any external consequence. And he is the same dead as alive. In one of the most original scenes in our recent drama, the two "lost souls," Daisy and Zero, play in their minds with the thoughts of life. But their life-thoughts do not come to speech:

"ZERO: Your hair's gettin' gray. You don't wear them shirt-waists any more with the low collars. When you'd bend down to pick somethin up——

DAISY: I wish I knew what to ask for. Girl takes

mercury after all-night party. Woman in ten-story death leap.

ZERO: I wonder where she'll go when she gets out. Gee, I'd like to make a date with her. Why didn't I go over there the night my wife went to Brooklyn? She never would 'a' found out.

DAISY: I saw Pauline Frederick do it once. Where could I get a pistol, though?

ZERO: I guess I didn't have the nerve.

DAISY: I'll bet you'd be sorry, then, that you'd been so mean to me. How do I know, though? Maybe you wouldn't.

ZERO: Nerve? I got as much nerve as anybody. I'm on the level, that's all. I'm a married man and I'm on the level.

DAISY: Anyhow, why ain't I got a right to live? I'm as good as anybody else. I'm too refined, I guess. That's the whole trouble.

ZERO: The time the wife had pneumonia I thought she was going to pass out. But she didn't. The doctor's bill was eighty-seven dollars. (*Looking up.*) Hey, wait a minute! Didn't you say eighty-seven dollars?

DAISY (*looking up*): What?

ZERO: Was the last you said, eighty-seven dollars?

DAISY (*consulting the slip*): Forty-two fifty.

ZERO: Well, I made a mistake. Wait a minute! (*He busies himself with an eraser.*) All right. Shoot!

DAISY: Six dollars, three-fifteen. Two-twenty-

five. Sixty-five cents. A dollar-twenty. You talk
to me as if I was dirt."

In such plays as these, where the externals of
events are shredded entirely apart from the internal
reality, we have the first tentatives of playwrights
to get below the surface to the hidden reality beneath.
Baffling these tentatives must be as they approach
the border line of mystery. Having gained poise
and discipline in the handling of the reality of sense
and bodily form, the playwright presses onward into
zones where reality begins to break into the unknown.

END

INDEX

321

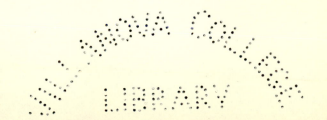

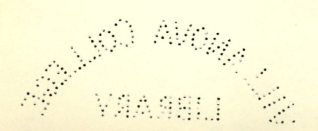